TOLKIEN

A biography

Also by Humphrey Carpenter

A Thames Companion
(with Mari Prichard)

TOLKIEN

A biography

BY HUMPHREY CARPENTER

Illustrated with photographs

Houghton Mifflin Company Boston

For information about permission to reproduce selections from this book, write to
Permissions, Houghton Mifflin Company, 2 Park Street, Boston, Massachusetts
02108.

Library of Congress Cataloging-in-Publication Data

Carpenter, Humphrey.
    Tolkien : a biography.
        Reprint. Originally published: J.R.R. Tolkien.
London : G. Allen & Unwin, 1977.
        Bibliography: p.
        Includes index.
        1. Tolkien, J. R. R. (John Ronald Reuel), 1892–1973 —
Biography.   2. Authors, English — 20th century — Biography.
I. Title.
PR6039.032Z62   1988   828'.91209   [B]   88-11908
ISBN 0-395-25360-8
ISBN 0-395-48676-9 (pbk.)

Printed in the United States of America

P   10 9 8 7 6 5 4 3 2 1

Dedicated to the memory of
'The T.C.B.S.'

Dedicated to the memory of
The I.C.B.S.

CONTENTS

Contents

ILLUSTRATIONS

(following page 148)

Author's note

This book is based upon the letters, diaries, and other papers of the late Professor J. R. R. Tolkien, and upon the reminiscences of his family and friends.

Tolkien himself did not entirely approve of biography. Or rather, he disliked its use as a form of literary criticism. 'One of my strongest opinions,' he once wrote, 'is that investigation of an author's biography is an entirely vain and false approach to his works.' Yet he was undoubtedly aware that the remarkable popularity of his fiction made it highly likely that a biography would be written after his death; and indeed he appears to have made some preparation for this himself, for in the last years of his life he annotated a number of old letters and papers with explanatory notes or other comments. He also wrote a few pages of recollections of his childhood. It may thus be hoped that this book would not be entirely foreign to his wishes.

In writing it I have tried to tell the story of Tolkien's life without attempting any critical judgements of his works of fiction. This is partly in deference to his own views, but in any case it seems to me that the first published biography of a writer is not necessarily the best place to make literary judgements, which will after all reflect the character of the critic just as much as that of his subject. I have however tried to delineate some of the literary and other influences that came to bear on Tolkien's imagination, in the hope that this may shed some light on his books.

H. C.
Oxford, 1976

I

A visit

I

A visit

I

A visit

It is mid-morning on a spring day in 1967. I have driven from the centre of Oxford, over Magdalen Bridge, along the London road, and up a hill into the respectable but dull suburb of Headington. Near a large private school for girls I turn left into Sandfield Road, a residential street of two-storey brick houses, each with its tidy front garden.

Number seventy-six is a long way down the road. The house is painted white and is partially screened by a tall fence, a hedge, and overhanging trees. I park the car, open the arched gate, go up the short path between rose bushes, and ring the front door bell.

For a long time there is silence, except for the rumble of distant traffic in the main road. I am beginning to think of ringing again or of turning away when the door is opened by Professor Tolkien.

He is slightly smaller than I expected. Tallness is a quality of which he makes much in his books, so it is a little surprising to see that he himself is slightly less than the average height – not much, but just enough to be noticeable. I introduce myself, and (since I made this appointment in advance and am expected) the quizzical and somewhat defensive look that first met me is replaced by a smile. A hand is offered and my own is firmly grasped.

Behind him I can see the entrance-hall, which is small and tidy and contains nothing that one would not expect in the house of a middle-class elderly couple. W. H. Auden, in an injudicious re-mark quoted in the newspapers, has called the house 'hideous', but that is nonsense. It is simply ordinary and suburban.

Mrs Tolkien appears for a moment, to greet me. She is smaller than her husband, a neat old lady with white hair bound close to her head, and dark eyebrows. Pleasantries are exchanged, and then the Professor comes out of the front door and takes me into his 'office' at the side of the house.

This proves to be the garage, long abandoned by any car – he explains that he has not had a car since the beginning of the Second World War – and, since his retirement, made habitable and given over to the housing of books and papers formerly kept in his college room. The shelves are crammed with dictionaries, works on etymology and philology, and editions of texts in many languages, predominant among which are Old and Middle English and Old Norse; but there is also a section devoted to translations of *The Lord of the Rings* into Polish, Dutch, Danish, Swedish, and Japanese; and the map of his invented 'Middle-earth' is pinned to the window-ledge. On the floor is a very old portmanteau full of letters, and on the desk are ink-bottles, nibs and pen-holders, and two typewriters. The room smells of books and tobacco smoke.

It is not very comfortable, and the Professor apologises for receiving me here, but he explains that there is no space in the study-bedroom in the house where he actually does his writing. He says that in any case this is all temporary: soon he will, he hopes, manage to finish at least the major part of the work promised to his publishers, and then he and Mrs Tolkien will be able to move to more comfortable quarters and congenial surroundings, away from visitors and intrusions. He looks slightly embarrassed after the last remark.

I climb past the electric fire and, at his bidding, seat myself in a wheel-back chair, as he takes his pipe from the pocket of his tweed jacket and launches into an explanation of his inability to spare me more than a few minutes. A shiny blue alarm clock ticks noisily across the room as if to emphasise the point. He says that he has to clear up an apparent contradiction in a passage of *The Lord of the Rings* that has been pointed out in a letter from a reader; the matter requires his urgent consideration as a revised edition of the book is about to go to press. He explains it all in great detail, talking about his book not as a work of fiction but as a chronicle of actual events; he seems to see himself not as an author who has made a slight error that must now be corrected or explained away, but as a historian who must cast light on an obscurity in a historical document.

Disconcertingly, he seems to think that I know the book as well as he does. I have read it many times, but he is talking about details that mean little or nothing to me. I begin to fear that he will throw some penetrating question at me that will reveal my ignorance – and indeed now he does ask me a question, but fortunately it is rhetorical and clearly requires no more than the answer 'yes'.

I am still nervous that there will be other and harder questions, doubly nervous because I cannot hear everything that he is saying. He has a strange voice, deep but without resonance, entirely English but with some quality in it that I cannot define, as if he had come from another age or civilisation. Yet for much of the time he does not speak clearly. Words come out in eager rushes. Whole phrases are elided or compressed in the haste of emphasis. Often his hand comes up and grasps his mouth, which makes it even harder to hear him. He speaks in complex sentences, scarcely hesitating – but then there comes a long pause in which I am surely expected to reply. Reply to what? If there was a question, I did not understand it. Suddenly he resumes (never having finished his sentence) and now he reaches an emphatic conclusion. As he does so, he jams his pipe between his teeth, speaks on through clenched jaws, and strikes a match just as the full stop is reached.

Again I struggle to think of an intelligent remark, and again he resumes before I can find one. Following some slender connecting thread, he begins to talk about a remark in a newspaper that has made him angry. Now I feel that I can contribute a little, and I say something that I hope sounds intelligent. He listens with courteous interest, and answers me at some length, turning my remark (which was really very trivial) to excellent use, and so making me feel that I have said something worth saying. Then he is off on some tangential topic, and I am once more out of my depth, able to contribute no more than a monosyllable of agreement here and there; though it does occur to me that I am perhaps valued just as much as a listener as a participant in the conversation.

As he talks he moves unceasingly, pacing about the dark little room with an energy that hints at restlessness. He waves his pipe in the air, knocks it out in an ashtray, fills it, strikes a match, but scarcely ever smokes for more than a few puffs. He has small, neat, wrinkled hands, with a plain wedding-ring on the third finger of the left hand. His clothes are a little rumpled, but they sit well on him, and though he is in his seventy-sixth year there is only a suggestion of tubbiness behind the buttons of his coloured waistcoat.

I cannot for long keep my attention from his eyes, which may wander about the room or stare out of the window, yet now and then will return to dart a glance at me or rest a steady gaze as some vital point is made. They are surrounded by wrinkles and folds that change with and emphasise each mood.

The flood of words has dried up for a moment and the pipe is being lit again. I perceive my opportunity, and state my business, which now seems unimportant. Yet he turns to it immediately with enthusiasm, and listens to me attentively. Then, when this part of the conversation is done, I get up to go; but for the moment my departure is evidently neither expected nor desired, for he has started to talk again. Once more he refers to his own mythology. His eyes fix on some distant object, and he seems to have forgotten that I am there as he clutches his pipe and speaks through its stem. It occurs to me that in all externals he resembles the archetypal Oxford don, at times even the stage *caricature* of a don. But that is exactly what he is not. It is rather as if some strange spirit had taken on the guise of an elderly professor. The body may be pacing this shabby little suburban room, but the mind is far away, roaming the plains and mountains of Middle-earth.

Then it is all over, and I am being ushered out of the garage and taken to the garden gate – the smaller one opposite the front door: he explains that he has to keep the garage gates padlocked to stop football spectators parking their cars in his drive when they attend matches at the local stadium. Rather to my surprise, he asks me to come and see him again. Not for the moment, as neither he nor Mrs Tolkien has been well, and they are going on holiday to Bournemouth, and his work is many years behind-hand, and letters are piling up unanswered. But some time, soon. He shakes my hand and is gone, a little forlornly, back into the house.

II

1892–1916 : Early years

1
Bloemfontein

On a March day in 1891 the steamer *Roslin Castle* left dock to sail from England to the Cape. Standing on the stern deck, waving to the family she would not see again for a long time, was a slim good-looking girl of twenty-one. Mabel Suffield was going to South Africa to marry Arthur Tolkien.

It was in every way a dividing point in her life. Behind her lay Birmingham, foggy days, and family teas. Ahead was an unknown country, eternal sunshine, and marriage to a man thirteen years her senior.

Although Mabel was so young, there had been a long engagement, for Arthur Tolkien had proposed to her and she had accepted three years earlier, soon after her eighteenth birthday. However, her father would not permit a formal betrothal for two years because of her youth, and so she and Arthur could only exchange letters in secret and meet at evening parties where the family eye was upon them. The letters were entrusted by Mabel to her younger sister Jane, who would pass them to Arthur on the platform of New Street Station in Birmingham, when she was catching a train home from school to the suburb where the Suffields lived. The evening parties were generally musical gatherings at which Arthur and Mabel could only exchange covert glances or at most the touch of a sleeve, while his sisters played the piano.

It was a Tolkien piano, of course, one of the upright models manufactured by the family firm that had made what money the Tolkiens once possessed. On the lid was inscribed: 'Irresistible Piano-Forte: Manufactured Expressly for Extreme Climates'; but the piano firm was in other hands now, and Arthur's father was bankrupt, without a family business to provide employment for his sons. Arthur had tried to make a career in Lloyds Bank, but promotion in the Birmingham office was slow, and he knew that if he was to support a wife and family he would have to look elsewhere. He turned his eye to South Africa, where the gold and diamond discoveries were making banking into an expanding business with good prospects for employees. Less than a year after proposing to Mabel he had obtained a post with the Bank of Africa, and had sailed for the Cape.

Arthur's initiative had soon been justified. For the first year he had been obliged to travel extensively, for he was sent on temporary postings to many of the principal towns between the Cape and Johannesburg. He acquitted himself well, and at the end of 1890 he was appointed manager of the important branch at Bloemfontein, capital of the Orange Free State. A house was provided for him, the income was adequate, and so at last marriage was possible. Mabel celebrated her twenty-first birthday at the end of January 1891, and only a few weeks later she was on board *Roslin Castle* and sailing towards South Africa and Arthur, their betrothal now blessed with her father's approval.

Or perhaps 'tolerance' would be a better word, for John Suffield was a proud man, especially in the matter of the ancestry which in many ways was all he had left to be proud of. Once he had owned a prosperous drapery business in Birmingham, but now like Arthur Tolkien's father he was bankrupt. He had to earn his living as a commercial traveller for Jeyes disinfectant; yet the failure of his fortunes had only strengthened his pride in the old and respectable Midland family from which he was descended. What were the Tolkiens in comparison? Mere German immigrants, English by only a few generations – scarcely a fit pedigree for his daughter's husband.

If such reflections occupied Mabel during her three-week voyage, they were far from her mind on the day early in April when the ship sailed into harbour at Cape Town, and she caught sight at last of a white-suited, handsome, and luxuriantly-moustached figure on the quay, scarcely looking his thirty-four years as he peered anxiously through the crowd for a glimpse of his darling 'Mab'.

Arthur Reuel Tolkien and Mabel Suffield were married in Cape Town Cathedral on 16 April 1891, and spent their honeymoon in a hotel at nearby Sea Point. Then came an exhausting railway journey of nearly seven hundred miles to the capital of the Orange Free State, and the house which was to be Mabel's first and only home with Arthur.

Bloemfontein had begun life forty-five years earlier as a mere hamlet. Even by 1891 it was of no great size. Certainly it did not present an impressive spectacle to Mabel as she and Arthur got off the train at the newly built railway station. In the centre of the town was the market square where the Dutch-speaking farmers from the veldt trundled in aboard great ox-wagons to unload and sell the bales of wool that were the backbone of the State's economy. Around the square were clustered solid indications of civilisation: the colonnaded Parliament House, the two-towered Dutch Reformed church, the Anglican cathedral, the hospital, the public library, and the Presidency. There was a club for European residents (German, Dutch, and English), a tennis club, a law court, and a sufficiency of shops. But the trees that had been planted by the first settlers were still sparse, and the town's park was, as Mabel observed, no more than about ten willows and a patch of water. Only a few hundred yards beyond the houses was the open veldt where wolves, wild dogs, and jackals roamed and menaced the flocks, and where after dark a post-rider might be attacked by a marauding lion. From these treeless plains the wind blew into Bloemfontein, stirring the dust of the broad dirt-covered streets. Mabel, writing to her family, summed up the town as 'Owlin' Wilderness! Horrid Waste!'

However for Arthur's sake she must learn to like it, and meanwhile the life she found herself leading was by no means uncomfortable. The premises of the Bank of Africa, in Maitland Street just off the market square, included a solidly built residence with a large garden. There were servants in the house, some black or coloured, some white immigrants; and there was company enough to be chosen from among the many other English-speaking residents, who organised a regular if predictable round of dances and dinner-parties. Mabel had much time to herself, for when Arthur was not busy in the bank he was attending classes to learn Dutch, the language in which all government and legal documents were worded; or he was making useful acquaintances in the club. He could not afford to take life easy, for although there was only one other bank in Bloemfontein, this was the National, native to the Orange Free State; whereas the Bank of Africa of which Arthur

11

was manager was an outsider, a *uitlander*, and was only tolerated by a special parliamentary decree. To make matters worse, the previous manager of the Bank of Africa had gone over to the National, and Arthur had to work doubly hard to make sure that valuable accounts did not follow him. Then there were new projects in the locality which might be turned to the advantage of his bank, schemes connected with the Kimberley diamonds to the west or the Witwatersrand gold to the north. It was a crucial stage in Arthur's career, and, moreover, Mabel could see that he was intensely happy. His health had not been consistently good since he arrived in South Africa, but the climate seemed to suit his temperament; seemed, as Mabel noticed with the faintest apprehension, positively to appeal to him, whereas after only a few months she herself came to dislike it heartily. The oppressively hot summer and the cold, dry, dusty winter tried her nerves far more than she liked to admit to Arthur, and 'home leave' seemed a very long way off, for they would not be entitled to visit England until they had been in Bloemfontein for another three years.

Yet she adored Arthur, and she was always happy when she could entice him from his desk and they could go for walks or drives, play a game of tennis or a round of golf, or read aloud to each other. Soon there was something else to occupy her mind: the realisation that she was pregnant.

On 4 January 1892 Arthur Tolkien wrote home to Birmingham:

My dear Mother,
    I have good news for you this week. Mabel gave me a beautiful little son last night (3 January). It was rather before time, but the baby is strong and well and Mabel has come through wonderfully. The baby is (of course) lovely. It has beautiful hands and ears (very long fingers) very light hair, 'Tolkien' eyes and very distinctly a 'Suffield' mouth. In general effect immensely like a very fair edition of its Aunt Mabel Mitton. When we first fetched Dr Stollreither yesterday he said it was a false alarm and told the nurse to go home for a fortnight but he was mistaken and I fetched him again about eight and then he stayed till 12.40 when we had a whisky to drink luck to the boy. The boy's first name will be 'John' after its grandfather, probably John Ronald Reuel altogether. Mab wants to call it Ronald and I want to keep up John and Reuel . . .

'Reuel' was Arthur's own second name, but there was no family precedent for 'Ronald'. This was the name by which Arthur and Mabel came to address their son, the name that would be used by his relatives and later by his wife. Yet he sometimes said that he did not feel it to be his real name; indeed people seemed to feel faintly uncomfortable when choosing how to address him. A few close school-friends called him 'John Ronald', which sounded grand and euphonious. When he was an adult his intimates referred to him (as was customary at the time) by his surname, or called him 'Tollers', a hearty nickname typical of the period. To those not so close, especially in his later years, he was often known as 'J.R.R.T.' Perhaps in the end it was those four initials that seemed the best representation of the man.

John Ronald Reuel Tolkien was christened in Bloemfontein Cathedral on 31 January 1892, and some months later he had his photograph taken in the garden of Bank House, in the arms of the nurse who had been engaged to look after him. His mother was clearly in excellent health, while Arthur, always something of a dandy, posed in a positively jaunty manner in his white tropical suit and boater. Behind stood two black servants, a maid and a house-boy named Isaak, both looking pleased and a little surprised to be included in the photograph. Mabel found the Boer attitude to the natives objectionable, and in Bank House there was tolerance, most notably over the extraordinary behaviour of Isaak, who one day stole little John Ronald Reuel and took him to his kraal where he showed off with pride the novelty of a white baby. It upset everybody and caused a great turmoil, but Isaak was not dismissed, and in gratitude to his employer he named his own son 'Isaak Mister Tolkien Victor', the last being in honour of Queen Victoria.

There were other disturbances in the Tolkien household. One day a neighbour's pet monkeys climbed over the wall and chewed up three of the baby's pinafores. Snakes lurked in the wood-shed and had to be avoided. And many months later, when Ronald was beginning to walk, he stumbled on a tarantula. It bit him, and he ran in terror across the garden until the nurse snatched him up and sucked out the poison. When he grew up he could remember a hot day and running in fear through long, dead grass, but the memory of the tarantula itself faded, and he said that the incident left him with no especial dislike of spiders. Nevertheless, in his stories he wrote more than once of monstrous spiders with venomous bites. For the most part life at Bank House maintained an orderly pattern. In the early morning and late afternoon the child would be taken into the garden, where he could watch his father tending the vines or planting saplings in a piece of walled but unused ground. During the first year of the boy's life Arthur Tolkien made a small grove of cypresses, firs, and cedars. Perhaps this had something to do with the deep love of trees that would develop in Ronald.

From half past nine to half past four the child had to remain indoors, out of the blaze of the sun. Even in the house the heat could be intense, and he had to be clothed entirely in white. 'Baby does look such a fairy when he's *very* much dressed-up in white frills and white shoes,' Mabel wrote to her husband's mother. 'When he's very much *un*dressed I think he looks more of an elf still.'

There was more company for Mabel now. Soon after the baby's first birthday, her sister and brother-in-law May and Walter Incledon arrived from England. Walter, a Birmingham merchant in his early thirties, had business interests in the South African gold and diamond mines, and he left May and their small daughter Marjorie at Bank House and travelled on to the mining areas. May Incledon had arrived in time to keep her sister cheerful through the bitterness of another wintry summer in Bloemfontein, a season more hard to bear because Arthur too was away for some weeks on business. It was intensely cold, and the two sisters huddled round the dining-room stove while Mabel knitted garments for the baby and she and May talked about Birmingham days. Mabel was making little secret of her irritation with Bloemfontein life, its climate, its endless social calls, and its tedious dinner-parties. Home leave could be taken soon now, in a year or so – though Arthur was always suggesting reasons for postponing their visit to England. 'I will not let him put it off too long,' wrote Mabel. 'He does grow too fond of this climate to please me. I wish I could like it better, as I'm sure he'll never settle in England again.'

In the end the trip *had* to be postponed. Mabel found that she was pregnant again, and on 17 February 1894 she gave birth to another son. He was christened Hilary Arthur Reuel.

Hilary proved to be a healthy child who flourished in the Bloemfontein climate, but his elder brother was not doing so well.

14

Ronald was sturdy and handsome, with his fair hair and blue eyes – 'quite a young Saxon', his father called him. By now he was talking volubly and entertaining the bank clerks on his daily visit to his father's office downstairs, where he would demand pencil and paper and scribble away at crude drawings. But teething upset him badly and made him feverish, so that the doctor had to be called in day after day and Mabel was soon worn out. The weather was at its worst: an intense drought arrived, ruined trade, spoilt tempers, and brought a plague of locusts that swarmed across the veldt and destroyed a fine harvest. Yet despite all this, Arthur wrote to his father the words that Mabel had dreaded to hear: 'I think I shall do well in this country and do not think I should settle down well in England again for a permanency.'

Whether they were to stay or not, it was clear that the heat was doing a great deal of harm to Ronald's health. Something must be done to get him to cooler air. So in November 1894 Mabel took the two boys the many hundreds of miles to the coast near Cape Town. Ronald was nearly three now, old enough to retain a faint memory of the long train journey and of running back from the sea to a bathing hut on a wide flat sandy shore. After this holiday Mabel and the children returned to Bloemfontein, and preparations were made for their visit to England. Arthur had booked a passage and had engaged a nurse to travel with them. He badly wanted to accompany them himself; but he could not afford to be away from his desk, for there were railway schemes on hand that concerned the bank, and as he wrote to his father: 'In these days of competition one does not like to leave one's business in the hands of others.' Moreover time spent away would be on half pay, and he could not easily afford this in addition to the expense of the voyage. So he decided to stay in Bloemfontein for the time being and to join his wife and children in England a little later. Ronald watched his father painting *A. R. Tolkien* on the lid of a family trunk. It was the only clear memory of him that the boy retained.

The S.S. *Guelph* carried Mabel and the boys from South Africa at the beginning of April 1895. In Ronald's mind there would remain no more than a few words of Afrikaans and a faint recollection of a dry dusty barren landscape, while Hilary was too young even to remember this. Three weeks later, Mabel's little sister Jane, now a grown woman, met them at Southampton; and in a few hours they were all in Birmingham and cramming into the tiny family house in King's Heath. Mabel's father was as jolly as ever, cracking jokes and making dreadful puns, and her mother was kind and understanding. They stayed on, and the spring and summer passed with a marked improvement in Ronald's health; but though Arthur wrote to say that he missed his wife and children very badly and was longing to come and join them, there was always something to detain him.

Then in November came the news that he had contracted rheumatic fever. He had already partially recovered, but he could not face an English winter and would have to regain his health before he could make the journey. Mabel spent a desperately anxious Christmas, though Ronald enjoyed himself and was fascinated by the sight of his first Christmas tree, which was very different from the wilting eucalyptus that had adorned Bank House the previous December.

When January came, Arthur was reported to be still in poor health, and Mabel decided that she must go back to Bloemfontein and care for him. Arrangements were made, and an excited Ronald dictated a letter to his father which was written out by the nurse.

9 Ashfield Road, King's Heath, February 14th 1896.
My dear Daddy,
   I am so glad I am coming back to see you it is such a long time since we came away from you I hope the ship will bring us all back to you Mamie and Baby and me. I know you will be so glad to have a letter from your little Ronald it is such a long time since I wrote to you I am got such a big man now because I have got a man's coat and a man's bodice Mamie says you will not know Baby or me we have got such big men we have got such a lot of Christmas presents to show you Auntie Gracie has been to see us I walk every day and only ride in my mailcart a little bit. Hilary sends lots of love and kisses and so does your loving
                                            Ronald.

This letter was never sent, for a telegram arrived to say that Arthur had suffered a severe haemorrhage and Mabel must expect the worst. Next day, 15 February 1896, he was dead. By the time a full account of his last hours had reached his widow, his body had been buried in the Anglican graveyard at Bloemfontein, five thousand miles from Birmingham.

2
Birmingham

When the first state of shock was over, Mabel Tolkien knew that she must make decisions. She and the two boys could not stay for ever in her parents' crowded little suburban villa, yet she scarcely had the resources to establish an independent household. For all his hard work and conscientious saving, Arthur had only amassed a modest sum of capital which was chiefly invested in Bonanza Mines, and though the dividend was high it would not bring her an income of more than thirty shillings a week, scarcely sufficient to maintain herself and two children even at the lowest standard of living. There was also the question of the boys' education. Probably she could manage this herself for some years, for she knew Latin, French, and German, and could paint, draw, and play the piano. Later when Ronald and Hilary were old enough they must take the entrance examination for King Edward's School, Birmingham, which Arthur had attended and which was the best grammar school in the city. Meanwhile she must find cheap accommodation that she could rent. There were plenty of lodgings to be had in Birmingham, but the boys needed fresh air and the countryside, a home that could make them happy despite their poverty. She began to search through the advertisements.

Ronald, now in his fifth year, was slowly adjusting to life under his grandparents' roof. He had almost forgotten his father, whom he would soon come to regard as belonging to an almost legendary past. The change from Bloemfontein to Birmingham had confused him, and sometimes he expected to see the verandah of Bank House jutting out from his grandparents' home in Ashfield Road; but as the weeks passed and memories of South Africa began to fade, he took more notice of the adults around him. His Uncle Willie and his Aunt Jane were still living at home, and there was also a lodger, a sandy-haired insurance clerk who sat on the stairs singing 'Polly-Wolly-Doodle' to the accompaniment of a banjo, and making eyes at Jane. The family thought him common, and they were horrified when she became engaged to him. Ronald secretly longed for a banjo.

In the evening his grandfather would return from a day spent tramping the streets of Birmingham and cajoling orders for Jeyes Fluid from shopkeepers and factory managers. John Suffield had a long beard and seemed very old. He was sixty-three, and he vowed that he would live to be a hundred. A very jolly man, he did not seem to object to earning his living as a commercial traveller, even though he had once managed his own drapery shop in the city centre. Sometimes he would take a sheet of paper and a pen with an extra fine nib. Then he would draw a circle around a sixpence, and in this little space would write in fine copperplate the words of the entire Lord's Prayer. His ancestors had been engravers and plate-makers, which was perhaps why he had inherited this skill; he would talk with pride about how King William IV had given the family a coat of arms because they did fine work for him, and how Lord Suffield was a distant relative (which was not true).

So it was that Ronald began to learn the ways of the Suffield family. He came to feel far closer to them than to the family of his dead father. His Tolkien grandfather lived only a little way up the road, and sometimes Ronald was taken to see him; but John Benjamin Tolkien was eighty-nine and had been badly shaken by his son's death. Six months after Arthur died, the old man was in his own grave, and another of the boy's links with the Tolkiens was severed.

There was, however, Ronald's Aunt Grace, his father's younger sister, who told him stories of the Tolkien ancestors; stories which sounded improbable but which were, said Aunt Grace, firmly based on fact. She alleged that the family name had originally been 'von Hohenzollern', for they had emanated from the Hohenzollern district of the Holy Roman Empire. A certain George von Hohenzollern had, she said, fought on the side of Archduke Ferdinand of Austria at the Siege of Vienna in 1529. He had shown great daring in leading an unofficial raid against the Turks and capturing the

Sultan's standard. This (said Aunt Grace) was why he was given the nickname *Tollkühn*, 'foolhardy'; and the name stuck. The family was also supposed to have connections with France and to have intermarried with the nobility in that country, where they acquired a French version of their nickname, *du Téméraire*. Opinion differed among the Tolkiens as to why and when their ancestors had come to England. The more prosaic said it was in 1756 to escape the Prussian invasion of Saxony, where they had lands. Aunt Grace preferred the more romantic (if implausible) story of how one of the du Téméraires had fled across the Channel in 1794 to escape the guillotine, apparently then assuming a form of the old name, 'Tolkien'. This gentleman was reputedly an accomplished harpsichordist and clock-repairer. Certainly the story – typical of the kind of tale that middle-class families tell about their origins – gave colour to the presence of Tolkiens in London at the beginning of the nineteenth century, making their living as clock and watch manufacturers and piano-makers. And it was as a piano-maker and music-seller that John Benjamin Tolkien, Arthur's father, had come to Birmingham and set up business some years later.

The Tolkiens always liked to tell stories that gave a romantic colouring to their origins; but whatever the truth of those stories the family was at the time of Ronald's childhood entirely English in character and appearance, indistinguishable from thousands of other middle-class tradespeople who populated the Birmingham suburbs. In any case Ronald was more interested in his mother's family. He soon developed a strong affection for the Suffields and for what they represented. He discovered that though the family was now to be found chiefly in Birmingham, its origins were in the quiet Worcestershire town of Evesham, where Suffields had lived for many generations. Being in a sense a homeless child – for his journey from South Africa and the wanderings that now began gave him a sense of rootlessness – he held on to this concept of Evesham in particular and the whole West Midland area in general as being his true home. He once wrote: 'Though a Tolkien by name, I am a Suffield by tastes, talents and upbringing.' And of Worcestershire he said: 'Any corner of that county (however fair or squalid) is in an indefineable way "home" to me, as no other part of the world is.'

By the summer of 1896 Mabel Tolkien had found somewhere

cheap enough for herself and the children to live independently, and they moved out of Birmingham to the hamlet of Sarehole, a mile or so beyond the southern edge of the city. The effect of this move on Ronald was deep and permanent. Just at the age when his imagination was opening out, he found himself in the English countryside.

The house they came to was 5 Gracewell, a semi-detached brick cottage at the end of a row. Mabel Tolkien had rented it from a local landowner. Outside the gate the road ran up a hill into Moseley village and thence on towards Birmingham. In the other direction it led towards Stratford-upon-Avon. But traffic was limited to the occasional farm cart or tradesman's wagon, and it was easy to forget the city that was so near.

Over the road a meadow led to the River Cole, little more than a broad stream, and upon this stood Sarehole Mill, an old brick building with a tall chimney. Corn had been ground here for three centuries, but times were changing. A steam-engine had been installed to provide power when the river was low, and now the mill's chief work was the grinding of bones to make manure. Yet the water still tumbled over the sluice and rushed beneath the great wheel, while inside the building everything was covered with a fine white dust. Hilary Tolkien was only two and a half, but soon he was accompanying his elder brother on expeditions across the meadow to the mill, where they would stare through the fence at the water-wheel turning in its dark cavern, or run round to the yard where the sacks were swung down on to a waiting cart. Sometimes they would venture through the gate and gaze into an open doorway, where they could see the great leather belts and pulleys and shafts, and the men at work. There were two millers, father and son. The old man had a black beard, but it was the son who frightened the boys with his white dusty clothes and sharp-eyed face. Ronald named him 'the White Ogre'. When he yelled at them to clear off they would scamper away from the yard, and run round to a place behind the mill where there was a silent pool with swans swimming on it. At the foot of the pool the dark waters suddenly plunged over the sluice to the great wheel below: a dangerous and exciting place.

Not far from Sarehole Mill, a little way up the hill towards Moseley, was a deep tree-lined sandpit that became another favourite haunt for the boys. Indeed, explorations could be made in many directions, though there were hazards. An old farmer who once chased Ronald for picking mushrooms was given the nickname 'the Black Ogre' by the boys. Such delicious terrors were the essence of those days at Sarehole, here recalled (nearly eighty years later) by Hilary Tolkien:

'We spent lovely summers just picking flowers and trespassing. The Black Ogre used to take people's shoes and stockings from the bank where they'd left them to paddle, and run away with them, make them go and ask for them. And then he'd thrash them! The White Ogre wasn't quite so bad. But in order to get to the place where we used to blackberry (called the Dell) we had to go through the white one's land, and he didn't like us very much because the path was narrow through his field, and we traipsed off after corn-cockles and other pretty things. My mother got us lunch to have in this lovely place, but when she arrived she made a deep voice, and we both ran!'

There were few houses at Sarehole beside the row of cottages where the Tolkiens lived, but Hall Green village was only a little distance away down a lane and across a ford. Ronald and Hilary would sometimes buy sweets from an old woman with no teeth who kept a stall there. Gradually they made friends with the local children. This was not easy, for their own middle-class accents, long hair and pinafores were the subject of mockery, while they in their turn were unused to the Warwickshire dialect and the rough ways of the country boys. But they began to pick up something of the local vocabulary, adopting dialect words into their own speech: 'chawl' for a cheek of pork, 'miskin' for dustbin, 'pikelet' for crumpet, and 'gamgee' for cotton wool. This last owed its origins to a Dr Gamgee, a Birmingham man who had invented 'gamgee-tissue', a surgical dressing made from cotton wool. His name had become a household term in the district.

Mabel soon began to educate her sons, and they could have had no better teacher – nor she an apter pupil than Ronald, who could read by the time he was four and had soon learnt to write proficiently. His mother's own handwriting was delightfully unconventional. Having acquired the skill of penmanship from her father, she chose an upright and elaborate style, ornamenting her capitals with delicate curls. Ronald soon began to practise a hand that was, though different from his mother's, to become equally elegant and idiosyncratic. But his favourite lessons were those that concerned languages. Early in his Sarehole days his mother introduced him to the rudiments of Latin, and this delighted him. He was just as interested in the sounds and shapes of the words as in their meanings, and she began to realise that he had a special aptitude for language. She began to teach him French. He liked this much less, not for any particular reason; but the sounds did not please him as much as the sounds of Latin and English. She also tried to interest him in playing the piano, but without success. It seemed rather as if words took the place of music for him, and that he enjoyed listening to them, reading them, and reciting them, almost regardless of what they meant.

He was good at drawing too, particularly when the subject was a landscape or a tree. His mother taught him a great deal of botany, and he responded to this and soon became very knowledgeable. But again he was more interested in the shape and feel of a plant than in its botanical details. This was especially true of trees. And though he liked drawing trees he liked most of all to be *with* trees. He would climb them, lean against them, even talk to them. It saddened him to discover that not everyone shared his feelings towards them. One incident in particular remained in his memory: 'There was a willow hanging over the mill-pool and I learned to climb it. It belonged to a butcher on the Stratford Road, I think. One day they cut it down. They didn't do anything with it: the log just lay there. I never forgot that.'

Outside the school-room hours his mother gave him plenty of story-books. He was amused by *Alice in Wonderland*, though he had no desire to have adventures like Alice. He did not enjoy *Treasure Island*, nor the stories of Hans Andersen, nor *The Pied Piper*. But he liked Red Indian stories and longed to shoot with a bow and arrow. He was even more pleased by the 'Curdie' books of George Macdonald, which were set in a remote kingdom where misshapen and malevolent goblins lurked beneath the mountains. The Arthurian legends also excited him. But most of all he found delight in the Fairy Books of Andrew Lang, especially the *Red Fairy Book*, for tucked away in its closing pages was the best story he had ever read. This was the tale of Sigurd who slew the dragon Fafnir: a strange and powerful tale set in the nameless North. Whenever he read it Ronald found it absorbing. 'I desired dragons with a profound desire,' he said long afterwards. 'Of course, I in my timid body did not wish to have them in the neighbourhood. But the world that contained even the imagination of Fafnir was richer and more beautiful, at whatever cost of peril.'

Nor was he content merely to *read* about dragons. When he was about seven he began to compose his own story about a dragon. 'I remember nothing about it except a philological fact,' he recalled. 'My mother said nothing about the dragon, but pointed out that one could not say "a green great dragon", but had to say "a great green dragon". I wondered why, and still do. The fact that I remember this is possibly significant, as I do not think I ever tried to write a story again for many years, and was taken up with language.'

The seasons passed at Sarehole. Queen Victoria's Diamond Jubilee was celebrated and the college on top of the hill in Moseley was illuminated with coloured lights. Somehow Mabel managed to feed and clothe the boys on her meagre income, eked out with occasional help from Tolkien or Suffield relatives. Hilary grew to look more and more like his father, while Ronald developed the long thin face of the Suffields. Occasionally a strange dream came to trouble him: a great wave towering up and advancing ineluctably over the trees and green fields, poised to engulf him and all around him. The dream was to recur for many years. Later he came to think of it as 'my Atlantis complex'. But usually his sleep was undisturbed, and through the daily worries of the family's poverty-stricken existence there shone his love for his mother and for the Sarehole countryside, a place for adventure and solace. He revelled in his surroundings with a desperate enjoyment, perhaps sensing that one day this paradise would be lost. And so it was, all too soon.

Christianity had played an increasingly important part in Mabel Tolkien's life since her husband's death, and each Sunday she had taken the boys on a long walk to a 'high' Anglican church. Then one Sunday Ronald and Hilary found that they were going by strange roads to a different place of worship: St Anne's, Alcester Street, in the slums near the centre of Birmingham. It was a Roman Catholic church.

Mabel had been thinking for some time about becoming a Catholic. Nor did she take this step alone. Her sister May Incledon had returned from South Africa, now with two children, leaving her husband Walter to follow when he had completed his business. Unknown to him she too had decided to become a Catholic. During the spring of 1900 May and Mabel received instruction at St

Anne's, and in June of the same year they were received into the Church of Rome.

Immediately the wrath of their family fell upon them. Their father John Suffield had been brought up at a Methodist school, and was now a Unitarian. That his daughter should turn papist was to him an outrage beyond belief. May's husband, Walter Incledon, considered himself to be a pillar of his local Anglican church, and for May to associate with Rome was simply out of the question. Returning to Birmingham he forbade her to enter a Catholic church again, and she had to obey him; though for consolation – or was it revenge? – she turned to spiritualism.

Walter Incledon had provided a little financial help for Mabel Tolkien since Arthur's death. But now there would be no more money from that source. Instead Mabel would have to face hostility from Walter and from other members of her family, not to mention the Tolkiens, many of whom were Baptists and strongly opposed to Catholicism. The strain that this induced, coupled with the additional financial hardship, did no good to her health; but nothing would shake her loyalty to her new faith, and against all opposition she began to instruct Ronald and Hilary in the Catholic religion.

Meanwhile it was time for Ronald to be sent to school. In the autumn of 1899 at the age of seven he took the entrance examination for King Edward's, his father's old school. He failed to obtain a place, for his mother had probably been too easy-going in her teaching. But a year later he took the examination again and passed, entering King Edward's in September 1900. A Tolkien uncle who was uncharacteristically well-disposed towards Mabel paid the fees, which then amounted to twelve pounds per annum. The school was in the centre of Birmingham, four miles from Sarehole, and for the first few weeks Ronald had to walk much of the way, for his mother could not afford the train fare and the trams did not run as far as his home. Clearly this could not continue, and regretfully Mabel decided that their days in the country would have to end. She found a house to rent in Moseley, nearer the centre of the city and on the tram route, and late in 1900 she and the boys packed their belongings and left the cottage where they had been so happy for four years. 'Four years,' wrote Ronald Tolkien, looking back in old age, 'but the longest-seeming and most formative part of my life.'

King Edward's School could scarcely be missed by a traveller arriving in Birmingham on the London & North Western Railway, for it rose majestically above the subterranean smoke and steam of New Street Station. Resembling the dining-hall of a rich Oxford college, it was a heavy and soot-blackened essay in Victorian gothic by Barry, architect of the rebuilt Houses of Parliament.[1] The school, founded by Edward VI, was generously endowed, and the governors had been able to open branch-schools in many of the poorer parts of the city. But the educational standard of King Edward's itself, the 'High School', was still unrivalled in Birmingham, and many of the hundreds of boys who sat on worn benches construing their Caesar while the railway engines whistled below went on to win awards at the major universities.

By 1900 King Edward's had almost outgrown its buildings and was cramped, crowded, and noisy. It presented a daunting prospect to a boy who had been brought up in a quiet country village, and not surprisingly Ronald Tolkien spent much of his first term absent from school because of ill health. But gradually he became accustomed to the rough-and-tumble and the noise, and indeed soon grew to like it, settling down happily to the routine of school, although he did not as yet show any outstanding aptitude in classwork.

Meanwhile, home life was very different from what he had known at Sarehole. His mother had rented a small house on the main road in the suburb of Moseley, and the view from the windows was a sad contrast to the Warwickshire countryside: trams struggling up the hill, the drab faces of passers-by, and in the distance the smoking factory chimneys of Sparkbrook and Small Heath. To Ronald the Moseley house remained in memory as 'dreadful'. And no sooner had they settled than they had to move: the house was to be demolished to make room for a fire-station. Mabel found a villa less than a mile away in a terrace row behind King's Heath Station. They were now not far from her parents' home, but what had dictated her choice was the presence in the road of the new Roman Catholic church of St Dunstan, corrugated outside and pitch-pine within.

Ronald was still desperately forlorn at being severed from the Sarehole countryside, but he found some comfort in his new home.

[1]Barry's building was demolished after the school had moved to new premises in the nineteen-thirties.

25

The King's Heath house backed on to a railway line, and life was punctuated by the roar of trains and the shunting of trucks in the nearby coal-yard. Yet the railway cutting had grass slopes, and here he discovered flowers and plants. And something else attracted his attention: the curious names on the coal-trucks in the sidings below, odd names which he did not know how to pronounce but which had a strange appeal to him. So it came about that by pondering over *Nantyglo, Senghenydd, Blaen-Rhondda, Penrhiwceiber,* and *Tredegar,* he discovered the existence of the Welsh language.

Later in childhood he went on a railway journey to Wales, and as the station names flashed past him he knew that here were words more appealing to him than any he had yet encountered, a language that was old and yet alive. He asked for information about it, but the only Welsh books that could be found for him were incomprehensible. Yet however brief and tantalising the glimpse, he had caught sight of another linguistic world.

Meanwhile his mother was becoming restless. She did not like the King's Heath house and she had discovered that she did not like St Dunstan's Church. So she began to search around, and once again she took the boys on long Sunday walks in search of a place of worship that appealed to her. Soon she discovered the Birmingham Oratory, a large church in the suburb of Edgbaston that was looked after by a community of priests. Surely she would find a friend and a sympathetic confessor among them? What was more, attached to the Oratory and under the direction of its clergy was the Grammar School of St Philip, where the fees were lower than King Edward's and where her sons could receive a Catholic education. And (a deciding factor) there was a house to let next door to the school. So, early in 1902, she and the boys moved from King's Heath to Edgbaston, and Ronald and Hilary, now aged ten and eight, were enrolled at St Philip's School.

The Birmingham Oratory had been established in 1849 by John Henry Newman, then a recent convert to the Catholic faith. Within its walls he had spent the last four decades of his life, dying there in 1890. Newman's spirit still presided over the high-ceilinged rooms of the Oratory House in the Hagley Road, and in 1902 the community still included many priests who had been his friends and had served under him. One of these was Father Francis Xavier Morgan, then aged forty-three, who shortly after the Tolkiens moved into the district took over the duties of parish priest and came to call. In him Mabel soon found not only a sympathetic priest but a valuable friend. Half Welsh and half Anglo-Spanish (his mother's family were prominent in the sherry trade), Francis Morgan was not a man of great intellect, but he had an immense fund of kindness and humour and a flamboyance that was often attributed to his Spanish connections. Indeed he was a very noisy man, loud and affectionate, embarrassing to small children at first but hugely lovable when they got to know him. He soon became an indispensable part of the Tolkien household.

Without his friendship, life for Mabel and her sons would have shown scant improvement on the previous two years. They were living at 26 Oliver Road, a house that was only one degree better than a slum. Around them were mean side-streets. St Philip's School was only a step from their front door, but its bare brick classrooms were a poor substitute for the gothic splendours of King Edward's, and its academic standard was correspondingly lower. Soon Ronald had outpaced his class-mates, and Mabel realised that St Philip's could not provide the education that he needed. So she removed him, and once again undertook his tuition herself: with much success, for some months later he won a Foundation Scholarship to King Edward's and returned there in the autumn of 1903. Hilary too had been removed from St Philip's, but he had so far failed to pass the entrance examination to King Edward's; 'not my fault,' his mother wrote to a relative, 'or that he didn't know the things; but he is so dreamy and slow at writing.' For the time being she continued to teach the younger boy at home.

On his return to King Edward's, Ronald was placed in the Sixth Class, about half way up the school. He was now learning Greek. Of his first contact with this language he later wrote: 'The fluidity of Greek, punctuated by hardness, and with its surface glitter captivated me. But part of the attraction was antiquity and alien remoteness (from me): it did not touch home.' In charge of the Sixth Class was an energetic man named George Brewerton, one of the few assistant masters at the school who specialised in the teaching of English literature. This subject scarcely featured in the curriculum, and when taught it was confined chiefly to a study of Shakespeare's plays, which Ronald soon found that he 'disliked cordially'. In later years he especially remembered 'the bitter disappointment and disgust from schooldays with the shabby use made in Shakespeare of the coming of "Great Birnam Wood to high Dunsinane hill": I longed to devise a setting by which the trees might really march to war.' But if Shakespeare failed to please him there was other meat more suited to his taste. By inclination his form-master Brewerton was a medievalist. Always a fierce teacher, he demanded that his pupils should use the plain old words of the English language. If a boy employed the term 'manure' Brewerton would roar out: 'Manure? Call it muck! Say it three times! *Muck, muck, muck!*' He encouraged his pupils to read Chaucer, and he recited the *Canterbury Tales* to them in the original Middle English. To Ronald Tolkien's ears this was a revelation, and he determined to learn more about the history of the language.

At Christmas 1903 Mabel Tolkien wrote to her mother-in-law:

My dear Mrs Tolkien,

You said you like one of the boys' drawings better than anything bought with their money so they've done these for you. Ronald has really done his splendidly this year – he has just been having quite an exhibition in Father Francis' room – he has worked hard since he broke up on December 16th, and so have I, to find fresh subjects: – I haven't been out for almost a *month* – not even to The Oratory! – but the nasty wet muggy weather is making me better and since Ronald broke up I have been able to rest in the mornings. I keep having whole *weeks* of utter sleeplessness, which added to the internal cold and sickness have made it almost impossible to go on.

I found a postal order for 2/6 which you sent the boys some time ago – a year at least – which has been mislaid. They've been in town all afternoon spending this and a little bit more on things they wanted to give. – They've done all my Xmas shopping – Ronald can match silk lining or any art shade like a true 'Parisian Modiste'. – Is it his Artist or Draper Ancestry coming out? – He is going along at a great rate at school – he knows far more Greek than I do Latin – he says he is going to do German with me these holidays – though at present I feel more like Bed.

One of the clergy, a young, merry one, is teaching Ronald to play chess – he says he has read *too* much, everything fit for a boy under fifteen, and he doesn't know any single classical thing to recommend him. Ronald is making his First Communion this Christmas – so it is a very great feast indeed to us this year. I

don't say this to vex you – only you say you like to know everything about them.
                    Yours always lovingly,
                        Mab.

The New Year did not begin well. Ronald and Hilary were confined to bed with measles followed by whooping-cough, and in
Hilary's case by pneumonia. The additional strain of nursing them
proved too much for their mother, and as she feared it proved
'impossible to go on'. By April 1904 she was in hospital, and her
condition was diagnosed as diabetes.

The Oliver Road house was closed, the scant furniture was
stored, and the boys were sent away to relatives, Hilary to his
Suffield grandparents and Ronald to Hove to stay with the family
of Edwin Neave, the sandy-haired insurance clerk who was now
married to his Aunt Jane. Insulin treatment was not yet available
for diabetic patients, and there was much anxiety over Mabel's
condition, but by the summer she had recovered sufficiently to be
discharged from hospital. Clearly she must undergo a long and
careful convalescence. A plan was proposed by Father Francis
Morgan. At Rednal, a Worcestershire hamlet a few miles beyond
the Birmingham boundary, Cardinal Newman had built a modest
country house which served as a retreat for the Oratory clergy.
On the edge of its grounds stood a little cottage occupied by the
local postman, whose wife could let them have a bedroom and
sitting-room, and could cook for them. It would be an ideal setting
for recuperation, and all three of them would benefit from the
renewed contact with country air. So, late in June 1904, the boys
rejoined their mother and they all went to Rednal for the summer.

It was as if they had come back to Sarehole. The cottage lay on
the corner of a quiet country lane, and behind it were the wooded
grounds of the Oratory House with the little cemetery adjoining
the chapel where the Oratory fathers and Newman himself were
buried. The boys had the freedom of these grounds, and further
afield they could roam the steep paths that led through the trees
to the high Lickey Hill. Mrs Till the postman's wife gave them
good meals, and a month later Mabel was writing on a postcard
to her mother-in-law: 'Boys look *ridiculously* well compared to the
weak white ghosts that met me on train 4 weeks ago!!! Hilary has
got tweed suit and his first Etons today! and looks *immense*. – We've

had perfect weather. Boys will write first wet day but what with Bilberry-gathering – Tea in Hay – Kite-flying with Fr. Francis – sketching – Tree Climbing – they've never enjoyed a holiday so much.'

Father Francis paid them many visits. He kept a dog at Rednal named 'Lord Roberts', and he used to sit on the ivy-covered verandah of the Oratory House smoking a large cherrywood pipe; 'the more remarkable', Ronald recalled, 'since he never smoked except there. Possibly my own later addiction to the Pipe derives from this.' When Father Francis was not in residence and there was no other priest staying at Rednal, Mabel and the boys would drive to mass in Bromsgrove sharing a hired carriage with Mr and Mrs Church, the gardener and caretaker for the Oratory fathers. It was an idyllic existence.

Too soon September brought the school term, and Ronald, now fit and well, had to return to King Edward's. But his mother could not yet bring herself to leave the cottage where they had been so happy, and go back to the smoke and dirt of Birmingham. So for the time being Ronald had to rise early and walk more than a mile to the station to catch a train to school. It was growing dark by the time he came home, and Hilary sometimes met him with a lamp.

Unnoticed by her sons, Mabel's condition began to deteriorate again. At the beginning of November she collapsed in a way that seemed to them sudden and terrifying. She sank into a diabetic coma, and six days later, on 14 November, with Father Francis and her sister May Incledon at her bedside in the cottage, she died.

3
'Private lang.'
– and Edith

'My own dear mother was a martyr indeed, and it is not to everybody that God grants so easy a way to his great gifts as he did to Hilary and myself, giving us a mother who killed herself with labour and trouble to ensure us keeping the faith.'

Ronald Tolkien wrote this nine years after his mother's death. It is some indication of the way in which he associated her with his membership of the Catholic Church. Indeed it might be said that after she died his religion took the place in his affections that she had previously occupied. The consolation that it provided was emotional as well as spiritual. Perhaps her death also had a cementing effect on his study of languages. It was she, after all, who had been his first teacher and who had encouraged him to take an interest in words. Now that she was gone he would pursue that path relentlessly. And certainly the loss of his mother had a profound effect on his personality. It made him into a pessimist.

Or rather, it made him into two people. He was by nature a cheerful almost irrepressible person with a great zest for life. He loved good talk and physical activity. He had a deep sense of humour and a great capacity for making friends. But from now onwards there was to be a second side, more private but predominant in his diaries and letters. This side of him was capable of bouts of profound despair. More precisely, and more closely related to his mother's death, when he was in this mood he had a deep sense of impending loss. Nothing was safe. Nothing would last. No battle would be won for ever.

Mabel Tolkien was buried in the Catholic churchyard at Bromsgrove. Over her grave Father Francis Morgan placed a stone cross

31

of the same design as that used for each of the Oratory clergy in their Rednal cemetery. In her will Mabel had appointed him to be guardian of her two sons, and it proved a wise choice, for he displayed unfailing generosity and affection to them. His generosity took a practical form, for he had a private income from his family's sherry business, and since as an Oratorian he was not obliged to surrender his property to the community he could use his money for his own purposes. Mabel had left only eight hundred pounds of invested capital with which to support the boys, but Father Francis quietly augmented this from his own pocket, and ensured that Ronald and Hilary did not go short of anything essential for their well-being.

Immediately after their mother's death he had to find somewhere for them to live: a tricky problem, for while ideally they should be housed by their own relatives there was a danger that the Suffield and Tolkien aunts and uncles might try to snatch them from the grasp of the Catholic Church. Already there had been some talk of contesting Mabel's will and of sending the boys to a Protestant boarding-school. There was however one relative, an aunt by marriage, who had no particular religious views and had a room to let. She lived in Birmingham near the Oratory, and Father Francis decided that her house would be as good a home as any for the moment. So a few weeks after their mother's death Ronald and Hilary (now aged thirteen and eleven) moved into their aunt's top-floor bedroom.

Her name was Beatrice Suffield. She lived in a dark house in Stirling Road, a long side-street in the district of Edgbaston. The boys had a large room to themselves, and Hilary was happy leaning out of the window and throwing stones at cats below. But Ronald, still numb from the shock of his mother's death, hated the view of almost unbroken rooftops with the factory chimneys beyond. The green countryside was just visible in the distance, but it now belonged to a remote past that could not be regained. He was trapped in the city. His mother's death had severed him from the open air, from Lickey Hill where he had gathered bilberries, and from the Rednal cottage where they had been so happy. And because it was the loss of his mother that had taken him away from all these things, he came to associate them with her. His feelings towards the rural landscape, already sharp from the earlier severance that had taken him from Sarehole, now became emotionally charged with personal bereavement. This love for the memory of the countryside of his youth was later to become a central part of his writing, and it was intimately bound up with his love for the memory of his mother.

Aunt Beatrice gave him and his brother board and lodging, but little more. She had been widowed not long before, and she was childless and poorly off. Sadly, she was also deficient in affection, and she showed little understanding of the boys' state of mind. One day Ronald came into her kitchen, saw a pile of ashes in the grate, and discovered that she had burnt all his mother's personal papers and letters. She had never considered that he might wish to keep them.

Fortunately the Oratory was near, and it soon became Ronald and Hilary's real home. Early in the morning they would hurry round to serve mass for Father Francis at his favourite side-altar in the Oratory church. Afterwards they would eat breakfast in the plain refectory, and then, when they had played their usual game of spinning the kitchen cat around in the revolving food-hatch, they would set off for school. Hilary had passed the entrance examination and was now at King Edward's, and the two boys would walk together down to New Street if there was time, or would take a horse-bus if the clock at Five Ways showed that they were late.

Ronald made many friends at school, and one boy in particular soon became an inseparable companion. His name was Christopher Wiseman. A year younger than Ronald, he was the son of a Wesleyan minister who lived in Edgbaston; he had fair hair, a broad good-natured face, and an energetically critical manner. The two boys met in the Fifth Class in the autumn of 1905, Tolkien achieving first place in the class – he was now showing distinct academic promise – and Wiseman coming second. This rivalry soon developed into a friendship based on a shared interest in Latin and Greek, a great delight in Rugby football ('soccer' was never played at King Edward's), and an enthusiasm for discussing anything and everything. Wiseman was a staunch Methodist, but the two boys found that they could argue about religion without bitterness.

Together they moved class by class up the school. Clearly Ronald Tolkien had an aptitude for languages – his mother had seen that – and King Edward's provided the ideal environment in which this aptitude could flourish. The study of Latin and Greek was the backbone of the curriculum, and both languages were taught particularly well in the First (or senior) Class, which Ronald reached shortly before his sixteenth birthday. The First Class was under the bright eye of the headmaster, Robert Cary Gilson, a remarkable man with a neat pointed beard who was an amateur inventor and an accomplished scientist as well as a skilled teacher of the classics; among his inventions were a windmill that charged batteries to provide electric light for his house, a species of hectograph which duplicated the school exam papers (illegibly, said the boys), and a small gun that could shoot golf balls. When teaching, he encouraged his pupils to explore the byways of learning and to be expert in everything that came their way: an example that made a great impression on Ronald Tolkien. But though he was discursive, Gilson also encouraged his pupils to make a detailed study of classical linguistics. This was entirely in keeping with Tolkien's inclinations; and, partly as a result of Gilson's teaching, he began to develop an interest in the general principles of language.

It was one thing to know Latin, Greek, French and German; it was another to understand *why* they were what they were. Tolkien had started to look for the bones, the elements that were common to them all: he had begun, in fact, to study philology, the science of words. And he was encouraged to do this even more when he made his acquaintance with Anglo-Saxon.

This was thanks to George Brewerton, the master who preferred *muck* to *manure*. Under his tuition Ronald Tolkien had shown an interest in Chaucerian English. Brewerton was pleased by this and offered to lend the boy an Anglo-Saxon primer. The offer was accepted eagerly.

Opening its covers, Tolkien found himself face to face with the language that was spoken by the English before the first Normans set foot in their land. Anglo-Saxon, also called Old English, was familiar and recognisable to him as an antecedent of his own language, and at the same time was remote and obscure. The primer explained the language clearly in terms that he could easily understand, and he was soon making light work of translating the prose examples at the back of the book. He found that Old English appealed to him, though it did not have the aesthetic charm of Welsh. This was rather a historical appeal, the attraction of studying the ancestor of his own language. And he began to find real excitement when he progressed beyond the simple passages in the primer and turned to the great Old English poem *Beowulf*. Reading this first in a translation and then in the original language, he found it to be one of the most extraordinary poems of all time: the tale of the warrior Beowulf, his fight with two monsters, and his death after battle with a dragon.

Now Tolkien turned back to Middle English and discovered *Sir Gawain and the Green Knight*. Here was another poem to fire his imagination: the medieval tale of an Arthurian knight and his search for the mysterious giant who is to deal him a terrible axe-blow. Tolkien was delighted by the poem and also by its language, for he realised that its dialect was approximately that which had been spoken by his mother's West Midland ancestors. He began to explore further in Middle English, and read the *Pearl*, an allegorical poem about a dead child which is believed to have been written by the author of *Sir Gawain*. Then he turned to a different language and took a few hesitant steps in Old Norse, reading line by line in the original words the story of Sigurd and the dragon Fafnir that had fascinated him in Andrew Lang's *Red Fairy Book* when he was a small child. By this time he had acquired a range of linguistic knowledge that was remarkable in a schoolboy.

He continued his search for the 'bones' behind all these languages, rummaging in the school library and exploring the remoter shelves of Cornish's bookshop down the road. Eventually he began to find – and to scrape together enough money to buy – German books on philology that were 'dry-as-dust' but which could provide him with the answers to his questions. Philology: 'the love of words'. For that was what motivated him. It was not an arid interest in the scientific principles of language; it was a deep *love* for the look and the sound of words, springing from the days when his mother had given him his first Latin lessons.

And as a result of this love of words, he had started to invent his own languages.

Most children make up their own words. Some even have rudimentary private languages that they share with each other. This was what Ronald's young cousins Mary and Marjorie Incledon had done. Their language was called 'Animalic', and it was constructed principally out of animal names; for instance

35

Dog nightingale woodpecker forty meant 'You are an ass'. The Incledons now lived outside Birmingham at Barnt Green, the neighbouring village to Rednal, and Ronald and Hilary usually spent part of their holidays there. Ronald learnt 'Animalic' and was amused by it. A little later Marjorie (the elder sister) lost interest in it, and when she dropped out Mary and Ronald collaborated to invent a new and more sophisticated language. This was called 'Nevbosh' or the New Nonsense, and it was soon sufficiently developed for the two cousins to chant limericks in it:

> *Dar fys ma vel gom co palt 'Hoc*
> *Pys go iskili far maino woc?*
> *Pro si go fys do roc de*
> *Do cat ym maino bocte*
> *De volt fact soc ma taimful gyroc!'*

(There was an old man who said 'How/Can I possibly carry my cow?/For if I were to ask it/ To get in my basket/ It would make such a terrible row!')

This kind of thing caused a good deal of amusement at Barnt Green, and as Ronald reached adolescence it gave him an idea. Already when beginning to learn Greek he had entertained himself by making up Greek-style words. Could he not take this further and invent a complete language, something more serious and properly organised than Nevbosh—most of which was only English, French, or Latin in disguise? Such a language might not have any particular use—though the invented language Esperanto was very popular at the time—but it would amuse him and allow him to put all his favourite sounds on paper. Certainly it seemed worth trying: if he had been interested in music he would very likely have wanted to compose melodies, so why should he not make up a personal system of words that would be as it were a private symphony?

In adult life Tolkien came to believe that his impulse towards linguistic invention was similar to that felt by many schoolchildren. He once remarked, while talking about the invention of languages: 'It's not that uncommon, you know. An enormously greater number of children have what you might call a creative element in them than is usually supposed, and it isn't necessarily limited to certain things: they may not want to paint or draw, or have much music, but they nevertheless want to create something. And if the main mass of education takes a linguistic form, their creation will take a linguistic form. It's so extraordinarily common, I once did think that there ought to be some organised research into it.'

When the young Tolkien first set to work at linguistic invention on an organised basis, he decided to take an existing language as a model or at least a starting-point. Welsh was not available to him in sufficient quantity, so he turned to another favourite source of words, the collection of Spanish books in Father Francis's room. His guardian spoke Spanish fluently and Ronald had often begged to be taught the language, but nothing came of it, though he was given the freedom of the books. Now he looked at them again and began work on an invented language that he called 'Naffarin'. It showed a great deal of Spanish influence, but it had its own system of phonology and grammar. He worked at it now and then, and he might have developed it still further had he not discovered a language that excited him far more than Spanish.

One of his school-friends had bought a book at a missionary sale, but found that he had no use for it and sold it to Tolkien. It was Joseph Wright's *Primer of the Gothic Language*. Tolkien opened it and immediately experienced 'a sensation at least as full of delight as first looking into Chapman's *Homer*'. Gothic ceased to be spoken with the decline of the Gothic peoples, but written fragments survived for posterity, and Tolkien found them immensely attractive. He was not content simply to learn the language, but began to invent 'extra' Gothic words to fill gaps in the limited vocabulary that survived, and to move on from this to the construction of a supposedly unrecorded but historical Germanic language. He communicated these enthusiasms to Christopher Wiseman, who was a sympathetic listener since he himself was studying Egyptian and its hieroglyphics. Tolkien also began to develop his invented languages *backwards*; that is, to posit the hypothetical 'earlier' words which he was finding necessary for invention by means of an organised 'historical' system. He was also working on invented alphabets; one of his notebooks from schooldays contains a system of code-symbols for each letter of the English alphabet. But it was languages that occupied him most, and on many days he closeted himself in the room he shared with Hilary and, as he wrote in his diary, 'Did a lot of private lang.'

Father Francis had done a good deal for the Tolkien boys since their mother's death. Every summer he had taken them on holiday to Lyme Regis, where they stayed at the Three Cups Hotel and paid visits to his friends in the neighbourhood. Ronald loved the scenery of Lyme and enjoyed sketching it on wet days, though when it was fine he was happiest rambling along the shore or visiting the spectacular landslip that had recently occurred on the cliffs near the town. Once he found a prehistoric jawbone there, which he supposed to be a piece of petrified dragon. On these holidays Father Francis talked a good deal to the boys, and he observed that they were not happy in the drab lodging that was provided for them by their Aunt Beatrice. Back in Birmingham he looked around for something better. He thought of Mrs Faulkner who lived in Duchess Road behind the Oratory. She gave musical soirées which several of the Fathers attended, and she also let rooms. He decided that her house might be a more pleasant home for Ronald and Hilary. Mrs Faulkner agreed to take them, and early in 1908 the boys moved to 37 Duchess Road.

It was a gloomy creeper-covered house, hung with dingy lace curtains. Ronald and Hilary were given a room on the second floor. The other occupants of the house were Mrs Faulkner's husband Louis (a wine-merchant with a taste for his own wares), their daughter Helen, Annie the maid, and another lodger, a girl of nineteen who lived on the first floor beneath the boys' bedroom and spent most of her time at her sewing-machine. Her name was Edith Bratt.

She was remarkably pretty, small and slim, with grey eyes, firm clear features and short dark hair. The boys learnt that she too was an orphan, her mother having died five years previously and her father some time before that. In fact she was illegitimate. Her mother, Frances Bratt, had given birth to Edith on 21 January 1889 in Gloucester, where she had perhaps gone to avoid scandal, for her home was in Wolverhampton where her family owned a boot and shoe manufacturing business. Frances was aged thirty at the time of Edith's birth. Afterwards she returned to the Birmingham district to brave the gossip of the neighbours and to bring up her daughter in the suburb of Handsworth. Frances Bratt never married, and the child's father was not named on the birth certificate, though Frances preserved his photograph, and his identity was known to the Bratt family. But if Edith knew the name of her father, she never passed it on to her own children.

Edith's childhood had been moderately happy. She was brought up in Handsworth by her mother and her cousin Jennie Grove. The Grove connection was much prized by the Bratts, for it linked them with the renowned Sir George Grove, editor of the musical dictionary. Edith herself proved to have a talent for music. She played the piano very well, and when her mother died she was sent to a girls' boarding-school that specialised in music. By the time she left school she was expected to be able to make a career as a piano teacher or just possibly a concert pianist. But her guardian, the family solicitor, did not seem to know what he should do next. He found a room for her at Mrs Faulkner's, supposing that her landlady's fondness for music would provide a sympathetic atmosphere as well as a piano for practising. But he had no further ideas; nor was there any urgency, for Edith had inherited a small amount of land in various parts of Birmingham, and this produced just enough income to keep her. Nothing more need be done for the moment; and nothing was done. Edith stayed on at Mrs Faulkner's, but she soon found that while her landlady was delighted to have a lodger who could play and accompany soloists at her soirées, the question of actually *practising* the piano was quite different. 'Now Edith dear,' Mrs Faulkner would say, sweeping into the room as soon as the scales and arpeggios began, *'that's enough for now!'* And Edith would go back sadly to her room and her sewing-machine.

Then the Tolkien brothers arrived in the house. She found them very pleasant. In particular she liked Ronald, with his serious face and perfect manners; while Ronald, though he was acquainted with few girls of his age, discovered that familiarity soon conquered any nervousness on his part. He and Edith struck up a friendship.

True, he was sixteen and she was nineteen. But he was old for his age and she looked young for hers, and she was neat and small and exceptionally pretty. Certainly she did not share his interest in languages, and she had received only a rather limited education. But her manner was very engaging. They became allies against 'the Old Lady', as they called Mrs Faulkner. Edith would persuade Annie the maid to smuggle titbits of food from the kitchen to the hungry boys on the second floor, and when the Old Lady was out, the boys would go to Edith's room for secret feasts.

Edith and Ronald took to frequenting Birmingham teashops, especially one that had a balcony overlooking the pavement. There they would sit and throw sugar-lumps into the hats of passers-by, moving to the next table when the sugar-bowl was empty. Later they invented a private whistle-call. When Ronald heard it in the early morning or at bedtime he would go to his window and lean out to see Edith waiting at her own window below.

With two people of their personalities and in their position, romance was bound to flourish. Both were orphans in need of affection, and they found that they could give it to each other. During the summer of 1909 they decided that they were in love.

Writing to Edith long afterwards, Ronald recalled 'my first kiss to you and your first kiss to me (which was almost accidental) + and our goodnights when sometimes you were in your little white nightgown, and our absurd long window talks; and how we watched the sun come up over town through the mist and Big Ben toll hour after hour, and the moths almost used to frighten you away – and our whistle-call – and our cycle-rides – and the fire talks – and the three great kisses.'

Ronald was now supposed to be working for an Oxford scholarship, but it was hard to concentrate on classical texts when one half of his mind was occupied with language-inventing and the other with Edith. There was also a new attraction for him at school: the Debating Society, highly popular with the senior boys. He had not yet spoken in debates, perhaps because of his still-squeaky adolescent voice and his reputation, already acquired, as an indistinct talker. But this term, spurred on by a new-found confidence, he made his maiden speech on a motion supporting the objects and tactics of the suffragettes. It was judged a good effort, though the school magazine thought that his talents as a debater were 'somewhat marred by a faulty delivery'. In another speech, on the motion (probably of his own devising) 'That this House deplores the occurrence of the Norman Conquest' he attacked (so the magazine reported) 'the influx of polysyllabic barbarities which ousted the more honest if humbler native words'; while in a debate on the authorship of Shakespeare's plays he 'poured a sudden flood of unqualified abuse upon Shakespeare, upon his filthy birthplace, his squalid surroundings, and his sordid character'. He also achieved much success on the Rugby football field. He was thin, almost scrawny, but he had already learnt to compensate for lack of weight by playing with ferocity. Now he made an extra effort, which was rewarded when he got into the school team. Once there, he played as he had never played before. Reflecting on this years later, he ascribed it directly to the impulse of chivalry: 'Having the romantic upbringing, I made a boy-and-girl affair serious, and made it the source of effort.'

Then one day towards the end of the autumn term of 1909 he arranged secretly with Edith that they should go for a bicycle ride into the countryside. 'We thought we had managed things very cleverly,' he wrote. 'Edith had ridden off on her bicycle nominally to visit her cousin Jennie Grove. After an interval I rode off "to the school sports-ground", but we reassembled and made for the Lickeys.' They spent the afternoon on the hills and then went into Rednal village in search of tea, which they were given at a house where Ronald had stayed some months previously while working for his scholarship. Afterwards they rode home, arriving separately at Duchess Road so as not to arouse suspicion. But they had reckoned without gossip. The woman who had given them tea told Mrs Church, the caretaker at the Oratory House, that Master Ronald had been to call and had brought an unknown girl with him. Mrs Church happened to mention it to the cook at the Oratory itself. And the cook, who always liked telling tales, told Father Francis.

Ronald's guardian had been as a father to him, and his feelings can be imagined when he learnt that the ward on whom he had lavished so much affection, care, and money, was not concentrating his abilities on vital school-work but was (as quickly became apparent upon investigation) conducting a clandestine love affair with a girl three years his senior who was living in the same house. Father Francis summoned Ronald to the Oratory, told him that he was deeply shaken, and demanded that the affair should stop. Then he made arrangements for Ronald and Hilary to move to new lodgings, so as to get Ronald away from the girl.

It may seem strange that Ronald did not simply disobey Father Francis and openly continue the romance. But the social conventions of the time demanded that young people should obey their parents or guardian; moreover Ronald had great affection for Father Francis, and depended on him for money. Nor was he a rebellious young man. Given all this, it is scarcely remarkable that he agreed to do as he was told.

At the height of the storm about Edith, Ronald had to go to Oxford to take the scholarship exam. If he had been in a calmer state of mind he would have revelled in his first view of Oxford. Seen from Corpus Christi College where he was staying, the towers and parapets offered him a prospect of which his school was but a poor shadow. Oxford was new to him in every way, for his ancestors had never been university people. Here now was his chance to win honour for the Tolkiens and the Suffields, to repay Father Francis's affection and generosity, and to prove that his love for Edith had not distracted him from his work. But it was not so easy. Looking at the notice-board after the examination, he saw that he had failed to obtain an award. He turned his back in misery on Merton Street and Oriel Square and walked to the railway station, perhaps wondering if he would ever return.

But in truth his failure was neither surprising nor disastrous. Competition for Oxford scholarships was always extremely severe, and this had been only his first attempt. He could try again next December, although by that time he would be nearly nineteen, and if he failed once more to win an award there would be no chance of his going to Oxford, for a commoner's fees would be beyond his guardian's pocket. Clearly he must work much harder.

'Depressed and as much in dark as ever,' he wrote in his diary on New Year's Day 1910. 'God help me. Feel weak and weary.' (It was the first time that he had kept a diary; or at least this is the first of his diaries that was preserved. Now, as later in life, he used it chiefly as a record of sorrow and distress, and when later in the year his gloom dissipated he ceased to keep up the diary entries.) He was faced with a dilemma, for though he and Hilary had moved to new lodgings they were not far from Mrs Faulkner's house, where Edith was still living. Father Francis had demanded that the love affair be broken off, yet he had not specifically forbidden Ronald to see Edith. Ronald hated to deceive his guardian, but he and Edith decided to meet clandestinely. They spent an afternoon together, taking a train into the countryside and discussing their plans. They also visited a jeweller's shop, where Edith bought Ronald a pen for his eighteenth birthday, and he purchased a ten-and-sixpenny wrist-watch for her twenty-first, which they celebrated in a tea-shop the next day. Edith had now decided to accept an invitation to go and live in Cheltenham with an elderly solicitor and his wife, who had befriended her. When she told this to Ronald he wrote 'Thank God' in his diary, for it was the best solution.

But once again they had been seen together. This time Father Francis made his attitude quite clear: Ronald must not meet or even write to Edith. He could only see her once more, to say good-bye on the day she left for Cheltenham. After that they must not communicate again until he was twenty-one, when his guardian would no longer be responsible for him. This meant a wait of three years. Ronald wrote in his diary: 'Three years is awful.'

A more rebellious young man might have refused to obey; even Ronald, loyal to Father Francis, found it hard to obey his guardian's wishes. On 16 February he wrote: 'Last night prayed would see E. by accident. Prayer answered. Saw her at 12.55 at Prince of Wales. Told her I could not write and arranged to see her off on Thursday fortnight. Happier but so much long to see her just once to cheer her up. Cannot think of anything else.' Then on 21 February: 'I saw a dejected little figure sloshing along in a mac and tweed hat and could not resist crossing and saying a word of love and cheerfulness. This cheered me up a little for a while. Prayed and thought hard.' And on 23 February: 'I met her coming from the Cathedral to pray for me.'

Though these meetings were accidental, there was the worst possible consequence. On 26 February Ronald 'had a dreadful letter from Fr. F saying I had been seen with a girl again, calling it evil and foolish. Threatening to cut short my University career if I did not stop. Means I cannot see E. Nor write at all. God help me. Saw E. at midday but would not be with her. I owe all to Fr. F and so must obey.' When Edith learnt what had happened she wrote to Ronald: 'Our hardest time of all has come.'

On Wednesday 2 March, Edith set out from Duchess Road to go to her new home in Cheltenham. In spite of his guardian's ban, Ronald prayed that he might catch a final glimpse of her. When the time for her departure came he searched the streets, at first in vain. But then: 'At Francis Road corner she passed me on bike on way to station. I shall not see her again perhaps for three years.'

4

'T.C., B.S., etc.'

Father Francis was not a clever man, and he did not perceive that by compelling Ronald and Edith to part he was transforming a boy-and-girl love-affair into a thwarted romance. Ronald himself wrote thirty years later: 'Probably nothing else would have hardened the will enough to give such an affair (however genuine a case of true love) permanence.'

In the weeks after Edith's departure he was morbid and depressed. There was little help to be gained from Father Francis, who was still deeply offended at the deception that had been practised upon him. At Easter, Ronald asked for his guardian's permission to write to Edith, and this was granted, though grudgingly. He wrote; and she replied, saying that she was happy in her new home, and that 'all that horrid time at Duchess Road seems only a dream now'.

Indeed she came to find life at Cheltenham to be most congenial. She was staying in the house of C. H. Jessop and his wife, whom she called 'Uncle' and 'Auntie' though they were not actually related to her. 'Uncle' was inclined to be grumpy but 'Auntie' always made up for this with kindness. There were few guests at the house beyond the vicar and elderly friends of the Jessops, but Edith could find companionship of her own age with her school-friend Molly Field whose family lived nearby. She practised the piano every day, took lessons on the organ, and began to play for services at the Anglican parish church, which she attended regularly. She involved herself in church affairs, assisting at the Boys' Club and the choir outings. She joined the Primrose League and went to Conservative Party meetings. She was making a life of her own, a better life than she had known before, which she would find it hard to relinquish when the time came.

For Ronald, school now became the centre of life. Relations with Father Francis were still strained, and the Oratory could not entirely retain its former place in his affections. But at King Edward's he found good company and friendship. It was a day-school, and there were no 'Tarts' or 'Bloods' such as revolted C. S. Lewis at his boarding-school (later described by him in *Surprised by Joy*). Certainly the older boys did have prestige in the eyes of the younger, but it was the prestige of age and achievement rather than of caste, while as to homosexuality Tolkien claimed that at nineteen he did not even know the word. Nevertheless it was into an all-male society that he now threw himself. At the age when many young men were discovering the charms of female company he was endeavouring to forget them and to push romance into the back of his mind. All the pleasures and discoveries of the next three years – and they were vital years in his development, as vital as the years with his mother – were to be shared not with Edith but with others of his sex, so that he came to associate male company with much that was good in life.

The school library was an important institution at King Edward's. Nominally under the control of an assistant master, it was in practice administered chiefly by a number of senior boys who were granted the title of Librarian. In 1911 these included Ronald Tolkien, Christopher Wiseman, R. Q. Gilson (son of the headmaster), and three or four others. This little clique formed itself into an unofficial group called the Tea Club. Here is Wiseman's account of its origins, told sixty-four years later:

'It started in the summer term, with very great daring. Exams went on for six weeks, and if you were not having an exam you really had nothing to do; so we started having tea in the school library. People used to bring "subventions": I remember someone brought a tin of fish and we didn't care for it, so up it went on a shelf on top of some books, and stayed there until it was nosed out a long time later! We used to boil a kettle on a spirit-stove; but the great problem was what you were to do with the tea-leaves. Well, the Tea Club often went on after school, and the cleaners would come round with their mops and buckets and brooms, throwing sawdust down and sweeping it all up; so we used to put the tea-leaves in their buckets. Those first teas were in the library cubbyhole. Then, as it was the summer term, we went out and had tea at Barrow's Stores in Corporation Street. In the Tea Room there was a sort of compartment, a table for six between two large settles, quite secluded; and it was known as the Railway Carriage. This became a favourite place for us, and we changed our title to the Barrovian Society, after Barrow's Stores. Later, I was editor of the School Chronicle, and I had to print a list of people who had gained various distinctions; so against the people in the list who were members I put an asterisk, and at the bottom of the page by the asterisk it said: "Also members of the T.C., B.S., etc." It was a seven-day wonder what it stood for!'

The membership of this curious and unofficial body fluctuated a little, but it soon achieved a constant nucleus in the persons of Tolkien, Wiseman, and Robert Quilter Gilson. 'R. Q.' had inherited from his father a lively face and a quick brain, but perhaps in reaction to the paternal enthusiasm for scientific invention he devoted his private energies to drawing and design, at which he displayed a talent. He was quiet-spoken but witty, fond of Renaissance painting and the eighteenth century. Here his tastes and expertise contrasted with those of the other two. Wiseman was knowledgeable about natural sciences and music; he had become an excellent mathematician and an amateur composer. 'John Ronald', as they called Tolkien, was versed in Germanic languages and philology, and had immersed himself thoroughly in Northern writings. Yet common to these three enthusiastic schoolboys was a thorough knowledge of Latin and Greek literature; and from this balance of similar and dissimilar tastes, shared and unshared knowledge, friendship grew.

Tolkien's contribution to the 'T.C.B.S.', as they came to call it, reflected the wide range of reading he had already encompassed. He delighted his friends with recitations from *Beowulf*, the *Pearl*, and *Sir Gawain and the Green Knight*, and recounted horrific episodes from the Norse *Völsungasaga*, with a passing jibe at Wagner whose interpretation of the myths he held in contempt. These erudite performances in no way struck his friends as odd; indeed, in Wiseman's words, 'the T.C.B.S. accepted it as yet another instance of the fact that the T.C.B.S. itself was odd'. Perhaps it was; though such coteries were (and are) not uncommon among well-educated adolescents, who are going through a stage of enthusiastic intellectual discovery.

Later a fourth member was added to the group. This was Geoffrey Bache Smith, a year younger than Gilson and nearly three years junior to Tolkien. He was not a classicist like the others, but came from the Modern side of the school. He lived with his brother and their widowed mother in West Bromwich and possessed what his friends considered to be a Midland wit. The T.C.B.S. took him into its ranks partly for this and partly because he had a qualification all too rare at King Edward's: he was knowledgeable about English literature, especially poetry; indeed he himself was a practising poet of some competence. Under the influence of 'G. B. S.' the T.C.B.S. began to wake up to the significance of poetry – as indeed Tolkien was already doing.

Only two masters at King Edward's made any serious attempt to teach English literature. One was George Brewerton and the other was R. W. Reynolds. Once a literary critic on a London journal, 'Dickie' Reynolds tried to instil into his pupils some idea of taste and style. He was not particularly successful with Ronald Tolkien, who preferred Latin and Greek poetry to Milton and Keats. But Reynolds's lessons may have had something to do with the fact that when he was eighteen Tolkien began tentatively to write verse. He did not write much, and it was not very good, certainly no better than the average juvenile efforts of the time. Indeed, there was only one sign of anything even faintly unlikely, and that came in July 1910 when he wrote a descriptive piece about a forest scene, entitled 'Wood-sunshine'. It included these lines:

> Come sing ye light fairy things tripping so gay,
> Like visions, like glinting reflections of joy
> All fashion'd of radiance, careless of grief,
> O'er this green and brown carpet; nor hasten away.
> O! come to me! dance for me! Sprites of the wood,
> O! come to me! Sing to me once ere ye fade!

Fairy spirits dancing on a woodland carpet seem a strange choice of subject for a rugger-playing youth of eighteen who had a strong taste for Grendel and the dragon Fafnir. Why should Tolkien want to write about them?

J. M. Barrie may have had a little to do with it. In April 1910 Tolkien saw *Peter Pan* at a Birmingham theatre, and wrote in his diary: 'Indescribable but shall never forget it as long as I live. Wish

E. had been with me.' But perhaps of more importance was his enthusiasm for the Catholic mystic poet Francis Thompson. By the end of his school career he was familiar with Thompson's verse, and later he became something of an expert on him. In 'Wood-sunshine' there is a distinct resemblance to an episode in the first part of Thompson's 'Sister Songs' where the poet sees first a single elf and then a swarm of woodland sprites in the glade; when he moves, they vanish. It may be that this was a source of Tolkien's interest in such things. Whatever their origins, dancing elves were to appear many times in his early poems.

His principal concern during 1910 was to work hard in preparation for a second attempt at the Oxford scholarship. He put in as many hours of private study as he could manage, but there were numerous distractions, not least Rugby football. He spent many afternoons on the muddy school sports ground in Eastern Road, from which there was a long ride home, often in the dark with the oil-lamp flickering on the back of his bicycle. Rugby sometimes led to injuries: he broke his nose in one match, and it never entirely regained its original shape; on another occasion he cut his tongue, and though the wound healed satisfactorily he later ascribed to it much of his indistinctness of speech. (Though in truth he was known as an indistinct speaker before he cut his tongue, and his poor articulation was really due to having too much to say rather than to experiencing any physical difficulty in saying it. He could and did recite poetry with the greatest clarity.) He was also spending a good deal of time working at languages, both historical and invented. In the Lent term of 1910 he delivered to the First Class at King Edward's a lecture with the weighty title: 'The Modern Languages of Europe – Derivations and Capabilities'. It took three one-hour lessons to read, and even then the master in charge stopped him before he could reach the 'Capabilities'. He also devoted much time to the Debating Society. There was a custom at King Edward's of holding a debate entirely in Latin, but that was almost too easy for Tolkien, and in one debate when taking the role of Greek Ambassador to the Senate he spoke entirely in Greek. On another occasion he astonished his schoolfellows when, in the character of a barbarian envoy, he broke into fluent Gothic; and on a third occasion he spoke in Anglo-Saxon. These activities occupied many hours, and he could not say that he had really spent long enough preparing for the scholarship. Nevertheless he set out for Oxford in December 1910 with rather more confidence in his chances.

This time he was successful. On 17 December 1910 he learnt that he had been awarded an Open Classical Exhibition to Exeter College. The result was not as pleasing as it might have been, for he was sufficiently accomplished to have won a valuable scholarship, and this Exhibition (a slightly inferior award) was worth only sixty pounds a year. However it was no mean achievement, and with the aid of a school-leaving bursary from King Edward's and additional help from Father Francis it would be possible for him to go up to Oxford.

Now that his immediate future was assured he was no longer under pressure in his school-work. But there was still plenty to occupy him in his final terms at King Edward's. He became a prefect, Secretary of the Debating Society, and Football Secretary. He read a paper to the school Literary Society on Norse Sagas, illustrating it with readings in the original language. And at about this time he discovered the Finnish *Kalevala* or Land of Heroes, the collection of poems which is the principal repository of Finland's mythology. Not long afterwards he wrote appreciatively of 'this strange people and these new gods, this race of unhypocritical low-brow scandalous heroes', adding 'the more I read of it, the more I felt at home and enjoyed myself'. He had discovered the *Kalevala* in W. H. Kirby's Everyman translation, and he determined to find an edition in the original Finnish as soon as possible.

The summer term of 1911 was his last at King Edward's. It ended as was usual with the performance of a Greek play with the choruses set to music-hall tunes. This time the choice was Aristophanes' *The Peace*, in which Tolkien took the part of Hermes. Afterwards (another King Edward's custom) the National Anthem was sung in Greek, and then the curtain dropped on his school career. 'The school-porter was sent by waiting relatives to find me,' he recalled years later. 'He reported that my appearance might be delayed. "Just now," he said, "he's the life and soul of the party." Tactful. In fact, having just taken part in a Greek play, I was clad in a himation and sandals, and was giving what I thought a fair imitation of a frenzied Bacchic dance.' But suddenly it was all over. He had loved his school, and now he hated leaving it. 'I felt,' he said, 'like a young sparrow kicked out of a high nest.'

49

In the summer holiday that followed, he made a journey to Switzerland. He and his brother Hilary were among a party organised by a family named Brookes-Smith, on whose Sussex farm Hilary was now working, having left school early to take up agriculture. There were about a dozen travellers: the Brookes-Smith parents, their children, Ronald and Hilary Tolkien and their Aunt Jane (now widowed), and one or two unattached schoolmistresses who were friends of Mrs Brookes-Smith. They reached Interlaken and set out, walking. Fifty-six years later Ronald recalled their adventures:

'We went on foot carrying great packs practically all the way from Interlaken, mainly by mountain paths, to Lauterbrunnen, and so to Mürren and eventually to the head of the Lauterbrunnenthal in a wilderness of morains. We slept rough – the men-folk – often in hayloft or cowbyre, since we were walking by map and avoided roads and never booked, and after a meagre breakfast we fed ourselves in the open. We must then have gone eastward over the two Scheidegge to Grindelwald, with Eiger and Münch on our right, and eventually reached Meiringen. I left the view of Jungfrau with deep regret, and the Silberhorn sharp against dark blue.

'We reached Brig on foot, a mere memory of noise: then a network of trams that screeched on their rails for it seemed at least twenty hours of the day. After a night of that we climbed up some thousands of feet to a "village" at the foot of the Aletsch glacier, and there spent some nights in a châlet inn under a roof and in beds (or rather under them: the *bett* being a shapeless bag under which you snuggled).

'One day we went on a long march with guides up the Aletsch glacier – when I came near to perishing. We had guides but either the effects of the hot summer were beyond their experience, or they did not much care, or we were late in starting. Anyway at noon we were strung out in file along a narrow track with a snow-slope on the right going up to the horizon, and on the left a plunge down into a ravine. The summer of that year had melted away much snow, and stones and boulders were exposed that (I suppose) were normally covered. The heat of the day continued the melting and we were alarmed to see many of them starting to roll down the slope at gathering speed: anything from the size of oranges to large footballs, and a few much larger. They were whizzing across our path and plunging into the ravine. They started slowly, and then usually held a straight line of descent, but the path was rough and one had also to keep an eye on one's feet. I remember the party just in front of me (an elderly schoolmistress) gave a sudden squeak and jumped forward as a large lump of rock shot between us. About a foot at most before my unmanly knees.

'After this we went on into Valais, and my memories are less clear; though I remember our arrival, bedraggled, one evening in Zermatt and the lorgnette stares of the French *bourgeoises dames*. We climbed with guides up to a high hut of the Alpine Club, roped (or I should have fallen into a snow-crevasse), and I remember the dazzling whiteness of the tumbled snow-desert between us and the black horn of the Matterhorn some miles away.'

Before setting off on the return journey to England, Tolkien bought some picture postcards. Among them was a reproduction of a painting by a German artist, J. Madelener. It is called *Der Berggeist*, the mountain spirit, and it shows an old man sitting on a rock under a pine tree. He has a white beard and wears a wide-brimmed round hat and a long cloak. He is talking to a white fawn that is nuzzling his upturned hands, and he has a humorous but compassionate expression; there is a glimpse of rocky mountains in the distance. Tolkien preserved this postcard carefully, and long afterwards he wrote on the paper cover in which he kept it: 'Origin of Gandalf'.

The travelling-party returned to England early in September. Back in Birmingham, Tolkien packed his possessions. Then at the end of the second week in October he accepted a generous lift from his old schoolmaster 'Dickie' Reynolds, who owned a motor car, and was driven to Oxford for the start of his first term.

5
Oxford

Already as the car bowled into Oxford he had decided that he would be happy there. This was a city that he could love and revere after the squalor and the drabness of Birmingham. Admittedly, to the eyes of a casual observer his own college, Exeter, was not the loveliest in the University. Its insipid frontage by George Gilbert Scott and its chapel, a tasteless copy of the Sainte Chapelle, were in truth no more remarkable than Barry's mock-gothic school in Birmingham. But a few yards away was the Fellows' Garden where the tall silver birch rose above the roof-tops and the plane and horse-chestnut stretched their branches over the wall into Brasenose Lane and Radcliffe Square. And to Ronald Tolkien it was his *own* college, his home, the first real home he had known since his mother's death. At the foot of his staircase was his name painted on a board, and up the uneven wooden steps with the broad black banister were his rooms, a bedroom and a plain but handsome sitting-room looking down to the narrow Turl Street. It was perfection.

The majority of undergraduates at Oxford in 1911 were from prosperous upper-class families. Many of them were members of the aristocracy. It was for this class of young man that the University (at this time) primarily catered; hence the comparatively luxurious lifestyle, with 'scouts' (college servants) waiting on undergraduates in their rooms. But besides the rich and aristocratic there was quite a different group of students: the 'poor scholars' who if not actually poor did not come from rich families, and who could only come to the university thanks to financial aid from scholarships. The first group did not always make life pleasant for the second, and had Tolkien (as a scholar from a middle-class background) found himself at one of the more fashionable colleges, he would probably have been the victim of a good deal of snobbery. By contrast, and fortunately for him, there was no such tradition of social distinction at Exeter College.

Yet it was as well for Tolkien that among the second-year men at his college were a couple of Catholics, who sought him out and made sure that he settled in. After that, he made friends quickly, though he had to be careful about money, for he only had a tiny income, and it was not easy to live economically in a society designed for the tastes of the rich. His 'scout' brought breakfast to his rooms every morning, and this could be restricted to a frugal meal of toast and coffee; but there was a tradition of entertaining one's friends to breakfast, and this demanded that something more substantial should be provided at one's own expense. Lunch was a mere 'commons' of bread, cheese, and beer, again brought to his rooms by the scout; while dinner, taken formally in Hall, was not an expensive meal; but it was pleasant at dinner to accept an offer of beer or wine from one's friends, and of course this gesture had to be returned. When the 'battel' or college account was presented for payment each Saturday morning it could be unpleasantly high. Then there were clothes to be bought, and a few pieces of furniture to be found for his rooms, for the college provided only the bare necessities. The cost soon mounted, and although Oxford tradesmen were accustomed to allowing almost unlimited credit they had to be paid in the end. After a year Tolkien wrote that he had 'a good few bills unaccounted for', and added: 'Money matters are not very cheerful.'

He had soon thrown himself wholeheartedly into university activities. He played rugger, though he did not become a leading figure in the college team. He did not row, for that sport above all at Oxford was the preserve of public-school men, but he joined the college Essay Club and the Dialectical Society. He also took part in the Stapeldon, the college debating society; and for good measure he started his own club. It was called the Apolausticks ('those devoted to self-indulgence') and it was chiefly composed of freshmen like himself. There were papers, discussions, and debates, and there were also large and extravagant dinners. It was one degree more sophisticated than the teas in the school library, but it was an expression of the same instinct that had helped to create the T.C.B.S. Indeed Tolkien was at his happiest in groups of cronies where there was good talk, plenty of tobacco (he was now firmly dedicated to a pipe, with occasional excursions into expensive cigarettes), and male company.

At Oxford the company had to be male. Admittedly there were a number of women students attending lectures, but they lived in ladies' colleges, grim enclaves on the outskirts of the city; and they had to be severely chaperoned whenever they approached a young man. In any case the men really preferred each other's company. The majority of them were fresh from the male preserves of the public school and they gladly accepted the masculine tone of Oxford.

They also used among themselves a curious slang, which converted breakfast to *brekker*, lecture to *lekker*, the Union to *the Ugger*, and a sing-song and a practical joke to *a sigger-sogger* and *a pragger-jogger*. Tolkien adopted this manner of speech, and he also joined enthusiastically in the Town versus Gown 'rags' that were popular at the time. Here is his account of a not untypical evening's entertainment:

'At ten to nine we heard a distant roar of voices and knew that there was something on foot so we dashed out of College and were in the thick of the fun for two hours. We "ragged" the town and the police and the proctors all together for about an hour. Geoffrey and I "captured" a bus and drove it up to Cornmarket making various unearthly noises followed by a mad crowd of mingled varsity and "townese". It was chockfull of undergrads before it reached the Carfax. There I addressed a few stirring words to a huge mob before descending and removing to the "maggers memugger" or the Martyr's Memorial where I addressed the crowd again. There were no disciplinary consequences of all this!'

This kind of behaviour, noisy, brash, and boorish, was more common among the upper-class undergraduates than among the 'poor scholars' like Tolkien, the majority of whom avoided such pranks and devoted themselves to their studies; but Tolkien was too sociable to be left out of anything lively that was happening. Partly as a result, he was not doing much work.

He was reading Classics, and he had to go to regular lectures and tutorials, but Exeter College had no resident classical tutor in his first two terms, and by the time the post was filled (by E. A. Barber, a good scholar but a dry teacher) Tolkien had got into slack ways.

By now he was bored with Latin and Greek authors and was far more excited by Germanic literature. He had no interest in lectures on Cicero and Demosthenes and was glad to escape to his rooms where he could go on working at his invented languages. Yet there was one area of the syllabus that interested him. For his special subject he had chosen Comparative Philology, and this meant that he attended classes and lectures given by the extraordinary Joseph Wright.

Joe Wright was a Yorkshireman, a truly self-made man who had worked his way up from the humblest origins to become Professor of Comparative Philology. He had been employed in a woollen-mill from the age of six, and at first this gave him no chance to learn to read and write. But by the time he was fifteen he was jealous of his workmates who could understand the newspapers, so he taught himself his letters. This did not take very long and only increased his desire to learn, so he went to night-school and studied French and German. He also taught himself Latin and mathematics, sitting over his books until two in the morning and rising again at five to set out for work. By the time he was eighteen he felt that it was his duty to pass on his knowledge to others, so he began a night-school in the bedroom of his widowed mother's cottage, charging his workmates twopence a week for tuition. When he was twenty-one he decided to use his savings to finance a term's study at a German university, so he took a boat to Antwerp and walked stage by stage to Heidelberg, where he became interested in philology. So this former mill-hand studied Sanskrit, Gothic, Old Bulgarian, Lithuanian, Russian, Old Norse, Old Saxon, Old and Middle High German, and Old English, eventually taking a doctorate. Returning to England he established himself in Oxford, where he was soon appointed Deputy Professor of Comparative Philosophy. He could afford the lease of a small house in Norham Road, where he engaged a housekeeper. He lived with the native economy of a true Yorkshireman: he used to drink beer which he bought in a small barrel, but he thought that it went too quickly, so he arranged with Sarah the housekeeper that she should buy it and he should pay for each glass as he consumed it. He continued to work without ceasing, beginning to write a series of language primers, among which was the Gothic book that proved such a revelation to Tolkien. Most important of all, he began his English Dialect Dictionary that was eventually published in six huge volumes. He himself had never lost his Yorkshire accent, and he remained fluent in the dialect of his native village. Nightly he sat up into the small hours working. His house was semi-detached, and in the other half of the building lived Dr Neubauer, Reader in Rabbinical Literature. Neubauer's eyes were bad and he could not work by artificial light. When Joe Wright went to bed at dawn he would knock on the wall to wake his neighbour, calling out 'Good morning!', and Neubauer would reply 'Good night!'

Wright married a former pupil. Two children were born to them, but both died in infancy. Nevertheless the Wrights carried on a stoic and lively existence in a huge house built to Joe's design in the Banbury Road. In 1912 Ronald Tolkien came to Wright as a pupil, and ever afterwards remembered 'the vastness of Joe Wright's dining-room table, when I sat alone at one end learning the elements of Greek philology from glinting glasses in the further gloom'. Nor was he ever likely to forget the huge Yorkshire teas given by the Wrights on Sunday afternoons, when Joe would cut gargantuan slices from a heavyweight plum cake, and Jack the Aberdeen terrier would perform his party trick of licking his lips noisily when his master pronounced the Gothic word for fig-tree, *smakka-bagms*.

As a teacher, Wright communicated to Tolkien his huge enthusiasm for philology, the subject that had raised him from penniless obscurity. Wright was always a demanding teacher, which was just what Tolkien needed. He had begun to feel a little superior to his fellow-classicists, with his wide-ranging knowledge of linguistics. But here was somebody who could tell him that he had a long way to go. At the same time Joe Wright encouraged him to show initiative. Hearing that Tolkien had an embryonic interest in Welsh, he advised him to follow it up – though he gave that advice in a characteristically Yorkshire manner: 'Go in for Celtic, lad; there's money in it.'

Tolkien followed this advice, though not exactly in the way that Joe Wright had intended. He managed to find books of medieval Welsh, and he began to read the language that had fascinated him since he saw a few words of it on coal-trucks. He was not disappointed; indeed he was confirmed in all his expectations of beauty. *Beauty:* that was what pleased him in Welsh; the appearance and sound of the words almost irrespective of their meaning. He once said: 'Most English-speaking people, for instance, will admit that *cellar door* is "beautiful", especially if dissociated from its sense (and its spelling). More beautiful than, say, *sky*, and far more beautiful than *beautiful*. Well then, in Welsh for me *cellar doors* are extraordinarily frequent.' Tolkien was so enthusiastic about Welsh that it is surprising that he did not visit Wales during his undergraduate days. But in a way this characterised his life. Though he studied the ancient literature of many countries he visited few of them, often through force of circumstance but perhaps partly through lack of inclination. And indeed the page of a medieval text may be more potent than the modern reality of the land that gave it birth.

During his undergraduate days Tolkien developed his childhood interest in painting and drawing and began to show some skill at it, chiefly in the sketching of landscapes. He also paid a great deal of attention to handwriting and calligraphy, and became accomplished in many styles of manuscript. This interest was a combination of his enthusiasm for words and his artist's eye, but it also reflected his many-sided personality, for as someone who knew him during these years remarked (with only slight exaggeration): 'He had a different style of handwriting for each of his friends.'

His first vacation from the University, at Christmas 1911, was spent in revisiting old haunts. The T.C.B.S. had survived his departure from King Edward's, and the club was now preparing for the biggest event in its short history, a performance of Sheridan's *The Rivals*. R. Q. Gilson, an enthusiast for the eighteenth century, had started it all, and as his father was headmaster there was no difficulty in obtaining permission, although a play by an English dramatist had never before been performed at the school. He and Christopher Wiseman, who were both still pupils at King Edward's, allocated parts to their friends. A clear choice for inclusion was G. B. Smith, not yet really regarded as a member of the T.C.B.S. but already much liked by them. And who was to take the crucial comic role of Mrs Malaprop? Who but their very own John Ronald. So Tolkien, at the end of his first term at Oxford, travelled to Birmingham and joined in the final rehearsals.

There was to be only one performance. As it happened the dress rehearsal finished long before curtain-up time, and, rather than hang about, the T.C.B.S. decided to go and have tea at Barrow's (the department store that had added the 'B' to 'T.C.B.S.') with coats over their costumes. The 'Railway Carriage' was empty when they arrived, so they removed the coats. The astonishment of the waitress and the shop-assistants remained in their memories for the rest of their lives.

Then came the performance. The school magazine reported: 'J. R. R. Tolkien's *Mrs Malaprop* was a real creation, excellent in every way and not least so in make-up. R. Q. Gilson as *Captain Absolute* was a most attractive hero, bearing the burden of what is a very heavy part with admirable spirit and skill; and as the choleric old *Sir Anthony*, C. L. Wiseman was extremely effective. Among the minor characters, G. B. Smith's rendering of the difficult and thankless part of *Faulkland* was worthy of high praise.' The occasion cemented Tolkien's friendship with G. B. Smith. The friendship was to be lasting and productive, and Smith was henceforth regarded as a full member of the T.C.B.S.

In the summer vacation of 1912 Tolkien went into camp for a fortnight with King Edward's Horse, a territorial cavalry regiment in which he had recently enrolled. He enjoyed the experience of galloping across the Kentish plains – the camp was near Folkestone – but it was a wet and windy fortnight and the tents were often blown down in the night. This taste of life on horseback and under canvas was enough for him, and he resigned from the regiment after a few months. When the camp had concluded he went on a walking holiday in Berkshire, sketching the villages and climbing the downs. And then, all too soon, his first year as an undergraduate was over.

He had done very little work and he was getting into lazy habits. At Birmingham he had attended mass several times a week, but without Father Francis to watch over him he found it all too easy to stay in bed in the mornings, particularly after sitting up late talking to friends and smoking in front of the fire. He recorded sadly that his first terms at Oxford had passed 'with practically none or very little practice of religion'. He tried to mend his ways, and he kept a diary for Edith in which he recorded all his misdemeanours and failings. But though she was a shining ideal to him – had they not vowed their love to each other, and did this not commit them to each other? – he was still forbidden to write to her or see her until he was twenty-one, and this would not happen for many months. In the meantime it was easy to while away the terms in expensive dinners, late-night conversations, and hours spent poring over medieval Welsh and invented languages.

At about this time he discovered Finnish. He had hoped to acquire some knowledge of the language ever since he had read the *Kalevala* in an English translation, and now in Exeter College library he found a Finnish grammar. With its aid he began an assault on the original language of the poems. He said afterwards: 'It was like discovering a wine-cellar filled with bottles of amazing wine of a kind and flavour never tasted before. It quite intoxicated me.'

He never learned Finnish well enough to do more than work through part of the original *Kalevala*, but the effect on his language-inventing was fundamental and remarkable. He abandoned neo-Gothic and began to create a private language that was heavily influenced by Finnish. This was the language that would eventually emerge in his stories as 'Quenya' or High-elven. That would not happen for many years; yet already a seed of what was to come was germinating in his mind. He read a paper on the *Kalevala* to a college society, and in it he began to talk about the importance of the type of mythology found in the Finnish poems. 'These mythological ballads,' he said, 'are full of that very primitive undergrowth that the literature of Europe has on the whole been steadily cutting and reducing for many centuries with different and earlier completeness among different people.' And he added: 'I would that we had more of it left – something of the same sort that belonged to the English.' An exciting notion; and perhaps he was already thinking of creating that mythology for England himself.

He spent Christmas 1912 with his Incledon relatives at Barnt Green near Birmingham. As usual in that family, the season was enlivened with theatricals, and this time Ronald himself wrote the play that they performed. It was called 'The Bloodhound, the Chef, and the Suffragette'. Later in life he professed to despise drama, but on this occasion he was not only the author but the leading actor, playing 'Professor Joseph Quilter, M.A., B.A., A.B.C., alias world-wide detective Sexton Q. Blake-Holmes, the Bloodhound', who is searching for a lost heiress named Gwendoline Goodchild. She meanwhile has fallen in love with a penniless student whom she meets while they are living in the same lodging-house, and she has to remain undiscovered by her father until her twenty-first birthday in two days' time, after which she will be free to marry.

This piece of family nonsense was even more topical than the Incledons realised. Not only was Ronald due to celebrate his own twenty-first a few days after the performance, but he also intended to reunite himself with Edith Bratt, for whom he had waited for nearly three years, and who he was quite certain had waited for him. As the clock struck midnight and marked the beginning of 3 January 1913, his coming of age, he sat up in bed and wrote a letter to her, renewing his declaration of love and asking her: 'How long will it be before we can be joined together before God and the world?'

But when Edith wrote in reply, it was to say that she was engaged to be married to George Field, brother of her school-friend Molly.

6
Reunion

He could have decided to forget all about her. His friends did not know of her existence and his aunts and uncles and cousins had never been told about her. Only Father Francis knew, and even though he was no longer Ronald's legal guardian he had no wish that the affair with Edith should begin again. So Ronald could have torn up Edith's letter and left her to marry George Field.

Yet there had been declarations and promises in the Duchess Road days that Ronald felt could not be lightly broken. Moreover Edith had been his ideal in the last three years, his inspiration and his hope for the future. He had nurtured and cultivated his love for her so that it grew in secret, even though it had to be fed solely on his memories of their adolescent romance and a few photographs of her as a child. He now perceived only one course of action: he must go to Cheltenham, beseech her to give up George Field, and ask her to marry him.

In truth he knew that she would say yes. She had hinted as much in her letter, explaining that she had only become engaged to George because he had been kind to her, and she felt 'on the shelf', and there was no other young man that she knew, and she had given up believing that Ronald would want to see her again after the three years had past. 'I began to doubt you, Ronald,' she told him in her letter, 'and to think you would cease to care for me.' But now that he had written to renew his vow of love, she indicated that everything had changed.

So on Wednesday 8 January 1913 he travelled by train to Cheltenham and was met on the platform by Edith. They walked out into the country and sat under a railway viaduct where they talked.

By the end of the day Edith had declared that she would give up George Field and marry Ronald Tolkien.

She wrote to George and sent him back his ring; and he, poor young man, was dreadfully upset at first and his family was insulted and angry. But eventually the matter ceased to be alluded to, and they all became friends once more. Edith and Ronald did not announce their engagement, being a little nervous of family reaction and wanting to wait until Ronald's prospects were more certain. But Ronald returned to his new term at Oxford in 'a bursting happiness'.

One of his first actions on arriving was to write to Father Francis explaining that he and Edith intended to be married. He was very nervous about this, but when Father Francis's reply came it was calm and resigned if far from enthusiastic. This was as well, for although the priest was no longer Ronald's legal guardian, he still gave him much-needed financial support; so it was essential that he tolerate the engagement.

Now that Ronald had been reunited with Edith he had to turn his full attention to Honour Moderations,[1] the first of the two examinations that would earn him his degree in Classics. He tried to cram into six weeks the work that he should have done during the previous four terms, but it was not easy to break the habit of sitting up late talking to friends, and he found it difficult to get up in the morning – though like many others before him he blamed this on the damp Oxford climate rather than on his own late hours. When Honour Moderations began at the end of February he was still poorly prepared for many papers. On the whole he was relieved when he learnt that he had at least managed to achieve a Second Class.

But he knew that he ought to have done better. A First in 'Mods' is not easy to achieve, but it is within the range of an able undergraduate who devotes himself to his work. Certainly it is expected of someone who intends to follow an academic career, and Tolkien already had such a career in mind. However he had achieved a 'pure alpha', a practically faultless paper, in his special subject, Comparative Philology. This was partly a tribute to the excellence of Joe Wright's teaching, but it was also an indication that Tolkien's

---

[1] Honour Moderations, like the majority of Oxford examinations, comprises a number of written papers covering various aspects of the candidate's subject. The classes awarded are (in descending order of merit) from First to Fourth.

greatest talents lay in this field; and Exeter College took note. The college was disappointed that as one of its award-holders he had missed a First, but suggested that if he had earned an alpha in philology he ought to become a philologist. Dr Farnell who was Rector of Exeter (the head of the college) knew that he was interested in Old and Middle English and other Germanic languages, so would it not be sensible if he changed to the English School? Tolkien agreed, and at the beginning of the summer term of 1913 he abandoned Classics and began to read English.

The Honour School of English Language and Literature was still young by Oxford standards, and it was split down the middle. On one side were the philologists and medievalists who considered that any literature later than Chaucer was not sufficiently challenging to form the basis of a degree-course syllabus. On the other were the enthusiasts for 'modern' literature (by which they meant literature from Chaucer to the nineteenth century) who thought that the study of philology and Old and Middle English was 'word-mongering and pedantry'. In some ways it was mistaken to try and squeeze both factions of opinion into the same Honours School. The result was that undergraduates who chose to specialise in 'Language' (that is, Old and Middle English and philology) were nevertheless compelled to read a good deal of modern literature, while those who wanted to read 'Literature' (the modern course) were also obliged to study texts in Sweet's Anglo-Saxon Reader and acquaint themselves with a certain amount of philology. Both courses were compromises, and neither side was entirely satisfied.

There was no question as to which side of the school would claim Tolkien. He would specialise in linguistic studies, and it was arranged that his tutor would be Kenneth Sisam, a young New Zealander who was acting as an assistant to A. S. Napier, the Professor of English Language and Literature. After meeting Sisam and surveying the syllabus Tolkien was 'seized with panic, because I cannot see how it is going to provide me with honest labour for two years and a term'. It all seemed too easy and familiar: he was already well acquainted with many of the texts he would have to read, and he even knew a certain amount of Old Norse, which he was going to do as a special subject (under the Icelandic expert W. A. Craigie). Moreover Sisam did not at first appear to be an inspiring tutor. He was a quiet-spoken man only four years older than Tolkien, certainly lacking the commanding presence of Joe Wright. But he was an accurate and painstaking scholar, and Tolkien soon came to respect and like him. As to the work, Tolkien spent more time at his desk than he had while studying Classics. It was not as easy as he had expected, for the standard of the Oxford English School was very high; but he was soon firmly in command of the syllabus and was writing lengthy and intricate essays on 'Problems of the dissemination of phonetic change', 'The lengthening of vowels in Old and Middle English times', and 'The Anglo-Norman element in English'. He was particularly interested in extending his knowledge of the West Midland dialect in Middle English because of its associations with his childhood and ancestry; and he was reading a number of Old English works that he had not previously encountered.

Among these was the *Crist* of Cynewulf, a group of Anglo-Saxon religious poems. Two lines from it struck him forcibly:

> *Eala Earendel engla beorhtast*
> *ofer middangeard monnum sended.*

'Hail Earendel, brightest of angels / above the middle-earth sent unto men.' *Earendel* is glossed by the Anglo-Saxon dictionary as 'a shining light, ray', but here it clearly has some special meaning. Tolkien himself interpreted it as referring to John the Baptist, but he believed that 'Earendel' had originally been the name for the star presaging the dawn, that is, Venus. He was strangely moved by its appearance in the Cynewulf lines. 'I felt a curious thrill,' he wrote long afterwards, 'as if something had stirred in me, half wakened from sleep. There was something very remote and strange and beautiful behind those words, if I could grasp it, far beyond ancient English.'

He found even more to excite his imagination when he studied his special subject. Old Norse (or Old Icelandic: the names are interchangeable) is the language that was brought to Iceland by the Norwegians who fled from their native land in the ninth century. Tolkien was already moderately acquainted with Norse, and he now made a thorough study of its literature. He read the sagas and the Prose or Younger Edda. He also studied the Poetic or Elder Edda; and so it was that he came upon the ancient storehouse of Icelandic myth and legend.

'The Elder Edda' is the name given to a collection of poems, some of them incomplete or textually corrupt, whose principal manuscript dates from the thirteenth century. But many of the poems themselves are more ancient, perhaps originating at a period earlier than the settlement of Iceland. Some are heroic, describing the world of men, while others are mythological, treating of the deeds of gods. Among the mythological lays in the Elder Edda none is more remarkable than the *Völuspa* or Prophecy of the Seeress, which tells the story of the cosmos from its creation, and foretells its doom. The most remarkable of all Germanic mythological poems, it dates from the very end of Norse heathendom, when Christianity was taking the place of the old gods; yet it imparts a sense of living myth, a feeling of awe and mystery, in its representation of a pagan cosmos. It had a profound appeal to Tolkien's imagination.

In the months following their reunion, the question of Edith's religion caused some concern to her and Ronald. If their marriage was to be blessed by his church she would have to become a Catholic. She was in theory quite happy to do this – indeed she believed that her family had long ago been Catholic. But it was not a simple matter. She was a member of the Church of England, and a very active member. During her separation from Ronald a large proportion of her life had centred on the parish church at her Cheltenham home, and she had made herself useful in church affairs. She had in consequence acquired some status in the parish; and it was a smart parish, typical of the elegant town. Now Ronald wanted her to renounce all this and to go to a church where nobody knew her; and looking at it from that point of view she did not relish the prospect. She was also afraid that her 'Uncle' Jessop in whose house she lived might be very angry, for like many others of his age and class he was strongly anti-Catholic. Would he allow her to go on living under his roof until her marriage if she 'poped'? It was an awkward situation, and she suggested to Ronald that the matter might be delayed until they were officially engaged or the time of their marriage was near. But he would not hear of this. He wanted her to act quickly. He despised the Church of England, calling it 'a pathetic and shadowy medley of half-remembered traditions and mutilated beliefs'. And if Edith were persecuted for her decision to become a Catholic, why then, that was precisely what had happened to his own dear mother, and *she* had endured it. 'I do so dearly believe,' he wrote to Edith, 'that no half-heartedness and no worldly fear must turn us aside from following the light unflinchingly.' (He himself was once more attending mass regularly and had perhaps chosen to forget his lapses of the previous year.) Clearly the question of Edith becoming a Catholic was an emotional matter to him; perhaps it was also in part, though he would not have admitted it, a test of her love after her unfaithfulness in becoming engaged to George Field.

So she did what he wanted. She told the Jessops that she intended to become a Catholic, and 'Uncle' reacted just as she had feared, for he ordered her to leave his house as soon as she could find some other accommodation. Faced with this crisis, Edith decided to set up home with her middle-aged cousin Jennie Grove, a tiny determined woman with a deformed back. Together they began to look for rooms. There seems to have been some suggestion that they might come to Oxford so that Edith could be near Ronald, but she does not appear to have wanted this. Perhaps she was resentful of the pressure he had brought to bear on her over the matter of Catholicism, and certainly she wanted to maintain an independent life until they were married. She and Jennie chose Warwick, which was not far from their native Birmingham but was far more attractive than that city. After a search they managed to find temporary rooms, and Ronald joined them there in June 1913.

He found Warwick, its trees, its hill, and its castle, to be a place of remarkable beauty. The weather was hot and he went punting with Edith down the Avon. Together they attended Benediction in the Roman Catholic church, 'from which' (he wrote) 'we came away serenely happy, for it was the first time that we had ever been able to go calmly side by side to church.' But they also had to spend some time searching for a house for Edith and Jennie, and when a suitable one was found there were innumerable arrangements to be made. Ronald found the hours that passed in domestic concerns to be rather irritating. Indeed he and Edith were not always happy when they were together. They no longer knew each other very well, for they had spent the three years of their separation in two totally different societies: the one all-male, boisterous, and academic; the other mixed, genteel, and domestic. They had grown up, but they had grown apart. From now on each would have to

make concessions to the other if they were to come to a real understanding. Ronald would have to tolerate Edith's absorption in the
daily details of life, trivial as they might seem to him. She would
have to make an effort to understand his preoccupation with his
books and his languages, selfish as it might appear to her. Neither
of them entirely succeeded. Their letters were full of affection but
also sometimes of mutual irritation. Ronald might address Edith
as 'little one' (his favourite name for her), and talk lovingly of her
'little house', but she was far from little in personality, and when
they were together their tempers would often flare. Part of the
trouble lay in Ronald's self-chosen role of sentimental lover, which
was quite unlike the face he showed to his male friends. There was
real love and understanding between him and Edith, but he often
wrapped it up in amatory cliché; while if he had shown her more
of his 'bookish' face and had taken her into the company of his male
friends, she might not have minded so much when these elements
loomed large in their marriage. But he kept the two sides of his life
firmly apart.

After his visit to Warwick Ronald set out for Paris with two
Mexican boys to whom he was to act as tutor and escort. In Paris
they met a third boy and two aunts, who spoke virtually no English. Ronald was ashamed that his own Spanish was only rudimentary, and he found that even his French deserted him when he
was faced with the necessity of speaking it. He loved much of Paris
and enjoyed exploring the city on his own, but he disliked the
Frenchmen he saw in the streets, and wrote to Edith about 'the
vulgarity and the jabber and spitting and the indecency'. Long
before this expedition he had conceived a dislike of France and the
French, and what he now saw did not cure him of his Gallophobia.
Certainly he had some justification for hating France after what
happened next. The aunts and the boys decided to visit Brittany,
and the prospect appealed to him, for the true Breton people are of
Celtic stock and speak a language that is in many respects similar
to Welsh. But in the event their destination proved to be Dinard,
a seaside resort like any other such place. 'Brittany!' Ronald wrote
to Edith. 'And to see nothing but trippers and dirty papers and
bathing machines.' There was worse to come. A few days after
their arrival he was walking in the street with one of the boys and
the older aunt. A car mounted the pavement and struck the aunt,
running her over and causing acute internal injury. Ronald helped

to take her back to the hotel but she died a few hours later. The holiday ended in distraught arrangements for the body to be shipped back to Mexico. Ronald brought the boys back to England, telling Edith: 'Never again except I am in the direst poverty will I take any such job.'

In the autumn of 1913 his friend G. B. Smith came up to Oxford from King Edward's School to be an Exhibitioner of Corpus Christi College where he was to read English. The T.C.B.S. was now equally represented at Oxford and Cambridge, for R. Q. Gilson and Christopher Wiseman were already at the latter university. The four friends occasionally met, but Tolkien had never mentioned to them the existence of Edith Bratt. Now that the time was approaching for her reception into the Catholic Church they had decided to be formally betrothed, and he would have to tell his friends. He wrote to Gilson and Wiseman, very uncertain as to what to say, and not even telling them his fiancée's name; clearly he felt that it all seemed to have little to do with the male comrade-ship of the T.C.B.S. The others congratulated him, though Gilson remarked with some insight: 'I have no fear at all that such a staunch T.C.B.S.-ite as yourself will ever be anything else.'

Edith was instructed in the Catholic faith by Father Murphy, the parish priest at Warwick, who did the job no more than adequately. Ronald was later to blame much on the poor teaching given her at this time. But he himself did not help her. He found it difficult to communicate to her the deep and passionate nature of his own faith, entwined as it was with the memory of his dead mother.

On 8 January 1914, Edith was received into the Roman Catholic Church. The date had been deliberately chosen by her and Ronald as it was the first anniversary of their reunion. Soon after her reception she and Ronald were officially betrothed in church by Father Murphy. Edith made her first confession and first communion, which she found to be 'a great and wonderful happiness'; and at first she continued in this state of mind, attending mass regularly and often making her communion. But the Catholic church at Warwick was a poor affair compared to the splendours of Chelten-ham (even Ronald called it 'sordid') and although Edith helped with a church club for working girls she made few friends in the congregation. She also began to dislike making her confession. It was therefore all too easy when she was worried about her health (which was often) to postpone going to mass. She reported to

Ronald that getting up to go to church early in the morning and fasting until she had made her communion did not agree with her. 'I want to go,' she told him, 'and wish I could go often, but it is quite impossible: my health won't stand it.'

She was leading a very dreary life. It was good to have her own house and the company of her cousin Jennie, but they often got on each other's nerves, and unless Ronald came for a visit there was no one else to talk to and nothing to do except keep house. She had her own piano and she could practise for hours, but she knew now that she would never make a career as a musician – marriage and raising a family would prevent it – so there was little incentive to do much playing. She was not needed as an organist at the Catholic church. She missed the social life of Cheltenham, and she did not have enough money for more than occasional visits to concerts or the theatre. So she was irritated to receive letters from Ronald describing a life at Oxford that was full of dinner-parties, 'rags', and visits to the cinematograph.

Ronald was becoming distinctly stylish. He bought furniture and Japanese prints for his rooms. He ordered two tailor-made suits, which he found looked very well on him. He started another club with his friend Colin Cullis; it was called the Chequers, and it met on Saturday nights to have dinner in his or Cullis's rooms. He was elected president of the college debating society (an influential body at Exeter) after a faction-fight which gave him his first taste of college politics, a taste that he liked very much. He punted, he played tennis, and now and then he did some work, enough to win the Skeat Prize for English awarded by his college in the spring of 1914. He used the five pounds of prize money to buy books of medieval Welsh and several of the works of William Morris: *The Life and Death of Jason*, Morris's translation of the *Völsungasaga*, and his prose-and-verse romance *The House of the Wolfings*.

Morris had himself been an undergraduate at Exeter College, and this connection had probably stimulated Tolkien's interest in him. But until now he had apparently not become acquainted with Morris's imaginative writings. Indeed his knowledge of modern literature in general was limited, for the Oxford English School syllabus did not require that he, as a linguist, should make more than a comparatively superficial study of post-Chaucerian writers. During this time he did make a few sketchy notes on Johnson, Dryden, and Restoration drama, but there is no indication that he had more than a passing interest in them. As to contemporary fiction, he wrote to Edith: 'I so rarely read a novel, as you know.' For him English literature ended with Chaucer; or to put it another way, he received all the enjoyment and stimulus that he could possibly require from the great poems of the Old and Middle English periods, and from the early literature of Iceland.

But that was the very reason that he now found *The House of the Wolfings* so absorbing. Morris's view of literature coincided with his own. In this book Morris had tried to recreate the excitement he himself had found in the pages of early English and Icelandic narratives. *The House of the Wolfings* is set in a land which is threatened by an invading force of Romans. Written partly in prose and partly in verse, it centres on a House or family-tribe that dwells by a great river in a clearing of the forest named Mirkwood, a name taken from ancient Germanic geography and legend. Many elements in the story seem to have impressed Tolkien. Its style is highly idiosyncratic, heavily laden with archaisms and poetic inversions in an attempt to recreate the aura of ancient legend. Clearly Tolkien took note of this, and it would seem that he also appreciated another facet of the writing: Morris's aptitude, despite the vagueness of time and place in which the story is set, for describing with great precision the details of his imagined landscape. Tolkien himself was to follow Morris's example in later years.

His own eye for landscape received a powerful stimulus during the summer of 1914 when, after visiting Edith, he spent a holiday in Cornwall, staying on the Lizard peninsula with Father Vincent Reade of the Birmingham Oratory. He found Cornwall exhilarating. He and Father Vincent went for long walks every day, and he wrote to Edith describing them: 'We walked over the moor-land on top of the cliffs to Kynance Cove. Nothing I could say in a dull old letter would describe it to you. The sun beats down on you and a huge Atlantic swell smashes and spouts over the snags and reefs. The sea has carved weird wind-holes and spouts into the cliffs which blow with trumpety noises or spout foam like a whale, and everywhere you see black and red rock and white foam against violet and transparent seagreen.' He never forgot this sight of the sea and the Cornish coastline, and it became an ideal landscape in his mind.

One day he and Father Vincent explored the villages that lie a short way inland from the Lizard promontory. He recorded of this expedition: 'Our walk home after tea started through rustic "Warwickshire" scenery, dropped down to the banks of the Helford river (almost like a fjord), and then climbed through "Devonshire" lanes up to the opposite bank, and then got into more open country, where it twisted and wiggled and wobbled and upped and downed until dusk was already coming on and the red sun just dropping. Then after adventures and redirections we came out on the bleak bare "Goonhilly" downs and had a four mile straight piece with turf for our sore feet. Then we got benighted in the neighbourhood of Ruan Minor, and got into the dips and waggles again. The light got very "eerie". Sometimes we plunged into a belt of trees, and owls and bats made you creep: sometimes a horse with asthma behind a hedge or an old pig with insomnia made your heart jump: or perhaps it was nothing worse than walking into an unexpected stream. The fourteen miles eventually drew to an end – and the last two miles were enlivened by the sweeping flash of the Lizard Lights and the sounds of the sea drawing nearer.'

At the end of the long vacation he travelled to Nottinghamshire to stay for a few days on the farm that his Aunt Jane was running with the Brookes-Smiths and his brother Hilary. While at the farm he wrote a poem. It was headed with the line from Cynewulf's *Crist* that had so fascinated him: *Eala Earendel engla beorhtast!* Its title was 'The Voyage of Earendel the Evening Star', and it began as follows:

> Earendel sprang up from the Ocean's cup
>   In the gloom of the mid-world's rim;
> From the door of Night as a ray of light
>   Leapt over the twilight brim,
> And launching his bark like a silver spark
>   From the golden-fading sand
> Down the sunlit breath of Day's fiery death
>   He sped from Westerland.

The succeeding verses describe the star-ship's voyage across the firmament, a progress that continues until the morning light blots out all sight of it.

This notion of the star-mariner whose ship leaps into the sky had grown from the reference to 'Earendel' in the Cynewulf lines. But the poem that it produced was entirely original. It was in fact the beginning of Tolkien's own mythology.

7
War

By the time that Tolkien wrote 'The Voyage of Earendel', in the late summer of 1914, England had declared war on Germany. Already young men were enlisting in their thousands, answering Kitchener's appeal for soldiers. But Tolkien's feelings were rather different: he was concerned to stay at Oxford until he could finish his degree, being hopeful of a First Class. So, though his aunts and uncles expected him to join up (his brother Hilary had already enlisted as a bugler) he went back to the University for the Michaelmas term.

At first he reported: 'It is awful. I really don't think I shall be able to go on: work seems impossible. Not a single man I know is up except Cullis.' But he became more cheerful when he learnt of the existence of a scheme whereby he could train for the army while at the University but defer his call-up until after he had taken his degree. He signed on for it.

Once he had decided what to do, life become more pleasant. He had now moved from his college rooms to 'digs' in St John's Street which he shared with Colin Cullis, who had not joined the army because of poor health. Tolkien found digs 'a delicious joy compared with the primitive life of college'. He was also delighted to discover that his T.C.B.S. friend G. B. Smith was still up at Oxford awaiting a commission. Smith was to join the Lancashire Fusiliers, and Tolkien resolved to try for a commission in the same regiment, if possible the same battalion.

A few days after the start of term he began to drill in the University Parks with the Officers' Training Corps. This had to be combined with his normal academic work, but he found that the double life suited him. 'Drill is a godsend,' he wrote to Edith. 'I have been up a fortnight nearly, and have not yet got a touch even of the real Oxford "sleepies".' He was also trying his hand at writing. His enthusiasm for William Morris had given him the idea of adapting one of the stories from the Finnish *Kalevala* into a Morris-style prose-and-verse romance. He chose the story of Kullervo, a hapless young man who unknowingly commits incest and, when he discovers, throws himself on to his sword. Tolkien began work on 'The Story of Kullervo' as he called it, and though it was little more than a pastiche of Morris it was his first essay in the writing of a legend in verse and prose. He left it unfinished.

At the beginning of the Christmas vacation of 1914 he travelled to London to attend a gathering of the T.C.B.S. Christopher Wiseman's family had moved south, and at their Wandsworth house there assembled all four members of the 'club': Tolkien, Wiseman, R. Q. Gilson, and G. B. Smith. They spent the weekend chiefly in sitting around the gas fire in the little upstairs room, smoking their pipes and talking. As Wiseman said, they felt 'four times the intellectual size' when they were together.

It was curious how they had gone on meeting and writing to each other, this little group of school-friends. But they had begun to hope that together they might achieve something of value. Tolkien once compared them to the Pre-Raphaelite Brotherhood, but the others scoffed at the idea. Yet they did feel that in some way they were destined to kindle a new light. Perhaps it was no more than the last spark of childhood ambition before it was snuffed out by experience of the world, but for Tolkien at least it had an important and practical result. He decided that he was a poet.

Afterwards he explained that this T.C.B.S. meeting late in 1914 had helped him to find 'a voice for all kind of pent up things', adding: 'I have always laid that to the credit of the inspiration that even a few hours with the four brought to us.'

Immediately following the weekend in London he began to write poems. They were in general not very remarkable, and certainly they were not always economical in their use of words. Here are some lines from 'Sea Chant of an Elder Day', written on 4 December 1914 and based on Tolkien's memories of his Cornish holiday a few months previously:

In a dim and perilous region, down whose great tempestuous ways
I heard no sound of men's voices; in those eldest of the days,

> I sat on the ruined margin of the deep voiced echoing sea
> Whose roaring foaming music crashed in endless cadency
> On the land besieged for ever in an aeon of assaults
> And torn in towers and pinnacles and caverned in great vaults.

When Tolkien showed this and other poems to Wiseman, his friend remarked that they reminded him of Symons's criticism of Meredith, 'when he compared M. to a lady who liked to put on all her jewelry after breakfast'. And Wiseman advised: 'Don't overdo it.'

Tolkien was more restrained in a poem describing his and Edith's love for each other, choosing a favourite image to express this:

> Lo! young we are and yet have stood
> like planted hearts in the great Sun
> of Love so long (as two fair trees
> in woodland or in open dale
> stand utterly entwined, and breathe
> the airs, and suck the very light
> together) that we have become
> as one, deep-rooted in the soil
> of Life, and tangled in sweet growth.

Among other poems written by Tolkien at this time was 'The Man in the Moon Came Down Too Soon' (which was eventually published in *The Adventures of Tom Bombadil*). He selected a similarly 'fairy' subject in 'Goblin Feet', a poem that he wrote to please Edith who said that she liked 'spring and flowers and trees, and little elfin people'. 'Goblin Feet' represents everything of this sort that Tolkien soon came to detest heartily, so it is scarcely fair to quote from it; yet it has an undeniable sureness of rhythm, and as it reached print in several anthologies at the time it can be said to be his first published work of any significance:

> I am off down the road
> Where the fairy lanterns glowed
> And the little pretty flittermice are flying:
> A slender band of grey
> It runs creepily away
> And the hedges and the grasses are a-sighing.

The air is full of wings
Of the blundering beetle-things
That go droning by a-whirring and a-humming.
O! I hear the tiny horns
Of enchanted leprechauns
And the padding feet of many gnomes a-coming.

O! the lights! O! the gleams: O! the little tinkling sounds:
O! the rustle of their noiseless little robes:
O! the echo of their feet, of their little happy feet:
O! their swinging lamps in little star-lit globes.

G. B. Smith read all Tolkien's verses and sent him criticisms. He was encouraging, but he remarked that Tolkien might improve his verse-writing by reading more widely in English literature. Smith suggested that he should try Browne, Sidney, and Bacon; later he recommended Tolkien to look at the new poems by Rupert Brooke. But Tolkien paid little heed. He had already set his own poetic course, and he did not need anyone else to steer him.

He soon came to feel that the composition of occasional poems without a connecting theme was not what he wanted. Early in 1915 he turned back to his original Earendel verses and began to work their theme into a larger story. He had shown the original Earendel lines to G. B. Smith, who had said that he liked them but asked what they were really about. Tolkien had replied: 'I don't know. I'll try to find out.' Not try to invent: *try to find out*. He did not see himself as an inventor of story but as a discoverer of legend. And this was really due to his private languages.

He had been working for some time at the language that was influenced by Finnish, and by 1915 he had developed it to a degree of some complexity. He felt that it was 'a mad hobby', and he scarcely expected to find an audience for it. But he sometimes wrote poems in it, and the more he worked at it the more he felt that it needed a 'history' to support it. In other words, you cannot have a language without a race of people to speak it. He was perfecting the language; now he had to decide to whom it belonged.

When talking about it to Edith he referred to it as 'my nonsense fairy language'. Here is part of a poem written in it, and dated 'November 1915, March 1916'. No translation survives, although the words *Lasselanta* ('leaf-fall', hence 'Autumn') and *Eldamar* (the 'elvenhome' in the West) were to be used by Tolkien in many other contexts :

> *Ai lintulinda Lasselanta*
> *Pilingeve suyer nalla ganta*
> *Kuluvi ya karnevalinar*
> *V'ematte singi Eldamar.*

During 1915 the picture became clear in Tolkien's mind. This, he decided, was the language spoken by the fairies or elves whom Earendel saw during his strange voyage. He began work on a 'Lay of Earendel' that described the mariner's journeyings across the world before his ship became a star. The Lay was to be divided into several poems, and the first of these, 'The Shores of Faery', tells of the mysterious land of Valinor, where Two Trees grow, one bearing golden sun-apples and the other silver moon-apples. To this land comes Earendel.

The poem bears comparatively little relation to Tolkien's later mythological concepts, but it includes elements that were to appear in *The Silmarillion*, and it deserves to be quoted as an indication of what was happening in his imagination at this time. It is here printed in its earliest form :

> West of the Moon, East of the Sun
> There stands a lonely Hill
> Its feet are in the pale green Sea;
> Its towers are white and still:
> Beyond Taníquetil
> In Valinor.
> No stars come there but one alone
> That hunted with the Moon,
> For there the Two Trees naked grow
> That bear Night's silver bloom;
> That bear the globéd fruit of Noon
> In Valinor.
> There are the shores of Faery
> With their moonlit pebbled strand
> Whose foam is silver music
> On the opalescent floor
> Beyond the great sea-shadows
> On the margent of the sand
> That stretches on for ever

From the golden feet of Kôr –
Beyond Taníquetil
In Valinor.

O! West of the Moon, East of the Sun
Lies the Haven of the Star;
The white town of the Wanderer
And the rocks of Eglamar:
There Wingelot is harboured
While Earendel looks afar
On the magic and the wonder
'Tween here and Eglamar –
Out, out beyond Taníquetil
In Valinor – afar.

While Tolkien's mind was occupied with the seeds of his mythology he was preparing himself for Schools, his final examination in English Language and Literature. The examination began in the second week of June 1915, and Tolkien was triumphant, achieving First Class Honours.

He could in consequence be reasonably certain of getting an academic job when the war was over; but in the meantime he had to take up his commission as a second lieutenant in the Lancashire Fusiliers. He was posted not as he had hoped to the 19th Battalion in which G. B. Smith was serving, but to the 13th. His training began in July at Bedford, where he was billeted in a house in the town with half a dozen other officers. He learnt to drill a platoon, and attended military lectures. He bought a motor bicycle which he shared with a fellow officer, and when he could get weekend leave he rode over to Warwick to visit Edith. He grew a moustache. For most of the time he looked and behaved like any other young officer.

In August he moved to Staffordshire, and during the succeeding weeks he and his battalion were shifted about from one camp to another with the apparent lack of plan which characterises troop-movements in wartime. Conditions were uniformly uncomfortable, and in the intervals between inedible meals, trench drill, and lectures on machine-guns, there was little to do except play bridge (which he enjoyed) and listen to ragtime on the gramophone (which he did not). Nor did he care for the majority of his fellow officers. 'Gentlemen are non-existent among the superiors,' he told Edith, 'and even human beings rare indeed.' He spent some of his time reading Icelandic – he was determined to keep up with his academic work during the war – but the time passed slowly. 'These grey days,' he wrote, 'wasted in wearily going over, over and over again, the dreary topics, the dull backwaters of the art of killing, are not enjoyable.'

By the beginning of 1916 he had decided to specialise in signalling, for the prospect of dealing with words, messages, and codes was more appealing than the drudgery and responsibility of commanding a platoon. So he learnt Morse code, flag and disc signalling, the transmission of messages by heliograph and lamp, the use of signal-rockets and field-telephones, and even how to handle carrier-pigeons (which were sometimes used on the battlefield). Eventually he was appointed battalion signalling officer.

Embarkation for France was now near, and he and Edith decided to get married before he left, for the appalling death-roll among the British troops made it clear that he might never return. They had in any case waited more than long enough, for he was twenty-four and she twenty-seven. They did not have much money, but at least he was earning regular pay in the Army, and he decided to ask Father Francis Morgan to transfer all of his modest share capital to his own name. He also hoped to get some income from his poetry. His poem 'Goblin Feet' had been accepted by Blackwells for the annual volume of *Oxford Poetry*, and encouraged by this he sent a selection of his verses to the publishers Sidgwick & Jackson. To add to his capital he also sold his share in the motorbike.

He went to Birmingham to see Father Francis about the money, and to tell him that he was going to marry Edith. He managed to arrange the money matters, but when it came to the point he could not bring himself to tell his old guardian about the marriage, and he left the Oratory without mentioning it; he could not forget Father Francis's opposition to the romance six years before. It was not until a fortnight before the wedding that he finally wrote and explained. The letter that came back was kindly; indeed Father Francis wished them both 'every blessing and happiness', and declared that he would conduct the ceremony himself in the Oratory Church. Alas, it was too late. Arrangements had already been made for the marriage to take place in the Catholic church at Warwick.

Ronald Tolkien and Edith Bratt were married by Father Murphy after early mass on Wednesday 22 March 1916. They had chosen a Wednesday because that was the day of the week on which they had been reunited in 1913. There was one unfortunate incident: Edith did not realise that when she signed the register she would have to give her father's name, and she had never told Ronald about her illegitimacy. Confronted by the register she panicked and wrote the name of an uncle, Frederick Bratt; but she could think of nothing to put under the heading 'Rank or profession of father', so she left it blank. Afterwards she told Ronald the truth. 'I think I love you even more tenderly because of all that, my wife,' he wrote to her, 'but we must as far as possible forget it and entrust it to God.' After the wedding they left by train for Clevedon in Somerset where they were to stay for a week, and in the compartment they both doodled (on the back of a greetings telegram) versions of Edith's new signature: *Edith Mary Tolkien . . . Edith Tolkien . . . Mrs Tolkien . . . Mrs J. R. R. Tolkien.* It looked splendid.

8

The breaking of the fellowship

When he got back from his honeymoon, Tolkien found a letter from Sidgwick & Jackson rejecting his poems. He had half expected this, but it was a disappointment. Edith returned to Warwick, but only to wind up her affairs in that town. They had decided that for the duration of the war she would not have a permanent home, but would live in furnished rooms as near as possible to Ronald's camp. She and her cousin Jennie (who was still living with her) came to Great Haywood, a Staffordshire village near the camp where Ronald was posted. There was a Catholic church in the village with a kindly priest, and Ronald had found good lodgings. But scarcely had he seen Edith settled than he received embarkation orders, and late on Sunday 4 June 1916 he set off for London and thence to France.

Everyone in England had known for some time that 'The Big Push' was imminent. A virtual stalemate had continued throughout 1915 on the Western Front, and neither poison-gas at Ypres nor mass slaughter at Verdun had altered the line by more than a few miles. But now that the hundreds of thousands of new recruits had filtered through the training camps and had emerged as a New Army, it was clear that something spectacular was about to happen.

Tolkien arrived at Calais on Tuesday 6 June and was taken to base camp at Étaples. Somehow on the journey his entire kit had been lost: camp-bed, sleeping-bag, mattress, spare boots, washstand, everything that he had chosen with care and bought at great expense had vanished without trace into the interstices of the army transport system, leaving him to beg, borrow, and buy replacements.

The days passed at Étaples, and nothing happened. The nervous excitement of embarkation relapsed into a weary boredom made worse by a total ignorance of what was going on. Tolkien wrote a poem about England, took part in training exercises, and listened to the seagulls wheeling overhead. Along with many of his fellow officers he was transferred to the 11th Battalion, where he found little congenial company. The junior officers were all recruits like himself, some less than twenty-one years old; while the older company commanders and adjutants were in many cases professional soldiers dug out of retirement, men with narrow minds and endless stories of India or the Boer War. These old campaigners were ready to take advantage of any slip made by a recruit, and Tolkien reported that they treated him like an inferior schoolboy. He had more respect for the 'men', the N.C.O.s and privates who made up the other eight hundred or so members of the battalion. A few of them were from South Wales but most were Lancashire men. Officers could not make friends among them, for the system did not permit it; but each officer had a batman, a servant who was detailed to look after his kit and care for him much in the manner of an Oxford scout. Through this, Tolkien got to know several of the men very well. Discussing one of the principal characters in *The Lord of the Rings* he wrote many years later: 'My "Sam Gamgee" is indeed a reflexion of the English soldier, of the privates and batmen I knew in the 1914 war, and recognised as so far superior to myself.'

After three weeks at Étaples the battalion set off for the Front. The train journey was almost unbelievably slow, interrupted by innumerable halts, and it was more than twenty-four hours before the flat featureless landscape of the Pas de Calais gave way to more hilly country where a canalised river with poplar-lined banks flowed alongside the railway. This was the Somme. And already they could hear gunfire.

Tolkien's battalion disembarked in Amiens, were given food from cookers in the main square, and then marched out of the town, heavily laden with their kit, stepping aside or halting when horses came by, pulling ammunition wagons or huge guns. Soon they were in the open Picardy countryside. By the sides of the straight road the houses gave way to fields of scarlet poppies or yellow mustard. It began to rain in torrents, and within moments the dusty surface of the road changed to a white chalky mud. The battalion marched on, dripping and cursing, to a hamlet called Rubempré, ten miles from Amiens. Here they were billeted for the night in conditions that they would soon be accustomed to: straw bunks in barns and sheds for the men, floor-space for camp beds in the farmhouses for the officers. The buildings were ancient and solid with warped beams and mud walls. Outside beyond the cross-roads and the low houses, fields of rain-swept cornflowers stretched away to the horizon. The war was inescapable: there were broken roofs and ruined buildings, while from the near distance came the sound that they had been approaching all day, the whine, crash, and boom of the Allied bombardment of German lines.

They stayed at Rubempré the next day, doing physical training and bayonet practice. On the Friday, 30 June, they moved to another hamlet nearer the front line. Early the next morning the attack began. They were not to be in it, for their task was to wait in reserve and go into battle several days later, by which time the Commander-in-Chief, Sir Douglas Haig, reckoned that the German line would be smashed open and the Allied troops would be able to penetrate deep into enemy territory. But that was not what happened.

At 7.30 a.m. on Saturday 1 July the troops in the British front line went over the top. Rob Gilson of the T.C.B.S., serving in the Suffolk regiment, was among them. They scrambled up ladders from the trenches and into the open, forming up in straight lines as they had been instructed, and beginning their slow tramp for-ward – slow because each man was carrying at least sixty-five pounds of equipment. They had been told that the German defences were already virtually destroyed and the barbed wire cut by the Allied barrage. But they could see that the wire was *not* cut, and as they approached it the German machine-guns opened fire on them.

Tolkien's battalion remained in reserve, moving to a village called Bouzincourt, where the majority bivouacked in a field while a few lucky ones (including Tolkien) slept in huts. There were clear signs that things had not gone according to plan on the battle-front: wounded men in their hundreds, many of them hideously mutilated; troops detailed for grave-digging; and a sinister smell of decay. The truth was that on the first day of battle twenty thousand Allied troops had been killed. The German defences had not been destroyed, the wire had scarcely been cut, and the enemy gunners had shot down the British and French, line after line, as they advanced with slow paces, forming a perfect target.

On Thursday 6 July the 11th Lancashire Fusiliers went into action, but only 'A' Company was sent down to the trenches, and Tolkien stayed at Bouzincourt with the remainder. He re-read Edith's letters with news from home and glanced once again at his collection of notes from the other members of the T.C.B.S. He was worried about Gilson and Smith, who had both been in the thick of the battle – and he was overwhelmingly relieved and delighted when later in the day G. B. Smith actually turned up at Bouzincourt alive and uninjured. Smith stayed for a few days' rest period before returning to the lines, and he and Tolkien met and talked as often as they could, discussing poetry, the war, and the future. Once they walked in a field where poppies still waved in the wind despite the battle that was turning the countryside into a featureless desert of mud. They waited anxiously for news of Rob Gilson. On the Sunday night 'A' Company came back from the trenches; a dozen of their number had been killed and more than a hundred wounded, and they told tales of horror. Then at last, on Friday 14 July, it was the turn of Tolkien and 'B' Company to go into action.

What Tolkien now experienced had already been endured by thousands of other soldiers: the long march at night-time from the billets down to the trenches, the stumble of a mile or more through the communication alleys that led to the front line itself, and the hours of confusion and exasperation until the hand-over from the previous company had been completed. For signallers such as Tolkien there was bitter disillusionment, as instead of the neat orderly conditions in which they had been trained they found a tangled confusion of wires, field-telephones out of order and covered with mud, and worst of all a prohibition on the use of wires for all but the least important messages (the Germans had tapped telephone lines and intercepted crucial orders preceding the attack). Even Morse code buzzers were prohibited, and instead the signallers had to rely on lights, flags, and at the last resort runners or even carrier-pigeons. Worst of all were the dead men, for corpses lay in every corner, horribly torn by the shells. Those that still had faces stared with dreadful eyes. Beyond the trenches no-man's-land was littered with bloated and decaying bodies. All around was desolation. Grass and corn had vanished into a sea of mud. Trees, stripped of leaf and branch, stood as mere mutilated and blackened trunks. Tolkien never forgot what he called the 'animal horror' of trench warfare.

His first day in action had been chosen by the Allied commanders for a major offensive, and his company was attached to the 7th Infantry Brigade for an attack on the ruined hamlet of Ovillers, which was still in German hands. The attack was unsuccessful, for once again the enemy wire had not been properly cut, and many of Tolkien's battalion were killed by machine-gun fire. But he survived unhurt, and after forty-eight hours without rest he was allowed some sleep in a dug-out. After another twenty-four hours his company was relieved of duty. On his return to the huts at Bouzincourt Tolkien found a letter from G. B. Smith:

15 July 1916.
My dear John Ronald,
    I saw in the paper this morning that Rob has been killed.
    I am safe but what does that matter?
    Do please stick to me, you and Christopher. I am very tired and most frightfully depressed at this worst of news.
    Now one realises in despair what the T.C.B.S. really was.
    O my dear John Ronald what ever are we going to do?
                            Yours ever,
                            G. B. S.

Rob Gilson had died at La Boisselle, leading his men into action on the first day of the battle, 1 July.

Tolkien wrote to Smith: 'I do not feel a member of a complete body now. I honestly feel that the T.C.B.S. has ended.' But Smith replied: 'The T.C.B.S. is not finished and never will be.'

Day now followed day in the same pattern: a rest period, back to the trenches, more attacks (usually fruitless), another rest period. Tolkien was among those who were in support at the storming of the Schwaben Redoubt, a massive fortification of German trenches. Prisoners were taken, among them men from a Saxon regiment that had fought alongside the Lancashire Fusiliers against the French at Minden in 1759. Tolkien spoke to a captured officer who had been wounded, offering him a drink of water; the officer corrected his German pronunciation. Occasionally there were brief periods of calm when the guns were silent. At one such moment (Tolkien later recalled) his hand was on the receiver of a trench telephone when a field-mouse emerged from hiding and ran across his fingers.

On Saturday 19 August Tolkien and G. B. Smith met again, at Acheux, They talked, and met again on the following days, on the last of which they had a meal together at Bouzincourt, coming under fire as they ate but surviving uninjured. Then Tolkien returned to the trenches.

Although there was no longer the same intensity of fighting as in the first days of the Battle of the Somme, British losses continued to be severe, and many of Tolkien's battalion were killed. He himself remained entirely uninjured, but the longer he stayed in the trenches the greater were his chances of being among the casualties. As to leave, it was ever imminent but never granted.

His rescuer was 'pyrexia of unknown origin', as the medical officers called it. To the soldiers it was simply 'trench fever'. Carried by lice, it caused a high temperature and other fever symptoms, and already thousands of men had reported sick with it. On Friday 27 October it struck Tolkien. He was billeted at Beauval at the time, twelve miles behind the lines. When he was taken ill they transported him to hospital a short distance away. A day later he was on a sick-train bound for the coast, and by the Sunday night a bed had been found for him in hospital at Le Touquet, where he remained for a week.

But the fever did not die down, and on 8 November he was put on board ship for England. Upon arrival he was taken by train to hospital in Birmingham. So in a matter of days he found himself transported from the horror of the trenches to white sheets and a view of the city that he knew so well.

He was reunited with Edith, and by the third week in December he was well enough to leave hospital and go to Great Haywood to spend Christmas with her. There he received a letter from Christopher Wiseman, who was serving in the Navy:

H.M.S. *Superb*. 16 December 1916.
My dear J. R.,
    I have just received news from home about G. B. S., who has succumbed to injuries received from shells bursting on

December 3rd. I can't say very much about it now. I humbly pray Almighty God I may be accounted worthy of him.

Chris.

Smith had been walking down the road in a village behind the lines when a shell burst near him; he was wounded in the right arm and thigh. An operation was attempted, but gas-gangrene had set in. They buried him in Warlencourt British Cemetery.

Not long before, he had written to Tolkien:

My chief consolation is that if I am scuppered tonight – I am off on duty in a few minutes – there will still be left a member of the great T.C.B.S. to voice what I dreamed and what we all agreed upon. For the death of one of its members cannot, I am determined, dissolve the T.C.B.S. Death can make us loathsome and helpless as individuals, but it cannot put an end to the immortal four! A discovery I am going to communicate to Rob before I go off to-night. And do you write it also to Christopher. May God bless you, my dear John Ronald, and may you say the things I have tried to say long after I am not there to say them, if such be my lot.

Yours ever,

G. B. S.

III

1917–1925: The making of a mythology

1
Lost Tales

May you say the things I have tried to say long after I am not there to say them. G. B. Smith's words were a clear call to Ronald Tolkien to begin the great work that he had been meditating for some time, a grand and astonishing project with few parallels in the history of literature. He was going to create an entire mythology.

The idea had its origins in his taste for inventing languages. He had discovered that to carry out such inventions to any degree of complexity he must create for the languages a 'history' in which they could develop. Already in the early Earendel poems he had begun to sketch something of that history; now he wanted to record it in full.

There was another force at work: his desire to express his most profound feelings in poetry, a desire that owed its origin to the inspiration of the T.C.B.S. His first verses had been unremarkable, as immature as the raw idealism of the four young men; but they were the first steps towards the great prose-poem (for though in prose it is a poetic work) that he now began to write.

And there was a third element playing a part: his desire to create a mythology *for England*. He had hinted at this during his undergraduate days when he wrote of the Finnish *Kalevala*: 'I would that we had more of it left – something of the same sort that belonged to the English.' This idea grew until it reached grand proportions. Here is how Tolkien expressed it, when recollecting it many years later: 'Do not laugh! But once upon a time (my crest has long since fallen) I had a mind to make a body of more or less connected legend, ranging from the large and cosmogonic to the level of romantic fairy-story – the larger founded on the lesser in contact with the earth, the lesser drawing splendour from the vast back-cloths – which I could dedicate simply: to England; to my country. It should possess the tone and quality that I desired, somewhat cool and clear, be redolent of our "air" (the clime and soil of the North West, meaning Britain and the hither parts of Europe; not Italy or the Aegean, still less the East), and, while possessing (if I could achieve it) the fair elusive beauty that some call Celtic (though it is rarely found in genuine ancient Celtic things), it should be "high", purged of the gross, and fit for the more adult mind of a land long steeped in poetry. I would draw some of the great tales in fullness, and leave many only placed in the scheme, and sketched. The cycles should be linked to a majestic whole, and yet leave scope for other minds and hands, wielding paint and music and drama. Absurd.'

Absurdly grand the concept may have seemed, but on his return from France, Tolkien determined to realise it. Here now was the time and place: he was once more with Edith and at Great Haywood, in the English countryside that was so dear to him. Even Christopher Wiseman far away at sea sensed that something was about to happen. He wrote to Tolkien: 'You ought to start the epic.' And Tolkien did. On the cover of a cheap notebook he wrote in thick blue pencil the title that he had chosen for his mythological cycle: 'The Book of Lost Tales'. Inside the notebook he began to compose what eventually became known as *The Silmarillion*.

No account of the external events of Tolkien's life can provide more than a superficial explanation of the origins of his mythology. Certainly the device that linked the stories in the first draft of the book (it was later abandoned) owes something to William Morris's *The Earthly Paradise*; for, as in that story, a sea-voyager arrives at an unknown land where he is to hear a succession of tales. Tolkien's voyager was called Eriol, a name that is explained as meaning 'One who dreams alone'. But the tales that Eriol hears, grand, tragic, and heroic, cannot be explained as the mere product of literary influences and personal experience. When Tolkien began to write he drew upon some deeper, richer seam of his imagination than he had yet explored; and it was a seam that would continue to yield for the rest of his life.

The first of the 'legends' that make up *The Silmarillion* tell of the creation of the universe and the establishing of the known world, which Tolkien, recalling the Norse *Midgard* and the equivalent words in early English, calls 'Middle-earth'. Some readers have taken this to refer to another planet, but Tolkien had no such intention. 'Middle-earth is *our* world,' he wrote, adding: 'I have (of course) placed the action in a purely imaginary (though not wholly impossible) period of antiquity, in which the shape of the continental masses was different.'

Later stories in the cycle deal chiefly with the fashioning of the 'Silmarilli' (the three great jewels of the elves which give the book its title), their theft from the blessed realm of Valinor by the evil power Morgoth, and the subsequent wars in which the elves try to regain them.

Some have puzzled over the relation between Tolkien's stories and his Christianity, and have found it difficult to understand how a devout Roman Catholic could write with such conviction about a world where God is not worshipped. But there is no mystery. *The Silmarillion* is the work of a profoundly religious man. It does not contradict Christianity but complements it. There is in the legends no worship of God, yet God is indeed there, more explicitly in *The Silmarillion* than in the work that grew out of it, *The Lord of the Rings*. Tolkien's universe is ruled over by God, 'The One'. Beneath Him in the hierarchy are 'The Valar', the guardians of the world, who are not gods but angelic powers, themselves holy and subject to God; and at one terrible moment in the story they surrender their power into His hands.

Tolkien cast his mythology in this form because he wanted it to be remote and strange, and yet at the same time *not to be a lie*. He wanted the mythological and legendary stories to express his own moral view of the universe; and as a Christian he could not place this view in a cosmos without the God that he worshipped. At the same time, to set his stories 'realistically' in the known world, where religious beliefs were explicitly Christian, would deprive them of imaginative colour. So while God is present in Tolkien's universe, He remains unseen.

When he wrote *The Silmarillion* Tolkien believed that in one sense he was writing the truth. He did not suppose that precisely such peoples as he described, 'elves', 'dwarves', and malevolent 'orcs', had walked the earth and done the deeds that he recorded. But he did feel, or hope, that his stories were in some sense an embodiment of a profound truth. This is not to say that he was writing an allegory: far from it. Time and again he expressed his distaste for that form of literature. 'I dislike allegory wherever I smell it,' he once said, and similar phrases echo through his letters to readers of his books. So in what sense did he suppose *The Silmarillion* to be 'true'?

Something of the answer can be found in his essay *On Fairy-Stories* and in his story *Leaf by Niggle*, both of which suggest that a man may be given by God the gift of recording 'a sudden glimpse of the underlying reality or truth'. Certainly while writing *The Silmarillion* Tolkien believed that he was doing more than inventing a story. He wrote of the tales that make up the book: 'They arose in my mind as "given" things, and as they came, separately, so too the links grew. An absorbing, though continually interrupted labour (especially, even apart from the necessities of life, since the mind would wing to the other pole and spread itself on the linguistics): yet always I had the sense of recording what was already "there", somewhere: not of "inventing".'

The first story to be put on paper – it was written out during Tolkien's convalescence at Great Haywood early in 1917 – actually occupies a place towards the end of the cycle. This is 'The Fall of Gondolin', which tells of the assault on the last elvish stronghold by Morgoth, the prime power of evil. After a terrible battle a group of the inhabitants of Gondolin make their escape, and among them is Earendel,[1] grandson of the king; here then is the link with the early Earendel poems, the first sketches for the mythology. The style of 'The Fall of Gondolin' suggests that Tolkien was influenced by William Morris, and it is not unreasonable to suppose that the great battle which forms the central part of the story may owe a little of its inspiration to Tolkien's experiences on the Somme – or rather to his reaction to those experiences, for the fighting at Gondolin has a heroic grandeur entirely lacking in modern warfare. But in any case these were only superficial 'influences': Tolkien used no models or sources for his strange and exciting tale. Indeed its two most notable characteristics are entirely his own device: the invented names, and the fact that the majority of the protagonists are elves.

Strictly speaking it could be said that the elves of *The Silmarillion* grew out of the 'fairy folk' of Tolkien's early poems, but really

[1]The spelling 'Earendil' was not adopted by Tolkien until some years later.

there is little connection between the two. Elves may have arisen in his mind as a result of his enthusiasm for Francis Thompson's 'Sister Songs' and Edith's fondness for 'little elfin people', but the elves of *The Silmarillion* have nothing whatever to do with the 'tiny leprechauns' of 'Goblin Feet'. They are to all intents and purposes *men*: or rather, they are Man before the Fall which deprived him of his powers of achievement. Tolkien believed devoutly that there had once been an Eden on earth, and that man's original sin and subsequent dethronement were responsible for the ills of the world; but his elves, though capable of sin and error, have not 'fallen' in the theological sense, and so are able to achieve much beyond the powers of men. They are craftsmen, poets, scribes, creators of works of beauty far surpassing human artefacts. Most important of all they are, unless slain in battle, immortal. Old age, disease, and death do not bring their work to an end while it is still unfinished or imperfect. They are therefore the ideal of every artist.

These, then, are the elves of *The Silmarillion*, and of *The Lord of the Rings*. Tolkien himself summed up their nature when he wrote of them: 'They are made by man in his own image and likeness; but freed from those limitations which he feels most to press upon him. They are immortal, and their will is directly effective for the achievement of imagination and desire.'

As to the names of persons and places in 'The Fall of Gondolin' and the other stories in *The Silmarillion*, they were constructed from Tolkien's invented languages. Since the existence of these languages was a *raison d'être* for the whole mythology, it is not surprising that he devoted a good deal of attention to the business of making up names from them. Indeed the name-making and the linguistic work associated with it came (as he said in the passage quoted above) to occupy just as much if not more of his attention than the writing of the stories themselves. So it is worthwhile (and interesting) to get some idea of how he went about this part of the work.

Tolkien had sketched a number of invented languages when he was an adolescent, and had developed several of them to a degree of some complexity. But ultimately only one of these early experiments had pleased him, and had come to express his personal linguistic taste. This was the invented language that had been heavily influenced by Finnish. He called it 'Quenya', and by 1917 it was very sophisticated, possessing a vocabulary of many hundreds of words (based albeit on a fairly limited number of word-stems). Quenya was derived, as any 'real' language would have been, from a more primitive language supposedly spoken in an earlier age; and from this 'Primitive Eldarin' Tolkien created a second elvish language, contemporary with Quenya but spoken by different peoples of the elves. This language he eventually called 'Sindarin', and he modelled its phonology on Welsh, the language that after Finnish was closest to his personal linguistic taste.

Besides Quenya and Sindarin, Tolkien invented a number of other elvish languages. Though these existed only in outline, the complexities of their inter-relationship and the elaboration of a 'family tree' of languages occupied much of his mind. But the elvish names in *The Silmarillion* were constructed almost exclusively from Quenya and Sindarin.

It is impossible in a few sentences to give an adequate account of how Tolkien used his elvish languages to make names for the characters and places in his stories. But briefly, what happened was this. When working to plan he would form all these names with great care, first deciding on the meaning, and then developing its form first in one language and subsequently in the other; the form finally used was most frequently that in Sindarin. However, in practice he was often more arbitrary. It seems strange in view of his deep love of careful invention, yet often in the heat of writing he would construct a name that sounded appropriate to the character without paying more than cursory attention to its linguistic origins. Later he dismissed many of the names made in this way as 'meaningless', and he subjected others to a severe philological scrutiny in an attempt to discover *how* they could have reached their strange and apparently inexplicable form. This, too, is an aspect of his imagination that must be grasped by anyone trying to understand how he worked. As the years went by he came more and more to regard his own invented languages and stories as 'real' languages and historical chronicles that needed to be elucidated. In other words, when in this mood he did not say of an apparent contradiction in the narrative or an unsatisfactory name: 'This is not as I wish it to be; I must change it.' Instead he would approach the problem with the attitude: 'What does this mean? I must *find out*.'

This was not because he had lost his wits or his sense of proportion. In part it was an intellectual game of Patience[1] (he was very fond of Patience cards), and in part it grew from his belief in the ultimate *truth* of his mythology. Yet at other times he would consider making drastic changes in some radical aspect of the whole structure of the story, just as any other author would do. There were of course contradictory attitudes; but here as in so many areas of his personality Tolkien was a man of antitheses.

This, then, was the remarkable work that he began while he was on sick-leave at Great Haywood early in 1917. Edith was glad to help him, and she made a fair copy of 'The Fall of Gondolin', writing it out in a large exercise-book. It was an interlude of rare contentment. In the evenings she played the piano and he recited his poetry or made sketches of her. At this time she conceived a child. But the idyll could not last; 'trench fever' amounted to little more than a high temperature and general discomfort, and a month in hospital at Birmingham had apparently cured Tolkien. Now his battalion wanted him back in service in France. He did not want to go, of course, and it would be tragic if his life were wiped out by a German gun just when he was beginning his great work. But what else could he do?

His health provided the answer. Towards the end of his leave at Great Haywood he was taken ill again. He got better after a few weeks and was posted temporarily to Yorkshire. Edith and her cousin Jennie packed their belongings and followed him north, moving into furnished lodgings a few miles from his camp, at Hornsea. But just after he had returned to duty he went sick once more, and was put into a Harrogate sanatorium.

He was not malingering. There is no doubt that he had real symptoms of illness. But as Edith wrote to him, 'Every day in bed means another day in England,' and he knew that recovery would almost inevitably lead to a return to the trenches. So, as happened with many other soldiers, his body responded and kept his temperature above normal, while the fact that he was spending day after day in bed being dosed with aspirin did nothing to improve his strength. By April he was passed fit again and was sent for further training at an army signalling school in the North-East. There was a good chance that if he passed an examination he might

[1]'Patience', the English term for one-player card games, is known elsewhere as 'Solitaire'.

be appointed Signals Officer at the Yorkshire camp, a post that would probably keep him from the trenches. He sat the examination in July, but failed. A few days later he was taken ill again, and by the second week in August he was back in hospital.

This time he was in thoroughly congenial surroundings, at the Brooklands Officers' Hospital in Hull. A pleasant group of fellow patients provided good company, and among them was a friend from the Lancashire Fusiliers. He was visited by nuns from a local Catholic convent, with one of whom he formed a friendship that was to continue till the end of her life. He could also get on with his writing. Meanwhile Edith, now heavily pregnant, was living with her cousin in miserable seaside lodgings. She had long ago regretted giving up her house in Warwick; Great Haywood had served very well, but now life was almost unbearable. There was no piano in the boarding-house, food was desperately short thanks to the sinking of British ships by U-boats, and she hardly ever saw Ronald – his hospital was a long and weary journey from Hornsea. The local Catholic church was a poor temporary affair set up in a cinema, so that she felt almost inclined to go to the Anglican parish church with Jennie, who was a member of the Church of England; and she was finding pregnancy exhausting. She decided to go back to Cheltenham, where she had lived for three years, and which was the only town she really liked. She could arrange to give birth in a comfortable hospital, and until the time came she and Jennie could stay in rooms. So to Cheltenham they went.

At about this time, perhaps while he was lying in hospital in Hull, Tolkien composed another major story for 'The Book of Lost Tales'. This was the tale of the hapless Túrin, which was eventually given the title 'The Children of Húrin'. Again one may detect certain literary influences: the hero's fight with a great dragon inevitably suggests comparison with the deeds of Sigurd and Beowulf, while his unknowing incest with his sister and his subsequent suicide were derived quite consciously from the story of Kullervo in the *Kalevala*. But again these 'influences' are only superficial. 'The Children of Húrin' is a powerful fusion of Icelandic and Finnish traditions, but it passes beyond this to achieve a degree of dramatic complexity and a subtlety of characterisation not often found in ancient legends.

On 16 November 1917 a son was born to Ronald and Edith Tolkien, in a Cheltenham nursing home. It was a difficult labour, and Edith's life was in danger. But although Ronald had been discharged from hospital he was required in camp and, much to his sorrow, he could not get leave to come south until almost a week after the birth, by which time Edith had begun to recover. They decided to name the child John Francis Reuel, 'Francis' being in honour of Father Francis Morgan, who came from Birmingham to baptise the baby. After the christening Ronald returned to duty, and Edith brought the child back to Yorkshire, moving into furnished rooms at Roos, a village north of the Humber estuary and not far from the camp where Ronald (promoted to full lieutenant) was now stationed. By this time it seemed unlikely that he would be posted overseas again.

On days when he could get leave, he and Edith went for walks in the countryside. Near Roos they found a small wood with an undergrowth of hemlock, and there they wandered. Ronald recalled of Edith as she was at this time: 'Her hair was raven, her skin clear, her eyes bright, and she could sing – and *dance*.' She sang and danced for him in the wood, and from this came the story that was to be the centre of *The Silmarillion*: the tale of the mortal man Beren who loves the immortal elven-maid Lúthien Tinúviel, whom he first sees dancing among hemlock in a wood.

This deeply romantic fairy-story encompasses a wider range of emotions than anything Tolkien had previously written, achieving at times a Wagnerian intensity of passion. It is also Tolkien's first quest-story; and the journey of the two lovers to Morgoth's terrible fortress, where they hope to cut a Silmaril from his Iron Crown, seems as doomed to failure as Frodo's attempt to carry the Ring to its destination.

Of all his legends, the tale of Beren and Lúthien was the one most loved by Tolkien, not least because at one level he identified the character of Lúthien with his own wife. After Edith's death more than fifty years later he wrote to his son Christopher, explaining why he wished to include the name 'Lúthien' on her tombstone: 'She was (and knew she was) my Lúthien. I will say no more now. But I should like ere long to have a long talk with you. For if as seems probable I shall never write any ordered biography – it is against my nature, which expresses itself about things deepest felt in tales and myths – someone close in heart to me should know something about things that records do not record: the dreadful sufferings of our childhoods, from which we rescued one another, but could not wholly heal wounds that later often proved disabling; the sufferings that we endured after our love began–all of which (over and above personal weaknesses) might help to make pardonable, or understandable, the lapses and darknesses which at times marred our lives – and to explain how these never touched our depths nor dimmed the memories of our youthful love. For ever (especially when alone) we still met in the woodland glade and went hand in hand many times to escape the shadow of imminent death before our last parting.'

Tolkien's time at Roos came to an end in the spring of 1918 when he was posted to Penkridge, one of the Staffordshire camps where he had trained before going to France. At about this time those of his battalion who were still serving in France were all killed or taken prisoner at Chemin des Dames.

Edith, the baby, and Jennie Grove travelled south to be with him. Edith was finding it a 'miserable wandering homeless sort of life'; and scarcely had they settled at Penkridge than he was posted back to Hull. This time Edith refused to move. She was wearied by looking after the baby and was often in pain – the effects of the difficult birth had been long-lasting – and she wrote bitterly to Ronald: 'I'll never go round with you again.' Meanwhile on his return to the Humber Garrison Ronald was taken ill yet again, and was sent back to the officers' hospital in Hull. 'I should think you ought never to feel tired again,' Edith wrote, 'for the amount of *Bed* you have had since you came back from France nearly two years ago is enormous.' In hospital, besides working on his mythology and the elvish languages, he was teaching himself a little Russian and improving his Spanish and Italian.

By October he had been discharged from hospital. Peace seemed a little nearer, and he went to Oxford to see if there was any chance of finding an academic job. The outlook was poor: the University was scarcely functioning, and nobody knew what would happen when peace came. But when he called on William Craigie who had taught him Icelandic, there was more encouraging news. Craigie was on the staff of the New English Dictionary, the later parts of which were still being compiled at Oxford, and he told Tolkien that he could find him a job as an assistant lexicographer. When the war came to an end on 11 November, Tolkien contacted the army authorities and obtained permission to be stationed at Oxford 'for the purposes of completing his education' until demobilisation. He found rooms near his old digs in St John's Street, and late in November 1918 he, Edith, the baby, and Jennie Grove took up residence in Oxford.

2
Oxford interlude

Tolkien had long dreamt of returning to Oxford. Throughout his war service he had suffered an ache of nostalgia for his college, his friends, and the way of life that he had led for four years. He was also uncomfortably conscious of wasted time, for he was now twenty-seven and Edith was thirty. But at last they could enjoy what they had long hoped for: 'Our home together'.

Realising that he had entered a new phase of his life, Tolkien began (on New Year's Day 1919) to keep a diary in which he recorded principal events and his thoughts on them. After starting it in ordinary handwriting he began instead to use a remarkable alphabet that he had just invented, which looked like a mixture of Hebrew, Greek, and Pitman's shorthand. He soon decided to involve it with his mythology, and he named it 'The Alphabet of Rúmil' after an elvish sage in his stories. His diary entries were all in English but they were now written in this alphabet. The only difficulty was that he could not decide on a final form of it; he kept on altering the letters and changing their use, so that a sign that was used for 'r' one week might be used for 'l' the next. Nor did he always remember to keep a record of these changes, and after a time he found it difficult to read earlier entries in the diary. Resolutions to stop altering the alphabet and leave it alone were of no avail: a restless perfectionism in this as in so much else made him constantly refine and adjust.

With patience, the diary can be deciphered; and it provides a detailed picture of Tolkien's new pattern of life. After breakfast he would set out from 50 St John's Street to the New English Dictionary work-room, which was in the Old Ashmolean building in nearby Broad Street. There, in what he called 'that great dusty workshop, that brownest of brown studies', a small group of experts laboured away at producing the most comprehensive dictionary of the English language ever to be compiled. Their work had begun in 1878, and by 1900 the sections covering the letters A to H had been published; but eighteen years later after delays caused by the war, U to Z was still incomplete. The original editor, Sir James Murray, had died in 1915, and the work was now supervised by Henry Bradley, a remarkable man who had spent twenty years as a clerk to a Sheffield cutler before devoting himself to full-time scholarship and becoming a distinguished philologist.[1]

Tolkien enjoyed working at the Dictionary, and liked his colleagues, especially the accomplished C. T. Onions. For his first weeks he was given the job of researching the etymology of *warm, wasp, water, wick (lamp)*, and *winter*. Some indication of the skill that this required may be gathered from a glance at the entry that was finally printed for *wasp*. It is not a particularly difficult word, but the paragraph dealing with it cites comparable forms in Old Saxon, Middle Dutch, Modern Dutch, Old High German, Middle Low German, Middle High German, Modern German, Old Teutonic, primitive pre-Teutonic, Lithuanian, Old Slavonic, Russian, and Latin. Not surprisingly, Tolkien found that this kind of work taught him a good deal about languages, and he once said of the period 1919–20 when he was working on the Dictionary: 'I learned more in those two years than in any other equal period of my life.' He did his job remarkably well, even by the standards of the Dictionary, and Dr Bradley reported of him: 'His work gives evidence of an unusually thorough mastery of Anglo-Saxon and of the facts and principles of the comparative grammar of the Germanic languages. Indeed, I have no hesitation in saying that I have never known a man of his age who was in these respects his equal.'

From the Dictionary it was only a short walk home for lunch, and, not long after, for tea. Dr Bradley was an undemanding taskmaster as far as hours were concerned, and in any case the work was scarcely supposed to occupy Tolkien's entire day. Like many others who were employed at the Dictionary he was expected to fill out his time and his income by teaching in the University. He made it known that he was willing to accept pupils, and one by one

---

[1]As a child, Bradley had first learnt to read *upside-down* by looking at the Bible on his father's knees during family prayers.

the colleges began to respond – chiefly the women's colleges, for Lady Margaret Hall and St Hugh's badly needed someone to teach Anglo-Saxon to their young ladies, and Tolkien had the advantage of being married, which meant that a chaperone did not have to be sent to his home when he was teaching them.

Soon he and Edith decided that they could afford the rent of a small house, and they found a suitable one just round the corner from their rooms, at 1 Alfred Street (now called Pusey Street). They moved into it in the late summer of 1919, and engaged a cook-housemaid. It was a great joy to have a house of their own. Edith's piano was brought back from store, and she could play regularly again for the first time in years. She was pregnant once more, but at least she could give birth in her own house and bring up the baby in a proper home. By the spring of 1920 Ronald was earning enough from tuition to give up work at the Dictionary.

Meanwhile he continued to write 'The Book of Lost Tales', and one evening he read 'The Fall of Gondolin' aloud to the Essay Club at Exeter College. It was well received by an undergraduate audience that included two young men named Nevill Coghill and Hugo Dyson.

Suddenly the family's plans changed. Tolkien applied for the post of Reader in English Language at the University of Leeds, scarcely expecting to be considered, but in the summer of 1920 he was asked to go for an interview. He was met at the station in Leeds by George Gordon, Professor of English at the university. Gordon had been a prominent member of the English School at Oxford before the war, but Tolkien did not know him, and conversation was a little stilted as they took the tram through the town and up to the university. They started to talk about Sir Walter Raleigh, Professor of English Literature at Oxford. Tolkien recalled the occasion: 'I did not in fact think much of Raleigh – he was not, of course, a good lecturer; but some kind spirit prompted me to say that he was "Olympian". It went well; though I only really meant that he reposed gracefully on a lofty pinnacle above my criticism. I knew privately before I left Leeds that I had got the job.'

3
Northern venture

Smoky, begrimed, hung about with a thick industrial fog, crowded with factories and terraced houses, Leeds offered little prospect of a good life. The late Victorian university buildings, constructed of variegated brick in the mock-Gothic style, were a sad contrast to what Tolkien had been used to. He had serious misgivings about his decision to accept the post, and to move to the north of England.

At first life was difficult for him. Just after the Leeds term began in October 1920, Edith gave birth to a second son, who was christened Michael Hilary Reuel; Tolkien, living in a bedsitter in Leeds during the week, had to make a journey to Oxford at week-ends to see his family. Not until the beginning of 1921 were Edith and the baby ready to move north, and even then Tolkien could only find temporary accommodation for them in furnished rooms in Leeds. However, at the end of 1921 they took the lease of 11 St Mark's Terrace, a small dark house in a side-street near the university, and here they established their new home.

The English Department at Leeds University was still small, but George Gordon was building it up. Gordon was an organiser rather than a scholar, but Tolkien found him 'the very master of men'; moreover Gordon displayed great kindness to his new assistant, making space for him in his own office, a bare room of glazed bricks and hot-water pipes already shared with the Professor of French, and showing concern for his domestic arrangements. More important, he handed over to Tolkien virtual responsibility for all the linguistic teaching in the department.

Gordon had decided to follow the Oxford pattern and divide the

Leeds English syllabus into two options, one for undergraduates wishing to specialise in post-Chaucerian literature and the other for those who wanted to concentrate their attention on Anglo-Saxon and Middle English. This latter course had only just been established, and Gordon wanted Tolkien to organise a syllabus that would be attractive to undergraduates and would provide them with a sound philological training. Tolkien immediately threw himself into the work. He was at first a little glum at the sight of solid and dour Yorkshire students, but he soon came to have a great admiration for many of them. He once wrote: 'I am wholly in favour of the "dull stodges". A surprisingly large proportion prove "educable": for which a primary qualification is the willingness *to do some work*.' Many of his students at Leeds worked very hard indeed, and were soon achieving excellent results.

Yet Tolkien very nearly did not remain at Leeds. During his first term there, he was invited to submit his name as a candidate for two professorships of the English Language: the Baines Chair at Liverpool and the new De Beers Chair at Cape Town. He sent in his applications. Liverpool turned him down, but at the end of January 1921 Cape Town offered him the post. In many ways he would have liked to accept. It would have meant a return to the land of his birth, and he had always wanted to see South Africa again. But he refused the job. Edith and the baby were in no fit state to travel, and he did not want to be separated from her. Yet he wrote in his diary twelve months later: 'I have often wondered since if that was not our chance that came then, and we had not the courage to seize it.' Events were to prove this fear unfounded.

Early in 1922 a new junior lecturer was appointed to the language side of the English Department at Leeds, a young man named E. V. Gordon. This small dark Canadian (who was unrelated to George Gordon) had been a Rhodes Scholar at Oxford, and Tolkien had tutored him during 1920. Now he made him very welcome in Leeds. 'Eric Valentine Gordon has come and got firmly established and is my devoted friend and pal,' he wrote in his diary.

Soon after Gordon's arrival the two men began to collaborate on a major piece of scholarship. Tolkien had been working for some time at a glossary for a book of Middle English extracts that his former tutor Kenneth Sisam had edited. This meant in effect compiling a small Middle English dictionary, a task that he undertook with infinite precision and much imagination. The glossary took a long time to complete, but it reached print early in 1922, by which time Tolkien wanted to turn his hand to something that would give greater scope to his scholarship. He and E. V. Gordon decided to compile a new edition of the Middle English poem *Sir Gawain and the Green Knight*, as there was none in print that was suitable for university students. Tolkien was to be responsible for the text and glossary while Gordon would provide the greater part of the notes.

Tolkien found that his collaborator was 'an industrious little devil', and he had to work fast to keep up with him. They finished the book in time for publication by the Clarendon Press early in 1925. It was a major contribution to the study of medieval literature – though Tolkien himself would often in later years entertain his audience at lectures by making disparaging references to some point of interpretation in the edition, as if he himself had nothing to do with it: 'Tolkien and Gordon were quite wrong, quite wrong when they said that! Can't imagine what they were thinking of!'

E. V. Gordon shared Tolkien's sense of humour. Together the two men helped to form a Viking Club among the undergraduates, which met to drink large quantities of beer, read sagas, and sing comic songs. These were mostly written by Tolkien and Gordon, who made up rude verses about the students, translated nursery rhymes into Anglo-Saxon, and sang drinking songs in Old Norse. Several of their verses were printed privately some years later as *Songs for the Philologists*. Not surprisingly, the Viking Club helped to make Tolkien and Gordon popular as teachers, and through this and the excellence of their teaching the language side of the English Department attracted more and more pupils. By 1925 there were twenty linguistic specialists among the undergraduates, more than a third of the total number in the department, and a far higher proportion than was usually enrolled at Oxford for the equivalent course.

Home life for the Tolkiens was generally happy. Edith found the atmosphere in the university refreshingly informal, and she made friends with other wives. Money was not plentiful and Tolkien was saving to buy a house, so family holidays were few, but in the summer of 1922 there was a visit of some weeks to Filey on the Yorkshire coast. Tolkien did not like the place; he called it 'a very nasty little suburban seaside resort', and while he was there he had to spend a good deal of time marking School Certificate examination papers, a chore that he now undertook annually to earn some extra money. But he also wrote several poems.

He had been composing a good deal of verse over the last few years. Much of it was concerned with his mythology. Some found its way into print in the Leeds university magazine *The Gryphon*, in a local series called *Yorkshire Poetry*, and in a book of verses by members of the English Department entitled *Northern Venture*. Now he began a series of poems that he called 'Tales and Songs of Bimble Bay'. One, suggested by his feelings about Filey, complains of the sordid noisy character of modern urban life. Another, 'The Dragon's Visit', describes the ravages of a dragon who arrives at Bimble Bay and encounters 'Miss Biggins'. A third, 'Glip', tells of a strange slimy creature who lives beneath the floor of a cave and has pale luminous eyes. All are glimpses of important things to come.

In May 1923 Tolkien caught a severe cold which lingered and turned into pneumonia. His grandfather John Suffield, then aged ninety, was staying with the family at the time, and Tolkien recalled a vision of him 'standing by my bedside, a tall thin black-clad figure, and looking at me and speaking to me in contempt – to the effect that I and my generation were degenerate weaklings. There was I gasping for breath, but he must now say goodbye, as he was off to catch a boat to go a trip by sea around the British Isles!' The old man lived for another seven years, spending much of his time with his youngest daughter, Tolkien's Aunt Jane. She had left Nottinghamshire and had taken a farm at Dormston in Worcestershire. It was at the end of a lane that led no further, and the local people used sometimes to refer to it as 'Bag End'.

When Tolkien had recovered from pneumonia he went with Edith and the children to stay with his brother Hilary, who after his war service had bought a small orchard and market garden near Evesham, ancestral town of the Suffields. The family were pressed into service to help on the land, and there were also hilarious games with giant kites, which the two brothers flew from the field opposite the house to amuse the children. Tolkien also managed to find time to do some work, and to turn again to his mythology.

'The Book of Lost Tales' was almost complete. At Oxford and at Leeds Tolkien had composed the stories that tell of the creation of the universe, the fashioning of the Silmarils, and their theft from the blessed realm of Valinor by Morgoth. The cycle still lacked a clear ending – it was to conclude with the voyage of Earendel's star-ship that had been the first element of the mythology to arise in Tolkien's mind – and some of the stories were only in synopsis; but a little more effort would bring the work to a conclusion. Nevertheless Tolkien did not press on towards this objective, but began instead to rewrite. It was almost as if he did not want to finish it. Perhaps he doubted whether it would ever find a publisher; certainly it was a most unconventional work. But it was no odder than the books of Lord Dunsany, which had proved very popular. So what was holding him back? Principally his desire for perfection, but perhaps it was also something that Christopher Wiseman had once said about the elves in his early poems: 'Why these creatures live to you is because you are still creating them. When you have finished creating them they will be as dead to you as the atoms that make our living food.' In other words, Tolkien did not want to finish because he could not contemplate the thought of having no more creating to do inside his invented world; 'sub-creation', he was later to call it.

So he did not complete *The Silmarillion* (as he came to call the book) but went back and altered and polished and revised. He also began to cast two of the principal stories as poems, an indication that he still aspired as much towards verse as towards prose. For the story of Túrin he chose a modern equivalent of the type of alliterative measure that is found in *Beowulf*, and for the story of Beren and Lúthien he elected to work in rhyming couplets. This latter poem he called 'The Gest of Beren and Lúthien'; later he renamed it 'The Lay of Leithian'.

Meanwhile his career at Leeds took an important step forward. In 1922 George Gordon had left to go back to Oxford as Professor of English Literature, and Tolkien was a candidate for the Leeds chair that Gordon had occupied. In the event Lascelles Abercrombie was appointed, but Michael Sadler the Vice-Chancellor promised Tolkien that the University would soon be able to create a new Professorship of the English Language especially for him. Sadler kept his word, and Tolkien became a professor in 1924 at the age of thirty-two, remarkably young by the standards of British universities. In the same year, he and Edith bought a house on the outskirts of Leeds, at 2 Darnley Road, West Park. It was a great

107

improvement on St Mark's Terrace, being of some considerable size, and it was surrounded by open fields where Tolkien could take the children for walks.

At the beginning of 1924 Edith was upset to find that she was pregnant again. She hoped that it might be a daughter, but when the child was born in November it proved to be a boy. He was baptised Christopher Reuel, the first name being in honour of Christopher Wiseman. The baby prospered and became an especial delight to his father, who wrote in his diary: 'Now I would not go without what God has sent.'

Early in 1925 came word that the Professorship of Anglo-Saxon at Oxford was shortly to fall vacant; Craigie, the holder, was leaving to go to America. The post was advertised, and Tolkien applied. In theory he did not stand a good chance, for there were three other candidates with excellent credentials: Allen Mawer of Liverpool, R. W. Chambers of London, and Kenneth Sisam. However Mawer decided not to apply and Chambers refused the chair, so it was whittled down to a fight between Tolkien and his old tutor Sisam.

Kenneth Sisam was now in a senior position at the Clarendon Press, and though he was not engaged in full-time scholarship he had a good reputation in Oxford and a number of supporters. Tolkien was backed by many people, including George Gordon, a master hand at intrigue. But at the election the votes came out equal, so Joseph Wells the Vice-Chancellor had to make the decision with his casting vote. He voted for Tolkien.

IV

1925–1949(i) : 'In a hole in the ground there lived a hobbit'

And after this, you might say, nothing else really happened. Tolkien came back to Oxford, was Rawlinson and Bosworth Professor of Anglo-Saxon for twenty years, was then elected Merton Professor of English Language and Literature, went to live in a conventional Oxford suburb where he spent the first part of his retirement, moved to a nondescript seaside resort, came back to Oxford after his wife died, and himself died a peaceful death at the age of eighty-one. It was the ordinary unremarkable life led by countless other scholars; a life of academic brilliance, certainly, but only in a very narrow professional field that is really of little interest to laymen. And that would be that – apart from the strange fact that during these years when 'nothing happened' he wrote two books which have become world best-sellers, books that have captured the imagination and influenced the thinking of several million readers. It is a strange paradox, the fact that *The Hobbit* and *The Lord of the Rings* are the work of an obscure Oxford professor whose specialisation was the West Midland dialect of Middle English, and who lived an ordinary suburban life bringing up his children and tending his garden.

Or is it? Is not the opposite precisely true? Should we not wonder instead at the fact that a mind of such brilliance and imagination should be happy to be contained in the petty routine of academic and domestic life; that a man whose soul longed for the sound of the waves breaking against the Cornish coast should be content to talk to old ladies in the lounge of a hotel at a middle-class watering-place; that a poet in whom joy leapt up at the sight and smell of logs crackling in the grate of a country inn should be willing to sit in front of his own hearth warmed by an electric fire with simulated glowing coal? What do we make of that?

Perhaps in his years of middle age and old age we can do no more than observe, and puzzle; or perhaps, slowly, we shall see a pattern emerge.

1
Oxford life

Until the late nineteenth century the holders of most college fellow-ships at Oxford, that is the majority of teachers in the University, had to take holy orders and were not permitted to marry while they remained in office. The reformers of that era introduced non-clerical fellowships and abolished the requirement of celibacy. In so doing they changed the face of Oxford, and changed it visibly; for in the years that followed a tide of brick flowed steadily north-wards from the old boundary of the city, covering the fields along the Banbury and Woodstock Roads as the speculators erected hundreds of homes for the new married dons. By the beginning of the twentieth century North Oxford was a concentrated colony of academics, their wives, their children and their servants, its in-habitants occupying a variety of mansions ranging from the gothic and palatial (complete with turrets and stained glass) to the frankly suburban villa. Churches, schools, and clusters of shops were erected to serve the needs of this strange community, and soon few acres were left unoccupied. There was, however, a small amount of building still in progress during the nineteen-twenties; and in one of the North Oxford streets Tolkien found and bought a modest new house, L-shaped and of pale brick, with one wing running towards the road. The family travelled down from Leeds at the beginning of 1926 and moved in.

Here, in Northmoor Road, they remained for twenty-one years. Later in 1929 a larger neighbouring house was vacated by Basil Blackwell the bookseller and publisher, and the Tolkiens decided to buy it, moving from number twenty-two to number twenty early in the next year. This second house was broad and grey, more

113

imposing than its neighbour, with small leaded windows and a high slate roof. Shortly before the move a fourth and last child was born, the daughter that Edith had long hoped for, and was christened Priscilla Mary Reuel.

Apart from these two incidents, the birth of Priscilla in 1929 and the change of houses in 1930, life at Northmoor Road was without major event; or rather it was a life of pattern, almost of routine, in which there were minor interruptions but no significant change. So perhaps the best way to describe it is to follow Tolkien through a typical (though entirely imaginary) day in the early nineteen-thirties.

It is a saint's day, so it begins early. The alarm rings at seven in Tolkien's bedroom, a back room that looks east over the garden. It is really a bathroom-cum-dressing-room, and there is a bath in one corner of it, but he sleeps here because Edith finds his snoring tiresome, and because he keeps late hours that do not harmonise with her habits. So they have their own rooms and do not disturb one another.

He gets up unwillingly (he has never been an early riser by nature), decides to shave after mass, and goes in his dressing-gown along the passage to the boys' bedrooms to wake Michael and Christopher. John, the eldest boy, is now aged fourteen and away at a Catholic boarding-school in Berkshire, but the two younger sons, aged eleven and seven respectively, are still living at home.

Going into Michael's bedroom, Tolkien nearly trips over a model railway engine that has been left in the middle of the floor. He curses to himself. Michael and Christopher have a passion for railways at the moment, and they have devoted a complete up-stairs room to a track layout. They also go to watch engines, and draw (with impressive precision) pictures of Great Western Railway locomotives. Tolkien does not understand or really approve of what he calls their 'railway-mania'; to him railways only mean noise and dirt and the despoiling of the countryside. But he tolerates the hobby, and can even be persuaded on occasions to take them on expeditions to a distant station to watch the Cheltenham Flyer pass through.

When he has woken the boys, he gets dressed in his usual week-day outfit of flannel trousers and tweed jacket. Then he and his sons, who are wearing their dark blue Dragon School jackets and

114

shorts, get their bicycles out of the garage and set off along the silent Northmoor Road, where the bedroom curtains are still drawn in other houses, up Linton Road, and into the broad Banbury Road where the occasional car or bus passes them on its way into the city. It is a spring morning and there is a fine display of blossom on the cherry-trees that hang over the pavements from the front gardens.

They bicycle three-quarters of a mile into the town, to St Aloysius' Catholic Church, an unlovely edifice next to the hospital in the Woodstock Road. Mass is at seven-thirty, so by the time they get home they are just a few minutes late for breakfast. This is always served punctually at eight – strictly speaking at seven fifty-five, since Edith likes to keep the clocks in the house five minutes fast. Phoebe Coles, the daily help, has just arrived in the kitchen and is clattering about with dishes. Phoebe, who wears a housemaid's cap and works in the house all day, has been with the family for a couple of years and shows every sign of staying for many more; which is a great blessing, since before her arrival there were endless difficulties over servants.

During breakfast, Tolkien glances at the newspaper, but only in the most cursory fashion. He, like his friend C. S. Lewis, regards 'news' as on the whole trivial and fit to be ignored, and they both argue (to the annoyance of many of their friends) that the only 'truth' is to be found in literature. However, both men enjoy the crossword.

When breakfast is over, Tolkien goes into his study to light the stove. It is not a warm day and the house (like most middle-class English houses at this time) has no central heating, so he will need to get a good blaze going to make the room habitable. He is in a hurry, for he has a pupil coming at nine and he wants to check his lecture notes for the morning, so he clears out the ashes from the previous night's fire rather hastily; they are still warm, for he did not finish work and go to bed until after two o'clock. When he has lit the fire he throws a good deal of coal on to it, shuts the doors of the stove, and opens the draught regulator to full. Then he hurries upstairs to shave. The boys go off to school.

He has not finished shaving when the front door bell rings. Edith answers it, but she calls him and he comes downstairs with half his face still covered in lather. It is only the postman, but he says that there is a great deal of smoke coming out of the study chimney, and ought Mr Tolkien to see if everything is all right? Tolkien rushes into the study and finds that, as so often happens, the fire has blazed up in the stove and is about to set the chimney alight. He damps it down, thanks the postman, and exchanges some remarks with him about the growing of spring vegetables. Then he begins to open the post, remembers that he has not finished shaving, and only makes himself presentable just in time for the arrival of his pupil.

This is a young woman graduate who is studying Middle English. By ten past nine she and Tolkien are hard at work in the study discussing the significance of an awkward word in the *Ancrene Wisse*. If you were to put your head around the study door you would not be able to see them, for inside the door is a tunnel of books formed by a double row of bookcases, and it is not until the visitor emerges from this that the rest of the room becomes visible. There are windows on two sides, so that the room looks southwards towards a neighbouring garden and west towards the road. Tolkien's desk is in the south-facing window, but he is not sitting at it; he is standing by the fireplace waving his pipe in the air while he talks. The pupil frowns slightly as she puzzles over the complexities of what he is saying, and the difficulty of hearing all of it clearly, for he is talking very fast and sometimes indistinctly. But she begins to see the shape of his argument and the point to which he is leading, and scribbles enthusiastically in her notebook. By the time her 'hour' of supervision finishes, late, at twenty to eleven, she feels that she has been given a new insight into the way in which a medieval author chose his words. She leaves on her bicycle, reflecting that if all Oxford philologists could teach in this fashion, the English School would be a livelier place.

When he has seen her to the gate, Tolkien hurries back to his study and gathers up his lecture notes. He did not have time to check through them after all, and he hopes that everything he needs is there. He also takes a copy of the text that he is to lecture on, the Old English poem *Exodus*, knowing that if the worst happens and his notes do fail him, he can always expound directly from it extempore. Then, with his briefcase and his M.A. gown in the basket of his bicycle, he rides down to the town.

Sometimes he lectures in his own college, Pembroke, but this morning (as is more often the case) his destination is the Examination Schools, an oppressively grandiose late Victorian building in the High Street. Lecturers on popular subjects are allocated a large hall, such as the East School, where today C. S. Lewis will be drawing a large audience for his series on medieval studies. Tolkien himself gets a good attendance for his general lectures on *Beowulf*, which are intended for the non-specialist undergraduates; but today he is talking about a text that is required reading only for those few men and women in the English School who have opted for the philological course, and consequently he goes along the passage to a small dark ground-floor room where a mere eight or ten undergraduates, knowing his punctual habits, are already waiting for him in their gowns. He puts on his own gown and begins to lecture exactly as the deep bell of Merton clock a quarter of a mile away strikes eleven.

He lectures fluently, chiefly from his notes, but with occasional impromptu additions. He works through the text line by line, discussing the significance of certain words and expressions, and the problems raised by them. The undergraduates in the audience know him well and are faithful followers of his lectures, not only because he provides an illuminating interpretation of the texts but also because they *like* him: they enjoy his jokes, are used to his quick-fire manner of speaking, and find him thoroughly humane, certainly more humane than some of his colleagues, who lecture with a total disregard for their audience.

He need not have worried that his notes will run out. The chimes for twelve o'clock and the noise of people in the passage bring him to a halt long before he can finish his prepared material. Indeed for the last ten minutes he has departed entirely from his notes, and has been talking about a particular point of relation between Gothic and Old English that was suggested by a word in the text. Now he gathers up his papers, converses briefly with one of the undergraduates, and then departs to make way for the next lecturer.

In the passage he catches up for a moment with C. S. Lewis, and has a brief conversation with him. He wishes it were a Monday, on which day he regularly has a pint of beer with Lewis and talks for an hour or so, but neither man has time today, and Tolkien has to do some shopping before going home for lunch. He leaves Lewis and bicycles up the High Street to the busy arcade known as the Covered Market, where he has to collect sausages from Lindsey the butcher; Edith forgot to include them in the week's order that was delivered the day before. He exchanges a joke with Mr

117

Lindsey, and also calls in at the stationer on the corner of Market Street to buy some pen nibs. Then he bicycles home up the Banbury Road, and manages to fit in fifteen minutes at a long-overdue letter to E. V. Gordon about their plans to collaborate on an edition of *Pearl*. He begins to type the letter on his Hammond typewriter, a big machine with interchangeable typefaces on a revolving disc; his model has italics and the Anglo-Saxon letters þ, ð, and æ. Edith rings the handbell for lunch before he can finish.

Lunch, at which all the family is present, is chiefly taken up with a discussion about Michael's dislike of swimming lessons at school, and whether or not a septic toe should be allowed to prevent the boy from bathing. After the meal, Tolkien goes into the garden to see how the broad beans are coming along. Edith brings Priscilla out to play on the lawn, and discusses with him whether they should dig up the remainder of the old tennis court, to increase the size of the vegetable plot. Then, leaving Edith to feed the canaries and budgerigars in her aviary at the side of the house, he gets on his bicycle once more and pedals down to the town, this time for a meeting of the English Faculty.

The meeting is in Merton College, for the Faculty has no premises of its own other than a cramped library in the attic of the Examination Schools, and Merton is the college most closely associated with it. Tolkien himself is a Fellow of Pembroke, but he is not much involved with his college, and like all professors his first responsibility is towards his Faculty. The meeting begins at half past two. Besides the other professors – Wyld, who holds the chair of English Language and Literature, and Nichol Smith, the professor of English Literature – there are about a dozen dons present, several of them women. Sometimes these meetings can be acrimonious, and Tolkien himself has attended many when, while trying to initiate reforms of the syllabus, he has been the target for bitter attacks from the 'literature' camp. But those days are passed, and his reforms have been accepted and put into practice. Today's meeting is mostly concerned with routine business such as the dates of examinations, minor details of the syllabus, and the question of funds for the Faculty library. It all takes time, and the meeting does not break up until nearly four, which just gives Tolkien a few minutes to call in at the Bodleian Library and look up something in a book that he ordered from the stack the previous day. Then he rides home again in time for the children's tea at half past four.

After tea he manages to put in an hour and a half at his desk, finishing the letter to E. V. Gordon and beginning to arrange his lecture notes for the next day. When life goes according to plan he manages to prepare an entire course of lectures before the beginning of term, but too often pressure of time forces him to leave the work until the last minute. Even now he does not get very much done, for Michael wants help with his Latin prose homework, and this occupies twenty minutes. All too soon it is half past six and he must change into a dinner-jacket. He does not dine out more than once or twice a week, but tonight there is a guest night at his college, Pembroke, and he has promised to be there to meet a friend's guest. He ties his black tie hastily and again mounts his bicycle, leaving Edith to an early supper at home.

He reaches college in time for sherry in the Senior Common Room. His position at Pembroke is somewhat anomalous, thanks to the confused and confusing administrative practices of Oxford. It could almost be said that the colleges *are* the University, for the majority of the teaching staff hold college fellowships, and their primary responsibility is to instruct undergraduates in their own college. But professors are in a different position. They are primarily outside the collegiate system, for they teach on a faculty basis, irrespective of what college their pupils may belong to. However, so that a professor shall not be deprived of the social facilities and other conveniences of college life, he is allocated to a college and given a fellowship in it *ex officio*. This sometimes leads to bad feeling, for in all other circumstances colleges elect their own fellows, whereas 'Professorial Fellows' such as Tolkien are to some extent wished upon them. Tolkien thinks that Pembroke resents him a little; certainly the atmosphere in the common room is unfriendly and austere. Fortunately there is a junior fellow, R. B. McCallum, a lively man several years younger than Tolkien, who is an ally; and he is waiting now to introduce his guest. Dinner proves to be enjoyable – and edible, since the food is plain without any suggestion of that tiresome French cooking which (Tolkien reflects with disgust) is beginning to invade the high tables of several colleges.

After dinner he makes his excuses and leaves early, crossing the town to Balliol College where there is to be a meeting of the Coalbiters in John Bryson's rooms. The *Kolbítar*, to give it the Icelandic title (meaning those who lounge so close to the fire in winter that they 'bite the coal'), is an informal reading club founded by Tolkien somewhat on the model of the Viking Club in Leeds, except that its members are all dons. They meet for an evening several times each term to read Icelandic sagas. Tonight there is a good turn-out: George Gordon, now the President of Magdalen, Nevill Coghill of Exeter, C. T. Onions from the Dictionary, Dawkins the Professor of Byzantine and Modern Greek, Bryson himself, and – Tolkien is glad to note – C. S. Lewis, who chides him noisily for being late. They are currently reading the *Grettis Saga*, and Tolkien himself begins, which is customary as he is easily the best Norse scholar of anyone in the club. He resumes at the point where they left off last time, improvising a fluent translation from the text that is spread open on his knees. After he has done a couple of pages Dawkins takes over. He too is fluent, though not quite as fluent as Tolkien, but when the others take their turn they proceed much more slowly, each of them translating no more than half a page, for none of them professes to be more than a beginner at the language. This however is the whole purpose of the Coalbiters, for Tolkien started the club to persuade his friends that Icelandic literature is worth reading in the original language; and he encourages their somewhat halting steps and applauds their efforts.

After an hour or so they reach a good stopping-place, and the whisky bottle is opened while they discuss the saga. Then they listen to a scurrilous and very funny poem that Tolkien has just written about another member of the English Faculty. It is after eleven when they break up. Tolkien walks with Lewis to the end of Broad Street, and then they go their separate ways, Lewis down Holywell Street towards Magdalen (for he is a bachelor and usually sleeps in college in term-time) and Tolkien on his bicycle back to Northmoor Road.

Edith has gone to bed and the house is in darkness when he gets home. He builds up the fire in the study stove and fills his pipe. He ought, he knows, to do some more work on his lecture notes for the next morning, but he cannot resist taking from a drawer the half-finished manuscript of a story that he is writing to amuse himself and his children. It is probably, he suspects, a waste of time; certainly if he is going to devote any attention to this sort of thing it ought to be to *The Silmarillion*. But something draws him back night after night to this amusing little tale – at least it seems to amuse the boys. He sits down at the desk, fits a new relief nib to his dip pen (which he prefers to a fountain pen), unscrews the ink bottle, takes a sheet of old examination paper (which still has a candidate's essay on the Battle of Maldon on the back of it), and begins to write: 'When Bilbo opened his eyes, he wondered if he had; for it was just as dark as with them shut. No one was anywhere near him. Just imagine his fright! . . .'

We will leave him now. He will be at his desk until half past one, or two o'clock, or perhaps even later, with only the scratching of his pen to disturb the silence, while around him Northmoor Road sleeps.

2
Photographs observed

These, then, were some of the externals of his life: domestic routine, teaching, preparation for teaching, correspondence, an occasional evening with friends – and it would in truth be a rare evening that included both a dinner in college and a meeting of the Coalbiters; these and other irregular events such as the Faculty meeting are here put under the umbrella of the same imaginary day simply as an indication of the range of his activities. A truly average day would be more dull.

Or perhaps to the reader the events here described are *all* dull, unredeemed by a flicker of excitement: the trivial activities of a man enclosed in a narrow way of life that holds no interest for anyone outside it. All this, says the reader, this account of lighting the stove and bicycling to lectures and feeling unwelcome in a college common room, all this says nothing about the man who wrote *The Silmarillion* and *The Hobbit* and *The Lord of the Rings*, does nothing to explain the nature of his mind and the way in which his imagination responded to his surroundings. Certainly Tolkien himself would have agreed with this. It was one of his strongest-held opinions that the investigation of an author's life reveals very little of the workings of his mind. Maybe; but before we abandon our task as utterly hopeless, we could perhaps move in a little closer than the viewpoint we adopted for the imaginary day, move in and observe, or at least hazard a few guesses about some of the more obvious aspects of his personality. And if after this we may not have any better idea *why* he wrote his book, then at least we should know a little more about the man who did write them.

Perhaps we could start with photographs. There are plenty of them, for the Tolkiens took and kept endless snapshots. At first we get nowhere. Photographs of Tolkien in middle age reveal virtually nothing. Facing the camera is an ordinary middle-class Englishman of light build and moderate height. He is mildly handsome, with a long face; and that is about all that can be said. Admittedly there is a keenness in the eyes which suggests a lively mind, but nothing else reveals itself – nothing except his clothes, which are exceptionally *ordinary*.

His manner of dressing was of course partly the result of circumstances, the necessity of bringing up a large family on a relatively small income that left nothing over for personal extravagances. Later, when he became a wealthy man, he did indulge in coloured waistcoats. But his choice of clothes in middle age was also the sign of a dislike of dandyism. This he shared with C. S. Lewis. Neither could abide any manner of affectation in dress, which seemed to them to smack of the unmasculine and hence of the objectionable. Lewis took this to extremes, not only buying indifferent clothes but wearing them indifferently; Tolkien, always the more fastidious, at least kept his trousers pressed. But fundamentally both men had the same attitude to their appearance, an attitude that was shared by many of their contemporaries. This preference for plain masculine clothing was in part perhaps a reaction to the excessive dandyism and implied homosexuality of the 'aesthetes', who had first made their mark on Oxford in the age of Wilde and whose successors lingered on in the nineteen-twenties and early thirties, affecting delicate shades of garment and ambiguous nuances of manner. Theirs was a way of life of which Tolkien and the majority of his friends would have none; hence their almost exaggerated preference for tweed jackets, flannel trousers, nondescript ties, solid brown shoes that were built for country walks, dull-coloured raincoats and hats, and short hair. Tolkien's manner of dress also reflected some of his positive values, his love of everything that was moderate and sensible and unflorid and English. But beyond that his clothes gave no idea of the delicate and complex inner nature of the man who wore them.

What else can we discover from photographs of him? There is in most of them something so obvious that we are likely to miss it: the almost unvarying ordinariness of the backgrounds. In one picture he is sitting in his garden having tea; in another, standing in the sunlight in the angle of his house; in another, digging with his children in the sands at some coastal resort. One begins to get the idea that he was entirely conventional in the places that he lived in, even in the places that he visited.

And this is true. He occupied a North Oxford house that was both inside and outside almost indistinguishable from many hundreds of others in that district – it was less flamboyant, indeed, than many of its neighbours. He took his family on holiday to ordinary places. During the central years of his life, the richest period of creativity, he made no journeys outside the British Isles. Again this was partly the product of circumstances, of limited means; nor did he entirely lack the desire to travel: for instance he would have liked to follow E. V. Gordon's example and visit Iceland. Later in life when he had more money and fewer family ties he did make a few journeys abroad. But travel never played a large part in his life – simply because his imagination did not need to be stimulated by unfamiliar landscapes and cultures. What is more surprising is that he also denied himself many of the stimuli of familiar and loved places nearer home. It is true that during the years when he owned and drove a car (from 1932 to the beginning of the Second World War) he loved to explore the villages of Oxfordshire, particularly those in the east of the county; but he was not by habit a long-distance walker, and only once or twice did he join C. S. Lewis for the cross-country walking tours that were such an important part of his friend's life. He knew the Welsh mountains, but he rarely visited them; he loved the sea, but his only expeditions to it took the form of conventional English family holidays at ordinary resorts. Here again pressure of domestic responsibility is one explanation, and here again it does not provide the whole answer. Gradually one forms the idea that he did not altogether care very much where he was.

In one sense this is not true, and in another sense it is. Certainly he was not indifferent to his surroundings, for man's destruction of the landscape moved him to profound anger. Here, from his diary, is his anguished description of a return to his childhood landscape of Sarehole Mill in 1933, when he was driving his family to visit relatives in Birmingham:

'I pass over the pangs to me of passing through Hall Green – become a huge tram-ridden meaningless suburb, where I actually lost my way – and eventually down what is left of beloved lanes of childhood, and past the very gate of our cottage, now in the midst of a sea of new red-brick. The old mill still stands, and Mrs Hunt's still sticks out into the road as it turns uphill; but the crossing beyond the now fenced-in pool, where the bluebell lane ran down into the mill lane, is now a dangerous crossing alive with motors and red lights. The White Ogre's house (which the children were excited to see) is become a petrol station, and most of Short Avenue and the elms between it and the crossing have gone. How I envy those whose precious early scenery has not been exposed to such violent and peculiarly hideous change.'

He was similarly sensitive to the damage that was inflicted on the Oxfordshire countryside by the construction of wartime aerodromes and the 'improvement' of roads. Later in life, when his strongest-held opinions began to become obsessions, he would see a new road that had been driven across the corner of a field and cry, 'There goes the last of England's arable!' By this time of his life he would maintain that there was not one unspoilt wood or hillside left in the land, and if there was, then he would refuse to visit it for fear of finding it contaminated by litter. The converse of this is that he chose to live in almost excessively man-made surroundings, in the suburbs of Oxford and later of Bournemouth, themselves almost as 'meaningless' as the red-brick wilderness that had once been Sarehole. How can we reconcile these viewpoints?

Again, part of the answer lies in circumstance. The places where he lived were not really chosen by him at all: they were simply the places where, for a number of reasons, he found himself. Maybe, but in this case why did not his soul cry out against them? To which the reply comes, sometimes it did, aloud to a few close friends or privately in his diary. But for much of the time it did *not*, and the explanation for this would seem to lie in his belief that we live in a fallen world. If the world were unfallen and man were not sinful, he himself would have spent an undisturbed childhood with his mother in a paradise such as Sarehole had in memory become to him. But his mother had been taken from him by the wickedness of the world (for he believed ultimately that she had died through the cruelty and neglect of her family), and now even the Sarehole landscape itself had been wantonly destroyed. In such a world, where perfection and true happiness were impossible, did it really matter in what surroundings one lived, any more than it really mattered what clothes one wore or what food one ate (providing it was plain food)? They were all temporary imperfections, and though imperfect were merely transient. It was in this sense a profoundly Christian and ascetic attitude to life.

There is another explanation for his apparently careless approach to the externals of existence. By the time he reached middle age his imagination no longer needed to be stimulated by experience; or rather, it had received all the stimulus it required in the early years of his life, the years of event and changing landscapes; now it could nourish itself upon these accumulated memories. Here is how he himself explained this process, when describing the creation of *The Lord of the Rings*:

'One writes such a story not out of the leaves of trees still to be observed, nor by means of botany and soil-science; but it grows like a seed in the dark out of the leaf-mould of the mind: out of all that has been seen or thought or read, that has long ago been forgotten, descending into the deeps. No doubt there is much selection, as with a gardener: what one throws on one's personal compost-heap; and my mould is evidently made largely of linguistic matter.'

Vegetable matter has to decompose for a long time before it has broken down sufficiently to be used to enrich the soil, and Tolkien is saying here that it was almost exclusively upon *early* experience, sufficiently broken down by time, that he nourished the seeds of his imagination. Further experience was not necessary, and it was not sought.

We seem to have found out a little about him as a result of looking at old photographs; so perhaps it might be worth our while to pass on from regarding his appearance and his surroundings to considering another external characteristic, his voice and his manner of speaking. From adolescence to the end of his life he was notable, almost notorious, for the speed and indistinctness of his way of talking. Actually it is easy to exaggerate this, to make him into a caricature of the comic professor muttering inaudibly to himself. In reality it was not much like that. He did speak fast and not very clearly, but once the listener was used to the mannerism there was little difficulty in understanding most of what he said. Or rather, the difficulty was not physical but intellectual. He moved on so fast from idea to idea and spoke so allusively, assuming an equal knowledge in his listener, that all but those with a comparable range of learning were left behind. Not that to speak too cleverly is necessarily more defensible than to speak too fast, and

Tolkien can be justly accused of overestimating the intellectual powers of his listeners. Alternatively one can say that he did not bother to make himself clear because he was really speaking to himself, airing his own ideas without any attempt at real conversation. Certainly this was often true of his later years, when he lived a life that was for the most part devoid of intellectual companionship; the result was that he was simply not used to conversation, and he tended to talk in monologues. But even in those days one could challenge him verbally, could engage him in real discourse, and he would listen and respond with enthusiasm.

Indeed he never bore the hallmark of the truly selfish man, the man who will not listen to anyone else. Tolkien always listened, always had a deep concern for the joys and sorrows of others. In consequence, though in many respects a shy man, he made friends easily. He liked to strike up a conversation with a Central European refugee on a train, a waiter in a favourite restaurant, or a hall porter in a hotel. In such company he was always entirely happy. He reported of a railway journey in 1953, when he was returning after lecturing on *Sir Gawain* at Glasgow: 'I travelled all the way from Motherwell to Wolverhampton with a Scotch mother and a wee lassie, whom I rescued from standing in the corridor of a packed train, and they were allowed to go "first" without payment since I told the inspector I welcomed their company. My reward was to be informed ere we parted that (while I was at lunch) the wee lassie had declared: "I like him but I canna understand a word he says." To which I could only lamely reply that the latter was universal but the former not so usual.'

During his later years he formed friendships with the taxi-drivers whose cars he used to hire, with the policeman who patrolled the streets around his Bournemouth bungalow, and with the college scout and his wife who looked after him at the end of his life. There was no element of condescension in these friendships; it was simply that he liked company, and these were the people nearest at hand. Nor was he without consciousness of class: the very opposite was true. But it was precisely because of his certainty of his own station in life that there was about him nothing of intellectual or social conceit. His view of the world, in which each man belonged or ought to belong to a specific 'estate', whether high or low, meant that in one sense he was an old-fashioned conservative. But in another sense it made him highly sympathetic to his fellow-men, for it is those who are unsure of their status in the world, who feel they have to prove themselves and if necessary put down other men to do so, who are the truly ruthless. Tolkien was, in modern jargon, 'right-wing' in that he honoured his monarch and his country and did not believe in the rule of the people; but he opposed democracy simply because he believed that in the end his fellow-men would not benefit from it. He once wrote: 'I am not a "democrat", if only because "humility" and equality are spiritual principles corrupted by the attempt to mechanize and formalize them, with the result that we get not universal smallness and humility, but universal greatness and pride, till some Orc gets hold of a ring of power – and then we get and are getting slavery.' As to the virtues of an old-fashioned feudal society, this is what he once said about respect for one's superiors: 'Touching your cap to the Squire may be damn bad for the Squire but it's damn good for you.'

What else can we observe? Perhaps the imaginary account of a typical day tells us something in that it starts with a journey to mass at St Aloysius'; and any close scrutiny of his life must take account of the importance of his religion. His commitment to Christianity and in particular to the Catholic Church was total. This is not to say that the practice of his faith was always a source of consolation to him: he set himself a rigorous code of behaviour, especially in the matter of making his confession before receiving communion, and when (as often happened) he could not bring himself to go to confession he would deny himself communion and live in a pathetic state of spiritual depression. Another source of unhappiness in his last years was the introduction of the vernacular mass, for the use of English in the liturgy rather than the Latin he had known and loved since boyhood pained him deeply. But even during an English mass in the bare modern church in Headington that he attended during his retirement, where he was sometimes irritated by the singing of the children's choir and the wailing of babies, he would, when receiving communion, experience a profound spiritual joy, a state of contentment that he could reach in no other way. His religion was therefore one of the deepest and strongest elements in his personality.

On one level his devotion to Catholicism is explicable solely as a spiritual matter; on another, it was bound up very closely with his love for the mother who had made him a Catholic and who had died (he believed) for her Catholicism. Indeed one can see his love for her memory as a governing motive throughout his life and writings. Her death made him a pessimist; or rather, it made him capable of violent shifts of emotion. Once he had lost her, there was no security, and his natural optimism was balanced by deep uncertainty. Perhaps as a result, he was never moderate: love, intellectual enthusiasm, distaste, anger, self-doubt, guilt, laughter, each was in his mind exclusively and in full force when he experienced it; and at that moment no other emotion was permitted to modify it. He was thus a man of extreme contrasts. When in a black mood he would feel that there was no hope, either for himself or the world; and since this was often the very mood that drove him to record his feelings on paper, his diaries tend to show only the sad side of his nature. But five minutes later in the company of a friend he would forget this black gloom and be in the best of humour.

Someone so strongly guided by his emotions is unlikely to be a cynic, and Tolkien was never cynical, for he cared too deeply about everything to adopt an intellectual detachment. He could, indeed, hold no opinion half-heartedly, could not be uncommitted about any topic that interested him. This sometimes led to strange attitudes. For example, his Gallophobia (itself almost inexplicable) made him angry not only about what he considered to be the pernicious influence of French cooking in England but about the Norman Conquest itself, which pained him as much as if it had happened in his lifetime. This strength of emotion was also reflected in his passion for perfection in any kind of written work, and in his inability to shrug off a domestic disaster philosophically. Again, he cared too much.

If he had been a proud man, his strong emotions would probably have made him unbearable. But he was in fact very humble. This is not to say that he was unaware of his own talents, for he had a perfectly accurate idea of what he could do, and a firm belief in his ability both as a scholar and a writer. But he did not consider that these talents were particularly important (with the result that in later years fame greatly puzzled him), and he certainly had no personal pride in his own character. Far from it: he took an almost tragic view of himself as a weak man – which was another cause of his deep troughs of pessimism. But there was a different result of his humility: a deep sense of comedy that sprang from his picture of himself as yet another feeble member of the human race.

He could laugh at anybody, but most of all at himself, and his complete lack of any sense of dignity could and often did make him behave like a riotous schoolboy. At a New Year's Eve party in the nineteen-thirties he would don an Icelandic sheepskin hearthrug and paint his face white to impersonate a polar bear, or he would dress up as an Anglo-Saxon warrior complete with axe and chase an astonished neighbour down the road. Later in life he delighted to offer inattentive shopkeepers his false teeth among a handful of change. 'I have,' he once wrote, 'a very simple sense of humour, which even my appreciative critics find tiresome.'

A strange and complex man, and this attempt to study his personality has not taught us very much. But as C. S. Lewis makes a character say in one of his novels, 'I happen to believe that you can't study men, you can only get to know them, which is quite a different thing.'

3

'He had been inside language'

If you are primarily interested in Tolkien as the author of *The Lord of the Rings*, you may take fright at the prospect of a chapter that discusses 'Tolkien the scholar and the teacher'. Expressed in that fashion, it certainly sounds very dull. So the first thing to be said is that it is *not* dull. There were not two Tolkiens, one an academic and the other a writer. They were the same man, and the two sides of him overlapped so that they were indistinguishable – or rather they were not two sides at all, but different expressions of the same mind, the same imagination. So if we are going to understand anything about his work as a writer we had better spend a short time examining his scholarship.

The first thing to understand is why he liked languages. We know a good deal about this from the account of his childhood. The fact that he was *excited* by the Welsh names on coal-trucks, by the 'surface glitter' of Greek, by the strange forms of the Gothic words in the book he acquired by accident, and by the Finnish of the *Kalevala*, shows that he had a most unusual sensitivity to the sound and appearance of words. They filled for him the place that music has in many people's lives. Indeed the response that words awakened in him was almost entirely emotional.

But why should he choose to specialise in early English? Someone so fond of strange words would be more likely to have concentrated his attention on foreign languages. The answer is again to be found in his capacity for *excitement*. We know already of his emotional response to Finnish, Welsh, and Gothic, and we ought to understand that something equally exciting happened when he first realised that a large proportion of the poetry and prose of

Anglo-Saxon and early medieval England was written in the dialect that had been spoken by his mother's ancestors. In other words it was remote, but at the same time intensely personal to him.

We already know that he was deeply attached to the West Midlands because of their associations with his mother. Her family had come from the town of Evesham, and he believed that this West Midland borough and its surrounding county of Worcestershire had been the home of that family, the Suffields, for countless generations. He himself had also spent much of his childhood at Sarehole, a West Midland hamlet. That part of the English countryside had in consequence a strong emotional attraction for him; and as a result so did its language.

He once wrote to W. H. Auden: 'I am a West-midlander by blood, and took to early West-midland Middle English as to a known tongue as soon as I set eyes on it.' *A known tongue:* something that already seemed familiar to him. One might dismiss this as a ludicrous exaggeration, for how could he 'recognise' a language that was seven hundred and fifty years old? Yet this was what he really believed, that he had inherited some faint ancestral memory of the tongue spoken by distant generations of Suffields. And once this idea had occurred to him, it was inevitable that he should study the language closely and make it the centre of his life's work as a scholar.

This is not to say that he only studied the early English of the West Midlands. He became well versed in all dialects of Anglo-Saxon and Middle English and (as we have seen) he also read widely in Icelandic. Moreover during 1919 and 1920 when he was working on the Oxford Dictionary he made himself acquainted with a number of other early Germanic languages. In consequence by the time he began work at Leeds University in 1920 he had a remarkably wide range of linguistic knowledge.

At Leeds and later at Oxford he proved to be a good teacher. He was not at his best in the lecture room, where his quick speech and indistinct articulation meant that pupils had to concentrate hard in order to hear him. Nor was he always very good at explaining himself in the clearest terms, for he found it difficult to scale down his own knowledge of the subject so that his pupils could understand everything he was saying. But he invariably brought the subject alive and showed that it mattered to him.

The most celebrated example of this, remembered by everyone

who was taught by him, was the opening of his series of lectures on *Beowulf*. He would come silently into the room, fix the audience with his gaze, and suddenly begin to declaim in a resounding voice the opening lines of the poem in the original Anglo-Saxon, commencing with a great cry of '*Hwæt!*' (the first word of this and several other Old English poems), which some undergraduates took to be 'Quiet!' It was not so much a recitation as a dramatic performance, an impersonation of an Anglo-Saxon bard in a mead hall, and it impressed generations of students because it brought home to them that *Beowulf* was not just a set text to be read for the purposes of an examination but a powerful piece of dramatic poetry. As one former pupil, the writer J. I. M. Stewart, expressed it: 'He could turn a lecture room into a mead hall in which he was the bard and we were the feasting, listening guests.' Another who sat in the audience at these lectures was W. H. Auden, who wrote to Tolkien many years later: 'I don't think I have ever told you what an unforgettable experience it was for me as an undergraduate, hearing you recite *Beowulf*. The voice was the voice of Gandalf.'

One reason for Tolkien's effectiveness as a teacher was that besides being a philologist he was a writer and poet, a man who not only studied words but who used them for poetic means. He could find poetry in the sound of the words themselves, as he had done since childhood; but he also had a poet's understanding of how language is used. This was expressed in a memorable phrase in *The Times* obituary of him (undoubtedly written by C. S. Lewis long before Tolkien's death) which talks of his 'unique insight at once into the language of poetry and into the poetry of language'. In practical terms this meant that he could show a pupil not just what the words meant, but *why* the author had chosen that particular form of expression and how it fitted into his scheme of imagery. He thus encouraged students of early texts to treat them not as mere exemplars of a developing language but as literature deserving serious appreciation and criticism.

Even when dealing solely with the technical matters of language, Tolkien was a vivid teacher. Lewis suggests in the obituary that this was in part the product of the long attention to private languages, the fact that he had been not merely a student of languages but a linguistic inventor: 'Strange as it may seem, it was undoubtedly the source of that unparalleled richness and concreteness which later distinguished him from all other philologists. He had been inside language.'

'Distinguished him from all other philologists' sounds like a sweeping statement, but it is entirely true. Comparative philology grew up in nineteenth-century Germany, and although its practitioners were painstaking in their accuracy their writing was almost unredeemed in its dullness. Tolkien's own mentor Joseph Wright had been trained in Germany, and while his books are invaluable for their contribution to the science of language they reflect almost nothing of Wright's vigorous personality. Much as he loved his old teacher, Tolkien was perhaps thinking partly of Wright when he wrote of 'the bespectacled philologist, English but trained in Germany, where he lost his literary soul'.

Tolkien never lost his literary soul. His philological writings invariably reflect the richness of his mind. He brought to even the most intricate aspects of his subject a grace of expression and a sense of the larger significance of the matter. Nowhere is this demonstrated to better advantage than in his article (published in 1929) on the *Ancrene Wisse*, a medieval book of instruction for a group of anchorites, which probably originated in the West Midlands. By a remarkable and subtle piece of scholarship, Tolkien showed that the language of two important manuscripts of the text (one in a Cambridge college, the other in the Bodleian Library at Oxford) was no mere unpolished dialect, but a literary language, with an unbroken literary tradition going back to before the Conquest. He expressed this conclusion in vivid terms – and it should be appreciated that he is here really talking about his beloved West Midland dialect as a whole:

'It is not a language long relegated to the "uplands" struggling once more for expression in apologetic emulation of its betters or out of compassion for the lewd, but rather one that has never fallen back into "lewdness", and has contrived in troublous times to maintain the air of a gentleman, if a country gentleman. It has traditions and some acquaintance with books and the pen, but it is also in close touch with a good living speech – a soil somewhere in England.'

This kind of writing, forceful in its imagery, characterised all his articles and lectures, however abstruse or unpromising the subject might seem. In this respect he almost founded a new school of philology; certainly there had been no one before him who brought such humanity, one might say such emotion, to the subject; and it was an approach which influenced many of his most able pupils who themselves became philologists of distinction.

It ought also to be said that he was immensely painstaking. Broad and powerful statements such as that quoted above may have characterised his work, yet they were no mere assertions, but the product of countless hours of research into the minutiae of the subject. Even by the usual scrupulous standards of comparative philology, Tolkien was extraordinary in this respect. His concern for accuracy cannot be overemphasised, and it was doubly valuable because it was coupled with a flair for detecting patterns and relations. 'Detecting' is a good word, for it is not too great a flight of fancy to picture him as a linguistic Sherlock Holmes, presenting himself with an apparently disconnected series of facts and deducing from them the truth about some major matter. He also demonstrated his ability to 'detect' on a simpler level, for when discussing a word or phrase with a pupil he would cite a wide range of comparable forms and expressions in other languages. Similarly in casual conversation he delighted in producing unexpected remarks about names, such as his observation that the name 'Waugh' is historically the singular of 'Wales'.

But probably all this sounds like the scholar in his ivory tower. What did he *do*? What, in practical terms, did it mean to be the Professor of Anglo-Saxon at Oxford? The simplest answer is that it meant a good deal of hard work. The statutes called upon Tolkien to give a minimum of thirty-six lectures or classes a year, but he did not consider this to be sufficient to cover the subject, and in the second year after being elected Professor he gave one hundred and thirty-six lectures and classes. This was partly because there were comparatively few other people to lecture on Anglo-Saxon and Middle English. Later he managed to get another philologist, an excellent if intimidating teacher named Charles Wrenn, appointed to assist him, and then he was able to set himself a slightly less strenuous programme. But throughout the nineteen-thirties he continued to give at least twice the statutory number of lectures and classes each year, considerably more than most of his colleagues undertook.

So lectures, and the preparation for them, took up a very large proportion of his time. In fact this heavy teaching load was sometimes more than he could manage efficiently, and occasionally he would abandon a course of lectures because of insufficient time to prepare it. Oxford seized gleefully on this sin and bestowed upon him the reputation of not preparing his lectures properly, whereas the truth was that he prepared them too thoroughly. His deep commitment to the subject prevented him from tackling it in anything less than an exhaustive manner, with the result that he often sidetracked himself into the consideration of subsidiary details, and never managed to finish the treatment of the main topic.

His job also required him to supervise post-graduate students, and to examine within the University. In addition he undertook a good deal of 'freelance' work as an external examiner to other universities, for with four children to bring up he needed to augment his income. During the nineteen-twenties and thirties he made frequent visits to many of the British universities as an examiner, and spent countless hours marking papers. After the Second World War he restricted this activity to examining regularly for the Catholic University of Ireland, touring Eire and making many friends there in the process. This was much to his taste. Less attractive, indeed an unredeemed chore, was the marking of School Certificate (the examination then set for British secondary schools) which he undertook annually in the pre-war years to earn extra money. His time would have been better devoted to research or writing, but his concern for the family income made him spend many hours in the summer at this irritating task.

A good deal of his attention was also taken up by administration. It should be understood that an Oxford professor, unlike those in many other universities, is not by virtue of his office necessarily in a position of power in his faculty. He has no authority over the college tutors who in all probability make up the majority of the faculty staff, for they are appointed by their colleges and are not answerable to him. So if he wishes to initiate some major change of policy he must adopt persuasive rather than authoritarian tactics. And, on his return to Oxford in 1925, Tolkien did wish to make a major change: he wanted to reform certain aspects of the Final Honour School of English Language and Literature.

The years since the First World War had widened the old rift between Language and Literature, and each faction in the English School—and they really were factions, with personal as well as academic animosities—delighted to interfere with the syllabus of the other. The 'Lang.' side made sure that the 'Lit.' students had to spend a good deal of their time studying the obscurer branches of English philology, while the 'Lit.' camp insisted that the 'Lang.' undergraduates must set aside many hours from their specialisation (Anglo-Saxon and Middle English) to study the works of Milton and Shakespeare. Tolkien believed that this should be remedied. What was even more regrettable to him was that the linguistic courses laid considerable emphasis on the study of theoretical philology without suggesting that undergraduates should read widely in early and medieval literature. His own love of philology had always been based firmly on a knowledge of literature, and he determined that this state of affairs should be changed. He also proposed that Icelandic should be given more prominence in the syllabus; this latter hope was one reason for the formation of the Coalbiters.

His proposals required the consent of the whole faculty, and at first he met with a good deal of opposition. Even C. S. Lewis, not yet a personal friend, was among those who originally voted against him. But as the terms passed, Lewis and many others came over to Tolkien's side and gave him their active support. By 1931 he had managed ('beyond my wildest hopes', he wrote in his diary) to obtain general approval for the majority of his proposals. The revised syllabus was put into operation, and for the first time in the history of the Oxford English School something like a real *rapprochement* was achieved between 'Lang.' and 'Lit.'.

Besides being responsible for teaching and administration, professors at Oxford as elsewhere are expected to devote much of their time to original research. Tolkien's contemporaries had high hopes of him in this respect, for his glossary to Sisam's book, his edition with E. V. Gordon of *Sir Gawain and the Green Knight*, and his article on the *Ancrene Wisse* manuscripts demonstrated that he had an unrivalled mastery of the early Middle English of the West Midlands; and it was expected that he would continue to contribute important work in this field. He himself had every intention of doing so: he promised an edition of the Cambridge manuscript of the *Ancrene Wisse* to the Early English Text Society, and he did a great deal of research into this branch of early medieval English, this language 'with the air of a gentleman, if a country gentleman' which he loved so much. But the edition was not completed for many years, while the greater part of his research work never reached print.

Lack of time was one cause. He had chosen to devote the major part of his working life at Oxford to teaching, and this in itself limited what he could do in the matter of original research. The marking of examination papers in order to provide necessary money also ate into his time. But besides this there was the matter of his perfectionism.

Tolkien had a passion for perfection in written work of any kind, whether it be philology or stories. This grew from his emotional commitment to his work, which did not permit him to treat it in any manner other than the deeply serious. Nothing was allowed to reach the printer until it had been revised, reconsidered, and polished – in which respect he was the opposite of C. S. Lewis, who sent manuscripts off for publication with scarcely a second glance at them. Lewis, well aware of this difference between them, wrote of Tolkien: 'His standard of self-criticism was high and the mere suggestion of publication usually set him upon a revision, in the course of which so many new ideas occurred to him that where his friends had hoped for the final text of an old work they actually got the first draft of a new one.'

This is the main reason why Tolkien only allowed a small proportion of his work to reach the printed page. But what he did publish during the nineteen-thirties was a major contribution to scholarship. His paper on the dialects of Chaucer's *Reeve's Tale* is required reading for anyone who wishes to understand the regional variations of fourteenth-century English. (It was read to the Philological Society in 1931 but not published until 1934, and then with a typical Tolkien apology for the lack of what the author considered to be a necessary amount of revision and improvement.) And his lecture *Beowulf: the Monsters and the Critics*, delivered to the British Academy on 25 November 1936 and published in the following year, is a landmark in the history of criticism of this great Western Anglo-Saxon poem.

Beowulf, said Tolkien in the lecture, *is* a poem and not (as other commentators had often suggested) merely a jumble of confused literary traditions, or a text for scholarly examination. And he described, in characteristically imaginative terms, the way that earlier critics had treated the *Beowulf* poet's work: 'A man inherited a field in which was an accumulation of old stone, part of an older hall. Of the old stone some had already been used in building the house in which he actually lived, not far from the old house of his fathers. Of the rest he took some and built a tower. But his friends coming perceived at once (without troubling to climb the steps) that these stones had formerly belonged to a more ancient building. So they pushed the tower over, with no little labour, in order to look for hidden carvings and inscriptions, or to discover whence the man's distant forefathers had obtained their building material. Some suspecting a deposit of coal under the soil began to dig for it, and forgot even the stones. They all said: "This tower is most interesting." But they also said (after pushing it over): "What a muddle it is in!" And even the man's descendants, who might have been expected to consider what he had been about, were heard to murmur: "He is such an odd fellow! Imagine his using these old stones just to build a nonsensical tower! Why did not he restore the old house? He had no sense of proportion." But from the top of that tower the man had been able to look out upon the sea.'

In his lecture Tolkien pleaded for the rebuilding of that tower. He declared that although *Beowulf* is about monsters and a dragon, that does not make it negligible as heroic poetry. 'A dragon is no idle fancy,' he told his audience. 'Even today (despite the critics) you may find men not ignorant of tragic legend and history, who have heard of heroes and indeed seen them, who have yet been caught by the fascination of the worm.'

This was Tolkien talking not primarily as a philologist or even a literary critic, but as a storyteller. Just as Lewis said of his philology, 'He had been inside language', so it might be remarked that when he talked of the *Beowulf* dragon he was speaking as the author of *The Silmarillion* and – by this time – of *The Hobbit*. He had been into the dragon's lair.

Since the lecture was first published, many readers of *Beowulf* have dissented from Tolkien's view of the poem's structure. But even one of the severest critics of his interpretation, his old tutor Kenneth Sisam, admitted that the lecture has a 'fineness of perception and elegance of expression' which distinguish it from so much else in this field.

The *Beowulf* lecture and the paper on the *Reeve's Tale* were the only major pieces of philological work published by Tolkien in the nineteen-thirties. He planned to do much more: besides his work on the *Ancrene Wisse* he intended to produce an edition of the Anglo-Saxon poem *Exodus*, and indeed he nearly completed this task, but it was never finished to his satisfaction. He also planned further joint editions with E. V. Gordon, in particular of *Pearl* (a natural companion-piece to their *Gawain*) and of the Anglo-Saxon elegies *The Wanderer* and *The Seafarer*. But Gordon and Tolkien were now geographically far apart. In 1931 Gordon, who had been appointed Tolkien's successor as professor at Leeds, moved from there to take up a chair at Manchester University, and though the two men met and corresponded frequently, collaboration proved technically less easy than when they had been in the same place. Gordon did a great deal of work on all three projects, using Tolkien as a consultant rather than as a full collaborator, but nothing had reached print by 1938.

In the summer of that year. Gordon went into hospital for an operation for gall-stones. It seemed to be successful, but his condition suddenly deteriorated, and he died from a previously unsuspected kidney disorder, at the age of forty-two.

Gordon's death robbed Tolkien not only of a close friend but also of the ideal professional collaborator; and by now it was clear that he *needed* a collaborator, if only to make him surrender any material to the printer.[1] As it happened, he had made the acquaintance of another philologist who proved to be a good working partner. This was Simonne d'Ardenne, a Belgian graduate who studied Middle English with him for an Oxford B.Litt. early in the nineteen-thirties. Tolkien contributed much to her edition of *The Life and Passion of St Juliene*, a medieval religious work written in the *Ancrene Wisse* dialect. Indeed the d'Ardenne *Juliene* paradoxically contains more of his views on early Middle English than anything he ever published under his own name. Mlle d'Ardenne became a professor at Liège, and she and Tolkien planned to collaborate on an edition of *Katerine*, another Western Middle English text of the same group. But the war intervened and made communication between them impossible for many years, and after 1945 nothing was achieved by them beyond a couple of short articles on topics concerned with the manuscript of the text. Although Tolkien was able to work with Mlle d'Ardenne when he was in Belgium to attend a philological congress in 1951, she realised sadly

[1]Tolkien intended to complete the *Pearl* edition, but he found himself unable to do so (by this time he was absorbed in writing *The Lord of the Rings*). It was eventually revised and completed for publication by Ida Gordon, the widow of E. V. Gordon, and herself a professional philologist.

that collaboration with him was now impossible, for his mind was entirely on his stories.

But even if one is to regard his failure to publish more in his professional field as a matter for regret, one should not fail to take account of his wide influence, for his theories and deductions have been quoted (with or without due acknowledgement) wherever English philology is studied.

Nor should one forget the translations he made of *Pearl, Sir Gawain and the Green Knight,* and *Sir Orfeo.* The *Pearl* translation was begun at Leeds in the nineteen-twenties; Tolkien was attracted to the task by the challenge of the poem's complex metrical and verbal structure. He had finished it by 1926, but he did nothing about publishing it until Basil Blackwell offered to put it into print in the nineteen-forties, in return for a sum to be credited to Tolkien's heavily overdue account at Blackwell's bookshop in Oxford. The translation was set into type, but Blackwell waited in vain for Tolkien to write the introduction to the volume, and eventually the project was abandoned. The translation of *Gawain,* probably begun during the nineteen-thirties or forties, was finished in time for it to be broadcast in dramatised form by the BBC in 1953, Tolkien himself recording a short introduction and a longer concluding talk. Following the success of *The Lord of the Rings* his publishers Allen & Unwin determined to issue the *Gawain* and *Pearl* translations in one volume. With this in view, Tolkien made extensive revisions of both translations, but once again an introduction was required, and he found it extremely difficult to write one, being uncertain as to what ought to be explained to the non-scholarly reader for whom the book was intended. Again the project lapsed, and it was not until after his death that the two translations were published, together with a modern English rendering of a third poem of the same period, *Sir Orfeo,* which Tolkien had originally translated for a wartime cadets' course at Oxford. The introduction to the volume was assembled by Christopher Tolkien out of such materials as could be found among his father's papers.

These translations were in effect Tolkien's last published philological work, for although they are accompanied by no notes or commentary they are the result of sixty years' minute study of the poems, and in many places they provide an informed and illuminating interpretation of hard and ambiguous passages in the originals. Most important of all, they bring these poems to an audience that could not have read them in Middle English. For this reason they are a fitting conclusion to the work of a man who believed that the prime function of a linguist is to interpret literature, and that the prime function of literature is to be enjoyed.

4
Jack

When Tolkien returned to Oxford in 1925 there was an element missing from his life. It had disappeared with the breaking of the T.C.B.S. in the Battle of the Somme, for not since those days had he enjoyed friendship to the same degree of emotional and intellectual commitment. He had continued to see something of the other surviving T.C.B.S. member, Christopher Wiseman, but Wiseman was now heavily involved with his duties as the headmaster of a Methodist public school,[1] and when the two men did meet they now found very little in common.

On 11 May 1926 Tolkien attended a meeting of the English Faculty at Merton College. Among the familiar faces a new arrival stood out, a heavily-built man of twenty-seven in baggy clothes who had recently been elected Fellow and Tutor in English Language and Literature at Magdalen College. This was Clive Staples Lewis, known to his friends as 'Jack'.

At first the two men circled warily around one another. Tolkien knew that Lewis, though a medievalist, was in the 'Lit.' camp and thus a potential adversary, while Lewis wrote in his diary that Tolkien was 'a smooth, pale, fluent little chap', adding 'No harm in him: only needs a smack or so.' But soon Lewis came to have a firm affection for this long-faced keen-eyed man who liked good talk and laughter and beer, while Tolkien warmed to Lewis's quick mind and the generous spirit that was as huge as Lewis's shapeless flannel trousers. By May 1927 Tolkien had enrolled Lewis into the

---

[1] Queen's College Taunton, which Tolkien's grandfather John Suffield had attended as one of its earliest pupils.

Coalbiters to join in the readings of Icelandic sagas, and a long and complex friendship had begun.

Anyone who wants to know something of what Tolkien and Lewis contributed to each other's lives should read Lewis's essay on Friendship in his book *The Four Loves*. Here it all is, the account of how two companions become friends when they discover a shared insight, how their friendship is not jealous but seeks out the company of others, how such friendships are almost of necessity between men, how the greatest pleasure of all is for a group of friends to come to an inn after a hard day's walking: 'Those are the golden sessions,' writes Lewis, 'when our slippers are on, our feet spread out towards the blaze and our drinks at our elbows; when the whole world, and something beyond the world, opens itself to our minds as we talk; and no one has any claim or responsibility for another, but all are freemen and equals as if we had first met an hour ago, while at the same time an Affection mellowed by the years enfolds us. Life – natural life – has no better gift to give.'[1]

This is what it was about, those years of companionship, the walking tours, the friends gathered in Lewis's rooms on Thursday nights. It was partly the spirit of the times – you may find something of the same sense of male companionship in the writings of Chesterton; and it was a feeling shared, though with less self-awareness, by many men of the day. It has precedents in ancient civilisations, and closer at hand it was in part the result of the First World War, in which so many friends had been killed that the survivors felt the need to stay close together. Friendship of this kind was remarkable, and at the same time entirely natural and inevitable. It was not homosexual (Lewis dismisses that suggestion with deserved ridicule), yet it excluded women. It is the great mystery of Tolkien's life, and we shall understand little of it if we try to analyse it. At the same time if we have ever enjoyed a friendship of that sort we shall know exactly what it was about. And even if that fails us, we can find something of it expressed in *The Lord of the Rings*.

How did it begin? Perhaps 'Northernness' was the shared insight that started it. Since early adolescence Lewis had been captivated by Norse mythology, and when he found in Tolkien another who delighted in the mysteries of the Edda and the complexities of the

---

[1] C. S. Lewis, *The Four Loves* (Fontana, 1963), p. 68.

Völsung legend it was clear that they would have a lot to share. They began to meet regularly in Lewis's rooms in Magdalen, sometimes sitting far into the night while they talked of the gods and giants of Asgard or discussed the politics of the English School. They also commented on each other's poetry. Tolkien lent Lewis the typescript of his long poem 'The Gest of Beren and Lúthien', and after reading it Lewis wrote to him: 'I can quite honestly say that it is ages since I have had an evening of such delight: and the personal interest of reading a friend's work had very little to do with it – I should have enjoyed it just as well if I'd picked it up in a bookshop, by an unknown author.' He sent Tolkien detailed criticisms of the poem, which he jestingly couched in the form of a mock textual criticism, complete with the names of fictitious scholars ('Pumpernickel', 'Peabody', and 'Schick') who suggested that weak lines in Tolkien's poem were simply the result of scribal inaccuracies in the manuscript, and could not be the authentic work of the original poet. Tolkien was amused by this, but he did not accept any of Lewis's suggested emendations. On the other hand he did rewrite almost every passage that Lewis had criticised, rewrote so extensively, in fact, that the revised 'Gest of Beren and Lúthien' was scarcely the same poem. Lewis soon discovered this to be characteristic of his friend. 'He has only two reactions to criticism,' he remarked. 'Either he begins the whole work over again from the beginning or else takes no notice at all.'

By this time – the end of 1929 – Lewis was supporting Tolkien's plans for changes within the English School. The two men intrigued and discussed. Lewis wrote conspiratorially to Tolkien: 'Forgive me if I remind you that there are disguised orcs behind every tree.' Together they waged a skilful campaign, and it was partly thanks to Lewis's support on the Faculty Board that Tolkien managed to get his reformed syllabus accepted in 1931.

In *Surprised by Joy* Lewis wrote that friendship with Tolkien 'marked the breakdown of two old prejudices. At my first coming into the world I had been (implicitly) warned never to trust a Papist, and at my first coming into the English Faculty (explicitly) never to trust a philologist. Tolkien was both.' Soon after the second prejudice had been overcome, the friendship moved into the area of the first.

Lewis, the son of a Belfast solicitor, had been brought up as an Ulster protestant. During adolescence he had professed agnosticism; or rather he had discovered that for him the greatest delight was to be found not in Christianity but in pagan mythologies. Yet already he had receded a little from this standpoint. During the middle nineteen-twenties, after taking a First Class in the English School (and earlier a double First in Classics) and while making a precarious living as a tutor, he had arrived at what he called his 'New Look', the belief that the Christian 'myth' conveys as much truth as most men can comprehend. By 1926 he had moved further and had come to the conclusion that in effect his search for the source of what he called Joy was a search for God. Soon it became apparent to him that he must accept or reject God. At this juncture he became friends with Tolkien.

In Tolkien he found a person of wit and intellectual verve who was nevertheless a devout Christian. During the early years of their friendship there were many hours when Tolkien would lounge in one of Lewis's plain armchairs in the centre of the big sitting-room in Magdalen New Buildings while Lewis, his heavy fist grasping the bowl of his pipe and his eyebrows raised behind a cloud of smoke, would pace up and down, talking or listening, suddenly swinging round and exclaiming '*Distinguo,* Tollers! *Distinguo!*' as the other man, similarly wreathed in pipe smoke, made too sweeping an assertion. Lewis argued, but more and more in the matter of belief he was coming to admit that Tolkien was right. By the summer of 1929 he had come to profess theism, a simple faith in God. But he was not yet a Christian.

Usually his discussions with Tolkien took place on Monday mornings, when they would talk for an hour or two and then conclude with beer at the Eastgate, a nearby pub. But on Saturday 19 September 1931 they met in the evening. Lewis had invited Tolkien to dine at Magdalen, and he had another guest, Hugo Dyson, whom Tolkien had first known at Exeter College in 1919. Dyson was now Lecturer in English Literature at Reading University, and he paid frequent visits to Oxford. He was a Christian, and a man of feline wit. After dinner, Lewis, Tolkien, and Dyson went out for air. It was a blustery night, but they strolled along Addison's Walk discussing the purpose of myth. Lewis, though now a believer in God, could not yet understand the function of Christ in Christianity, could not perceive the meaning of the Crucifixion and Resurrection. He declared that he had to understand the purpose of these events – as he later expressed it in a letter to a friend, 'how the life and death of Someone Else (whoever he was) two thousand years ago could help us here and now – except in so far as his *example* could help us'.

As the night wore on, Tolkien and Dyson showed him that he was here making a totally unnecessary demand. When he encountered the idea of sacrifice in the mythology of a pagan religion he admired it and was moved by it; indeed the idea of the dying and reviving deity had always touched his imagination since he had read the story of the Norse god Balder. But from the Gospels (they said) he was requiring something more, a clear meaning beyond the myth. Could he not transfer his comparatively unquestioning appreciation of sacrifice from the myth to the true story?

But, said Lewis, *myths are lies, even though lies breathed through silver.*[1]

No, said Tolkien, *they are not.*

And, indicating the great trees of Magdalen Grove as their branches bent in the wind, he struck out a different line of argument.

You call a tree a tree, he said, and you think nothing more of the word. But it was not a 'tree' until someone gave it that name. You call a star a star, and say it is just a ball of matter moving on a mathematical course. But that is merely how *you* see it. By so naming things and describing them you are only inventing your own terms about them. And just as speech is invention about objects and ideas, so myth is invention about truth.

We have come from God (continued Tolkien), and inevitably the myths woven by us, though they contain error, will also reflect a splintered fragment of the true light, the eternal truth that is with God. Indeed only by myth-making, only by becoming a 'sub-creator' and inventing stories, can Man ascribe to the state of perfection that he knew before the Fall. Our myths may be misguided, but they steer however shakily towards the true harbour, while materialistic 'progress' leads only to a yawning abyss and the Iron Crown of the power of evil.

In expounding this belief in the inherent *truth* of mythology, Tolkien had laid bare the centre of his philosophy as a writer, the creed that is at the heart of *The Silmarillion*.

[1]The account of this conversation is based on Tolkien's poem 'Mythopoeia', to which he also gave the titles 'Misomythos' and 'Philomyth to Misomyth'. One manuscript is marked 'For C. S. L.'.

Lewis listened as Dyson affirmed in his own way what Tolkien had said. You mean, asked Lewis, that the story of Christ is simply a true myth, a myth that works on us in the same way as the others, but a myth that *really happened*? In that case, he said, I begin to understand.

At last the wind drove them inside, and they talked in Lewis's rooms until three a.m., when Tolkien went home. After seeing him out into the High Street, Lewis and Dyson walked up and down the cloister of New Buildings, still talking, until the sky grew light.

Twelve days later Lewis wrote to his friend Arthur Greeves: 'I have just passed on from believing in God to definitely believing in Christ – in Christianity. I will try to explain this another time. My long night talk with Dyson and Tolkien had a great deal to do with it.'

Meanwhile Tolkien, invigilating in the Examination Schools, was composing a long poem recording what he had said to Lewis. He called it 'Mythopoeia', the making of myths. And he wrote in his diary: 'Friendship with Lewis compensates for much, and besides giving constant pleasure and comfort has done me much good from the contact with a man at once honest, brave, intellectual – a scholar, a poet, and a philosopher – and a lover, at least after a long pilgrimage, of Our Lord.'

Lewis and Tolkien continued to see much of each other. Tolkien read aloud to Lewis from *The Silmarillion*, and Lewis urged him to press on and finish writing it. Tolkien later said of this: 'The unpayable debt that I owe to him was not "influence" as it is ordinarily understood, but sheer encouragement. He was for long my only audience. Only from him did I ever get the idea that my "stuff" could be more than a private hobby.'

Lewis's conversion to Christianity marked the beginning of a new stage in his friendship with Tolkien. From the early nineteen-thirties onwards the two men depended less exclusively on each other's company and more on that of other men. In *The Four Loves* Lewis states that 'two, far from being the necessary number for Friendship, is not even the best', and he suggests that each friend added to a group brings out some special characteristic in the others. Tolkien had experienced this in the T.C.B.S.; and the knot of friends which now began to come together was the ultimate

1 (a). Family group, Bloemfontein, November 1892. Left to right: Arthur Tolkien; a servant; Mabel Tolkien (seated); Isaak the houseboy; nurse holding Ronald Tolkien aged ten months. The handwriting around the photograph is that of Mabel Tolkien.

(b). Maitland Street, Bloemfontein, in the eighteen-nineties. Bank House, where Tolkien was born, is the second building from the left, beyond the two shops.

2. Sarehole Mill.

3 (a). Left to right: Ronald and Hilary Tolkien in May 1905, aged thirteen and eleven respectively.

(b). Father Francis Morgan.

4 (a). Edith Bratt in 1906, aged seventeen.

(b). Ronald Tolkien in 1911, aged nineteen.

5 (a). King Edward's School rugby football First XV, 1909–10. Christopher Wiseman stands fourth from left in the back row, Ronald Tolkien fifth from left. The handwriting is Tolkien's.

(b). Joseph Wright.

6 (a). Exeter College, Oxford: the library and chapel from the Fellows' Garden.

(b). The Apolausticks, May 1912. Tolkien was co-founder of this undergraduate club at Exeter College. He sits second from right in the middle row, with Colin Cullis in the centre of the row.

7. Edith and Ronald Tolkien in 1916.

8 (a). Leeds University English Department, 1921. In the middle of the front row are (left to right) Tolkien and George Gordon.

(b). E. V. Gordon.

9 (a). Family group in the garden at Northmoor Road circa 1936.
Left to right: Priscilla, Michael, John, J.R.R.T., Christopher.

(b). 20 Northmoor Road.

10 (a). Family group, Northmoor Road, August 1942.
Left to right (standing): Christopher, John.
(Sitting): Edith, Priscilla, J.R.R.T.

(b). C. S. Lewis.

11. Countryside near Oxford.
(a). The Berkshire Downs from the Ridgeway, near White Horse Hill.

(b). Great Tew, an unspoilt Oxfordshire village.

16. At the conferment of an Honorary Doctorate of Letters by Oxford University, 4 June 1972.

13. Edith and Ronald Tolkien at the gate of 76 Sandfield Road, in 1966.

14 (a). Tolkien on the terrace of the Hotel Miramar, Bournemouth, 1961.

(b). The last photograph of Tolkien, taken next to one of his favourite trees (*Pinus Nigra*) in the Botanic Garden, Oxford, 9 August 1973.

15. In the study at Merton Street, 1972.

"What does the writing say?" asked Frodo, who was trying to decipher the ~~decipher the arch of letters~~ inscription on the arch. "I thought I knew the elf-letters, but ~~these are all entangled~~ cannot read these."

"The words are in the elf-tongue of ~~word~~ the West of Middle-earth in the Elder Days," said Gandalf. "But they do not say anything of importance to us. ~~for that we need is the opening spell, and that they do not reveal.~~ They say only: *The Doors of Durin Lord of Moria : Speak, friend, and enter.* And underneath small and faint is : ~~I~~ *Narvi made them. Celebrimbor of Hollin drew these signs.*"

This is an archaic use of the elvish characters: spelling :———

ENNYN ÐURIN ARAN·VÓRIA : PEDO MELLON A MINNO :
im Narvi hain echant. Celebrimbor o Eregion teithant i·núw thin.
(?K)

12. A page from the manuscript of *The Lord of the Rings,* showing an early drawing by Tolkien of the gate to the Mines of Moria.

expression of the T.C.B.S. principle, the 'clubbable' urge which Tolkien had felt since those adolescent days. This group was known as The Inklings.

It began to form itself at about the time (in the early nineteen-thirties) when the Coalbiters ceased to meet, having fulfilled their aim of reading all the principal Icelandic sagas and finally the Elder Edda. 'The Inklings' was originally the name of a literary society founded in about 1931 by a University College undergraduate named Tangye Lean. Lewis and Tolkien both attended its meetings, at which unpublished compositions were read and criticised. After Lean left Oxford the club lived on; or rather its name was transferred half jestingly to the circle of friends who gathered at regular intervals around Lewis.

The Inklings have now entered literary history, and a good deal has been written about them, much of it over-solemn. They were no more (and no less) than a number of friends, all of whom were male and Christian, and most of whom were interested in literature. Numbers of people have been stated to have been 'members' at this or that period, whereas in truth there was no system of membership. Some men attended more or less regularly at various periods, while others were only occasional visitors. Lewis was the invariable nucleus, without whom any gathering would have been inconceivable. A list of other names gives little idea of what the Inklings really were; but if names matter, besides Lewis and Tolkien (who was almost invariably present) among those who attended in the years before and during the war were Major Warren Lewis (C. S. Lewis's brother, known as 'Warnie'), R. E. Havard (an Oxford doctor who attended the Lewis and Tolkien households), Lewis's long-standing friend Owen Barfield (although, being a London solicitor, Barfield rarely came to meetings), and Hugo Dyson.

It was a thoroughly casual business. One should not imagine that the same people turned up week after week, or sent apologies if they were to be absent. Nevertheless there were certain invariable elements. The group, or various members of it, would meet on a weekday morning in a pub, generally on Tuesdays in the Eagle and Child (known familiarly as 'The Bird and Baby'); though during the war when beer was short and pubs crowded with servicemen their habits were more flexible. On Thursday nights they would meet in Lewis's big Magdalen sitting-room, congregating some time after nine o'clock. Tea would be made and pipes lit, and then Lewis would boom out: 'Well, has nobody got anything to read us?' Someone would produce a manuscript and begin to read it aloud – it might be a poem, or a story, or a chapter. Then would come criticism: sometimes praise, sometimes censure, for it was no mutual admiration society. There might be more reading, but soon the proceedings would spill over into talk of all kinds, sometimes heated debate, and would terminate at a late hour.

By the late nineteen-thirties the Inklings were an important part of Tolkien's life, and among his own contributions to gatherings were readings from the still-unpublished manuscript of *The Hobbit*. When war broke out in 1939 another man was recruited to the group of friends. This was Charles Williams, who worked for the Oxford University Press at their London office and who with the rest of their staff was now transferred to Oxford. Williams was in his fifties; his thought and writings – he was a novelist, poet, theologian, and critic – were already known and respected, albeit by a small circle of readers. In particular his 'spiritual thrillers' (as they have been called), novels which deal with supernatural and mystical events in a mundane setting, had found a small but enthusiastic public. Lewis had known and admired Williams for some time, but Tolkien had only met him once or twice. Now he came to develop a complex attitude to him.

Williams, with his curious face (half angel, half monkey, Lewis called it), his very un-Oxford-like blue suit, the cigarette dangling from his mouth, and a bundle of proofs wrapped in *Time & Tide* tucked under his arm, was a person of great natural charm. Tolkien recalled twenty years later: 'We liked one another and enjoyed talking (mostly in jest)'. But he added: 'We had nothing to say to one another at deeper (or higher) levels.' This was partly because, while Williams enjoyed the chapters from *The Lord of the Rings* that were then being read to the group, Tolkien did not like Williams's books, or those which he had read. He declared that he found them 'wholly alien, and sometimes very distasteful, occasionally ridiculous'. And perhaps his reservations about Williams, or Williams's place in the Inklings, were not entirely intellectual. Lewis believed, and declared in *The Four Loves*, that true friends cannot be jealous when another comes to join them. But here Lewis was talking about Lewis, not about Tolkien. Clearly there was a little jealousy or resentment on Tolkien's part, and not without cause, for now the limelight of Lewis's enthusiasm shifted almost imperceptibly from himself to Williams. 'Lewis was a very impressionable man,' Tolkien wrote long afterwards, and elsewhere he talked of the 'dominant influence' that he believed Williams had come to exercise over Lewis, especially over his third novel, *That Hideous Strength.*

So Williams's arrival in Oxford marked the beginning of a third phase in Tolkien's friendship with Lewis, a faint cooling on Tolkien's part which even Lewis probably hardly noticed as yet. Something else made him cooler, something even more subtle: the matter of Lewis's growing reputation as a Christian apologist. As Tolkien had played such an important part in his friend's return to Christianity he had always regretted that Lewis had not become a Catholic like himself, but had begun to attend his local Anglican church, resuming the religious practices of his childhood. Tolkien had a deep resentment of the Church of England which he sometimes extended to its buildings, declaring that his appreciation of their beauty was marred by his sadness that they had been (he considered) perverted from their rightful Catholicism. When Lewis published a prose allegory telling the story of his conversion under the title *The Pilgrim's Regress*, Tolkien thought the title ironical. 'Lewis would regress,' he said. 'He would not re-enter Christianity by a new door, but by the old one: at least in the sense that in taking it up again he would also take up again, or reawaken, the prejudices so sedulously planted in childhood and boyhood. He would become again a Northern Ireland protestant.'

By the mid nineteen-forties Lewis was receiving a good deal of publicity ('too much,' said Tolkien, 'for his or any of our tastes') in connection with his Christian writings, *The Problem of Pain* and *The Screwtape Letters*. Tolkien perhaps felt, as he observed his friend's increasing fame in this respect, rather as if a pupil had speedily overtaken his master to achieve almost unjustified fame. He once referred to Lewis, not altogether flatteringly, as 'Everyman's Theologian'.

But if these thoughts were at all in Tolkien's mind in the early nineteen-forties they were well below the surface. He still had an almost unbounded affection for Lewis – indeed perhaps still cherished the occasional hope that his friend might one day become a Catholic. And the Inklings continued to provide much delight and encouragement to him. '*Hwæt! we Inclinga,*' he wrote in parody of the opening lines of *Beowulf*, '*on ærdagum searopancolra snyttru gehierdon.*' 'Lo! we have heard in old days of the wisdom of the cunning-minded Inklings; how those wise ones sat together in their deliberations, skilfully reciting learning and song-craft, earnestly meditating. That was true joy!'

5
Northmoor Road

'What were the women doing meanwhile? How should I know? I am a man and never spied on the mysteries of the Bona Dea.' So writes C. S. Lewis in *The Four Loves* while speculating on the history of male friendship. This is the inevitable corollary of a life that centres on the company of men, and on groups such as the Inklings: women get left out of it.

Edith Tolkien had only been given a limited education at a girls' boarding-school which, while good in music, was indifferent in other subjects. She had spent a few years in a Birmingham lodging-house, then a period at Cheltenham in a markedly non-intellectual middle-class household, and then a long time living with her poorly educated middle-aged cousin Jennie. There had been no chance either to continue her education or to improve her mind. More than this, she had lost a good deal of her independence. She had been set for a career as a piano teacher and just possibly as a soloist, but this prospect had simply faded away, first of all because there had been no immediate need for her to earn a living, and then because she had married Ronald Tolkien. In those days there was in normal circumstances no question of a middle-class wife continuing to earn her living after marriage, for to do so would have been an indication that the husband could not earn enough by himself. So piano playing was reduced to a mere hobby, although she continued to play regularly until old age, and her music delighted Ronald. He did not encourage her to pursue any intellectual activity, partly because he did not consider it to be a necessary part of her role as wife and mother, and partly because his attitude to her in courtship (exemplified by his favourite term for her, 'little one')

153

was not associated with his own intellectual life; to her he showed a side of his personality quite different from that perceived by his male friends. Just as he liked to be a man's man among his cronies, so at home he expected to live in what was primarily a woman's world.

Despite this, Edith might have been able to make a positive contribution to his life in the University. A number of Oxford dons' wives managed to do this. A few lucky ones such as Joseph Wright's wife Lizzie were themselves expert in their husbands' subjects, and could assist in their work. But a number of other wives who, like Edith, did not have university degrees could by their expert management of the household make their home into something of a social centre for their husbands' friends, and so participate in much of their lives.

Unfortunately everything worked out rather differently for Edith. She was inclined to be shy, for she had led a very limited social life in childhood and adolescence, and when she came to live in Oxford in 1918 she was unnerved by what she found. She and Ronald and the baby (and her cousin Jennie, who was still with them, remaining until they moved to Leeds) lived in modest rooms in a side-street in the town; and, from her viewpoint as someone who did not know Oxford, the University seemed an almost impenetrable fortress, a phalanx of imposing buildings where important-looking men passed to and fro in gowns, and where Ronald disappeared to work each day. When the University deigned to cross her threshold it was in the person of polite but awkward young men, friends of Ronald's who did not know how to talk to women, and to whom she could think of nothing to say, for their worlds simply did not overlap. Worse still, the visitors might be dons' wives, such as the terrifying Mrs Farnell, wife of the Rector of Exeter, whose presence even frightened Ronald. These women only confirmed Edith in her belief that the University was unapproachable in its eminence. They came from their awesome college lodgings or their turreted mansions in North Oxford to coo condescendingly at baby John in his cot, and when they departed they would leave their calling-cards on the hall tray (*one* card bearing their own name, *two* cards bearing their husband's) to indicate that Mrs Tolkien was of course expected to *return* the call after a short interval. But Edith's nerve failed her. What could she say to these people if she went to their imposing houses? What possible conversation could she have with these stately women, whose talk was all of people of whom she had never heard, of professors' daughters and titled cousins and other Oxford hostesses? Ronald was worried, for he knew what a solecism would be committed if his wife did not follow the strict Oxford etiquette. He persuaded her to return one call, to Lizzie Wright, who although very learned was not at all like most dons' wives, having a great deal of her husband's openness and common sense; but even then Ronald had to take her to the Wrights' front door himself and ring the bell before hurrying away round the corner. All the other calling-cards gathered dust, the calls were left unreturned, and it became known that Mr Tolkien's wife *did not call* and must therefore be quietly excluded from the round of dinner-parties and At Homes.

Then the Tolkiens moved to Leeds, and Edith found that things were different there. People occupied ordinary modest houses, and there was no nonsense about calling-cards. Another university wife lived a few doors down in St Mark's Terrace and often called for a chat. Edith also began to see a good deal of Ronald's pupils who came in for tutorials or tea, and she liked many of them very much. Many of these pupils became family friends who kept in touch with her in later years and often came to visit. There were informal university dances which she enjoyed. Even the children (there were now John, Michael, and, at the end of their time in Leeds, Christopher) were not forgotten, for the university organised splendid Christmas parties at which the Vice-Chancellor used to dress up as Father Christmas. Later, Ronald managed to afford to buy a larger house in Darnley Road, away from the smoke and dirt of the city. They employed a maid and a nurse for the children. On the whole Edith was happy.

But then suddenly they were back in Oxford. The first house in Northmoor Road was bought by Ronald while Edith was still in Leeds, without her ever having seen it; and she thought it was too small. The older boys had caught ringworm from a public comb at a photographer's studio in Leeds, and they had to be given lengthy and expensive treatment. When they were sufficiently recovered to go to the Dragon School they were at first unhappy there among the rough-and-tumble of other boys. Then Edith became pregnant again. Not until after the birth of Priscilla in 1929 and the move to the larger house next door in 1930 could she feel settled.

Even then, family life never entirely regained the equilibrium it had achieved in Leeds. Edith began to feel that she was being ignored by Ronald. In terms of actual hours he was certainly in the house a great deal: much of his teaching was done there, and he was not often out for more than one or two evenings a week. But it was really a matter of his affections. He was very loving and considerate to her, greatly concerned about her health (as she was about his) and solicitous about domestic matters. But she could see that one side of him only came alive when he was in the company of men of his own kind. More specifically she noticed and resented his devotion to Jack Lewis.

On the occasions when Lewis came to Northmoor Road, the children liked him because he did not talk condescendingly to them; and he gave them books by E. Nesbit, which they enjoyed. But with Edith he was shy and ungainly. Consequently she could not understand the delight that Ronald took in his company, and she became a little jealous. There were other difficulties. She had only known a home life of the most limited sort in her own childhood, and she therefore had no example on which to base the running of her household. Not surprisingly she cloaked this uncertainty in authoritarianism, demanding that meals be precisely on time, that the children eat up every scrap, and that servants should perform their work impeccably. Underneath all this she was often very lonely, frequently being without company other than the servants and the children during that part of the day when Ronald was out or in his study. During these years Oxford society was gradually becoming less rigid; but she did not trust it, and she made few friends among other dons' families, with the exception of Charles Wrenn's wife, Agnes. She also suffered from severe headaches which could prostrate her for a day or more.

It quickly became clear to Ronald that Edith was unhappy with Oxford, and especially that she was resentful of his men friends. Indeed he perceived that his need of male friendship was not entirely compatible with married life. But he believed that this was one of the sad facts of a fallen world; and on the whole he thought that a man had a right to male pleasures, and should if necessary insist on them. To a son contemplating marriage he wrote: 'There are many things that a man feels are legitimate even though they cause a fuss. Let him not lie about them to his wife or lover! Cut them out – or if worth a fight: just insist. Such matters may arise frequently – the glass of beer, the pipe, the non writing of letters, the other friend, etc., etc. If the other side's claims really are unreasonable (as they are at times between the dearest lovers and most loving married folk) they are much better met by above board refusal and "fuss" than subterfuge.'

There was also the problem of Edith's attitude to Catholicism. Before they were married, Ronald had persuaded her to leave the Church of England and to become a Catholic, and she had resented this a little at the time. During the subsequent years she had almost given up going to mass. In the second decade of marriage her anti-Catholic feelings hardened, and by the time the family returned to Oxford in 1925 she was showing resentment of Ronald taking the children to church. In part these feelings were due to Ronald's rigid, almost medieval, insistence upon frequent confession; and Edith had always hated confessing her sins to a priest. Nor could he discuss her feelings with her in a rational manner, certainly not with the lucidity he demonstrated in his theological arguments with Lewis: to Edith he presented only his emotional attachment to religion, of which she had little understanding. Occasionally her smouldering anger about church-going burst into fury; but at last after one such outburst in 1940 there was a true reconciliation between her and Ronald, in which she explained her feelings and even declared that she wished to resume the practice of her religion. In the event she did not return to regular church-going, but for the rest of her life she showed no resentment of Catholicism, and indeed delighted to take an interest in church affairs, so that it appeared even to friends who were Catholics that she was an active church-goer.

To some extent Ronald and Edith lived separate lives at Northmoor Road, sleeping in different bedrooms and keeping different hours. He worked late, partly because he was short of time in the day, but also because it was not until she had gone to bed that he could stay at his desk without interruption. During the day he could not work for long before she summoned him to some domestic duty, or called him to come and have tea with a friend. These frequent interruptions, themselves no more than an understandable demand from Edith for affection and attention, were often an irritant to him, though he bore them patiently.

Yet it would be wrong to picture her as excluded totally from his work. During these years he did not share his writing with her anything like as fully as he had done long before at Great Haywood; not since then had she been encouraged to participate in his work, and of his manuscripts only the early pages of 'The Book of Lost Tales' are in her handwriting. Yet she inevitably shared in the family's interest when he was writing *The Hobbit* and *The Lord of the Rings*, and although she was not well acquainted with the details of his books and did not have a deep understanding of them, he did not shut her out from this side of his life. Indeed she was the first person to whom he showed two of his stories, *Leaf by Niggle* and *Smith of Wootton Major*; and he was always warmed and encouraged by her approval.

He and Edith shared many friends. Among these, some had academic connections, such as Rosfrith Murray (daughter of the original Oxford Dictionary editor Sir James Murray) and her nephew Robert Murray, and former pupils and colleagues such as Simonne d'Ardenne, Elaine Griffiths, Stella Mills, and Mary Salu. All these were family friends, as much a part of Edith's life as of Ronald's, and this itself was a binding force between them. She and Ronald did not always talk about the same things to the same people, and as they grew older each went his and her own way in this respect, Ronald discoursing on an English place-name apparently oblivious that the same visitor was simultaneously being addressed by Edith on the subject of a grandchild's measles. But this was something that regular guests learnt to cope with.

Those friends and others who knew Ronald and Edith Tolkien over the years never doubted that there was deep affection between them. It was visible both in the small things, the almost absurd degree to which each worried about the other's health, and the care with which they chose and wrapped each other's birthday presents; and in the large matters, the way in which Ronald willingly abandoned such a large part of his life in retirement to give Edith the last years at Bournemouth that he felt she deserved, and the degree to which she showed pride in his fame as an author.

A principal source of happiness to them was their shared love for their family. This bound them together until the end of their lives, and it was perhaps the strongest force in the marriage. They delighted to discuss and mull over every detail of the lives of their children, and later of their grandchildren. They were very proud when Michael won the George Medal in the Second World War for his action as an anti-aircraft gunner defending aerodromes in the Battle of Britain; and they felt similar pride when John was ordained a priest in the Catholic Church shortly after the war. Tolkien was immensely kind and understanding as a father, never shy of kissing his sons in public even when they were grown men, and never reserved in his display of warmth and love.

If to us, reading about it so many years later, life at Northmoor Road seems dull and uneventful, we should realise that this was not how the family felt it to be at the time. To them it was full of event. There was the unforgettable occasion in 1932 when Tolkien bought his first car, a Morris Cowley that was nicknamed 'Jo' after the first two letters of its registration. After learning to drive he took the entire family by car to visit his brother Hilary at his Evesham fruit farm. At various times during the journey 'Jo' sustained two punctures and knocked down part of a dry-stone wall near Chipping Norton, with the result that Edith refused to travel in the car again until some months later – not entirely without justification, for Tolkien's driving was daring rather than skilful. When accelerating headlong across a busy main road in Oxford in order to get into a side-street, he would ignore all other vehicles and cry *'Charge 'em and they scatter!'* – and scatter they did. 'Jo' was later replaced by a second Morris which did duty until the beginning of the Second World War, when petrol rationing made it impractical to keep it. By this time Tolkien perceived the damage that the internal combustion engine and new roads were doing to the landscape, and after the war he did not buy another car or drive again.

What else remained in the children's memories? Long summer hours digging up the asphalt of the old tennis-court at 20 Northmoor Road to enlarge the vegetable-plot, under the supervision of their father, who (like their mother) was an enthusiastic gardener, though he left much of the practical work of cultivating vegetables and pruning trees to John, preferring to concentrate his own attention on the roses and on the lawn, from which he would remove every possible weed. The early years at 22 Northmoor Road when there were a succession of Icelandic *au pair* girls, who told folk-tales about trolls. Visits to the theatre, which their father always seemed to enjoy, although he declared he did not approve of Drama. Bicycling to early mass at St Aloysius', or at St Gregory's up the Woodstock Road, or at the Carmelite convent nearby. The barrel of beer in the coal-hole behind the kitchen which dripped regularly and (said their mother) made the house smell like a brewery. July and August afternoons boating on the river Cherwell (which was only just down the road), floating in the family punt hired for the season down past the Parks to Magdalen Bridge, or better still poling up-river towards Water Eaton and Islip, where a picnic tea could be spread on the bank. Walks across the fields to Wood Eaton to look for butterflies, and then back along by the river where Michael would hide in the crack of an old willow; walks when their father seemed to have a boundless store of knowledge about trees and plants. Seaside summer holidays at Lyme Regis when old Father Francis Morgan came down from Birmingham to join them, embarrassing the children with his loud and boisterous ways just as he had embarrassed Ronald and Hilary at Lyme twenty-five years before. The family holiday at Lamorna Cove in Cornwall in 1932 with Charles Wrenn and his wife and daughter, when Wrenn and Tolkien held a swimming race wearing panama hats and smoking pipes while they swam. This was the holiday about which Tolkien later wrote: 'There was a curious local character, an old man who used to go about swapping gossip and weather-wisdom and such like. To amuse my boys I named him Gaffer Gamgee, and the name became part of family lore to fix on old chaps of the kind. The choice of Gamgee was primarily directed by alliteration; but I did not invent it. It was in fact the name when I was small (in Birmingham) for "cotton-wool".' Then there were the later holidays at Sidmouth, where there were hill walks and marvellous rock-pools by the sea, and where their father was already beginning to write *The Lord of the Rings*; the drives on autumn afternoons to the villages east of Oxford, to Worminghall or Brill or Charlton-on-Otmoor, or west into Berkshire and up White Horse Hill to see the ancient long-barrow known as Wayland's Smithy; the memories of Oxford, of the countryside, and of the stories that their father told them.

6
The storyteller

These stories had begun during the Leeds years. John, the eldest son, often found difficulty in getting to sleep. When he was lying awake his father would come and sit on his bed and tell him a tale of 'Carrots', a boy with red hair who climbed into a cuckoo clock and went off on a series of strange adventures.

In this fashion Tolkien discovered that he could use the imagination which was creating the complexities of *The Silmarillion* to invent simpler stories. He had an amiably childlike sense of humour, and as his sons grew older this manifested itself in the noisy games he played with them – and in the stories he told Michael when the younger boy was troubled with nightmares. These tales, invented in the early days at Northmoor Road, were about the irrepressible villain 'Bill Stickers', a huge hulk of a man who always got away with everything. His name was taken from a notice on an Oxford gate that said BILL STICKERS WILL BE PROSECUTED, and a similar source provided the name of the righteous person who was always in pursuit of Stickers, 'Major Road Ahead'.

The 'Bill Stickers' stories were never written down, but others were. When he was on holiday with the family at Filey in the summer of 1925, Tolkien composed a full-length tale for John and Michael. The younger boy lost a toy dog on the beach, and to console him his father began to invent and narrate the adventures of Rover, a small dog who annoys a wizard, is turned into a toy, and is then lost on the beach by a small boy. But this is only the beginning, for Rover is found by the sand-sorcerer Psamathos Psamathides who gives him the power to move again, and sends him on a visit to the Moon, where he has many strange adventures, most notably an encounter with the White Dragon. Tolkien wrote down this story under the title 'Roverandom'. Many years later he offered it to his publishers, very tentatively, as one of a number of possible successors to *The Hobbit*, but it was not thought suitable on that occasion, and Tolkien never offered it again.

The children's enthusiasm for 'Roverandom' encouraged him to write more stories to amuse them. Many of these got off to a good start but were never finished. Indeed some of them never progressed beyond the first few sentences, like the tale of Timothy Titus, a very small man who is called 'Tim Tit' by his friends. Among other stories begun but soon abandoned was the tale of Tom Bombadil, which is set in 'the days of King Bonhedig' and describes a character who is clearly to be the hero of the tale: 'Tom Bombadil was the name of one of the oldest inhabitants of the kingdom; but he was a hale and hearty fellow. Four foot high in his boots he was, and three feet broad. He wore a tall hat with a blue feather, his jacket was blue, and his boots were yellow.'

That was as far as the story ever reached on paper, but Tom Bombadil was a well-known figure in the Tolkien family, for the character was based on a Dutch doll that belonged to Michael. The doll looked very splendid with the feather in its hat, but John did not like it and one day stuffed it down the lavatory. Tom was rescued, and survived to become the hero of a poem by the children's father, 'The Adventures of Tom Bombadil', which was published in the *Oxford Magazine* in 1934. It tells of Tom's encounters with 'Goldberry, the River-woman's daughter', with the 'Old Man Willow' which shuts him up in a crack of its bole (an idea, Tolkien once said, that probably came in part from Arthur Rackham's tree-drawings), with a family of badgers, and with a 'Barrow-wight', a ghost from a prehistoric grave of the type found on the Berkshire Downs not far from Oxford. By itself, the poem seems like a sketch for something longer, and when possible successors to *The Hobbit* were being discussed in 1937 Tolkien suggested to his publishers that he might expand it into a more substantial tale, explaining that Tom Bombadil was intended to represent 'the spirit of the (vanishing) Oxford and Berkshire countryside'. This idea was not taken up by the publishers, but Tom and his adventures subsequently found their way into *The Lord of the Rings*.

The purchase of a car in 1932 and Tolkien's subsequent mishaps while driving it led him to write another children's story, 'Mr Bliss'. This is the tale of a tall thin man who lives in a tall thin house, and who purchases a bright yellow automobile for five shillings, with remarkable consequences (and a number of collisions). The story was lavishly illustrated by Tolkien in ink and coloured pencils, and the text was written out by him in a fair hand, the whole being bound in a small volume. 'Mr Bliss' owes a little to Beatrix Potter in its ironical humour and to Edward Lear in the style of its draw-ings, though Tolkien's approach is less grotesque and more deli-cate than Lear's. Like 'Roverandom' and the Bombadil poem it was shown to Tolkien's publishers in 1937, and it was received with much enthusiasm. Preliminary arrangements were made to publish it, not so much as a successor to *The Hobbit* but as an entertaining stop-gap until the true sequel was ready. However its multi-coloured pictures meant that printing would be very expen-sive, and the publishers asked Tolkien if he would re-draw them in a simpler style. He agreed, but he could not find the time to undertake the work, and the manuscript of 'Mr Bliss' was con-signed to a drawer, where it remained until many years later it was sold to Marquette University in America, along with the manu-scripts of Tolkien's published stories.[1]

The fact that 'Mr Bliss' was so lavishly illustrated – was con-structed indeed around the pictures – is an indication of how seriously Tolkien was taking the business of drawing and painting. He had never entirely abandoned this chilhood hobby, and during his undergraduate days he illustrated several of his own poems, using watercolours, coloured inks or pencils, and beginning to develop a style that was suggestive of his affection for Japanese prints and yet had an individual approach to line and colour. The war and his work interrupted him, but in about 1925 he began to draw again regularly, one of the first results being a series of illus-trations for 'Roverandom'. Later, during holidays at Lyme Regis in 1927 and 1928, he drew pictures of scenes from *The Silmarillion*. These show how clearly he visualised the landscapes in which his legends were set, for in several of the drawings the scenery of

[1]'Mr Bliss' was not the only composition by Tolkien owing its inspiration to motor transport. 'The Bovadium Fragments' (perhaps composed early in the nineteen-sixties) is a parable of the destruction of Oxford (*Bovadium*) by the *motores* manufactured by the *Daemon* of *Vaccipratum* (a reference to Lord Nuffield and his motor-works at Cowley) which block the streets, asphyxiate the inhabitants, and finally explode.

Lyme itself is absorbed into the stories and invested with mystery.

He was by now a very talented artist, although he had not the same skill at drawing figures as he had with landscapes. He was at his best when picturing his beloved trees, and like Arthur Rackham (whose work he admired) he could give to twisted root and branch a sinister mobility that was at the same time entirely true to nature.

Tolkien's talents as a storyteller and an illustrator were combined each December, when a letter would arrive for the children from Father Christmas. In 1920 when John was three years old and the family was about to move to Leeds, Tolkien had written a note to his son in shaky handwriting signed 'Yr loving Fr. Chr.'. From then onwards he produced a similar letter every Christmas. From simple beginnings the 'Father Christmas Letters' expanded to include many additional characters such as the Polar Bear who shares Father Christmas's house, the Snow Man who is Father Christmas's gardener, an elf named Ilbereth who is his secretary, snow-elves, gnomes, and in the caves beneath Father Christmas's house a host of troublesome goblins. Every Christmas, often at the last minute, Tolkien would write out an account of recent events at the North Pole in the shaky handwriting of Father Christmas, the rune-like capitals used by the Polar Bear, or the flowing script of Ilbereth. Then he would add drawings, write the address on the envelope (labelling it with such superscriptions as 'By gnome-carrier. Immediate haste!') and paint and cut out a highly realistic North Polar postage stamp. Finally he would deliver the letter. This was done in a variety of ways. The simplest was to leave it in the fireplace as if it had been brought down the chimney, and to cause strange noises to be heard in the early morning, which together with a snowy footprint on the carpet indicated that Father Christmas himself had called. Later the local postman became an accomplice and used to deliver the letters himself, so how could the children not believe in them? Indeed they went on believing until each in turn reached adolescence and discovered by accident or deduction that their father was the true author of the letters. Even then, nothing was said to destroy the illusion for the younger children.

Besides being entertained by their father's own stories, the Tolkien children were always provided with full nursery bookshelves. Much of their reading-matter consisted of Tolkien's own childhood favourites, such as George Macdonald's 'Curdie' stories and Andrew Lang's fairy-tale collections; but the nursery also housed more recent additions to children's literature, among them E. A. Wyke-Smith's *The Marvellous Land of Snergs*, which was published in 1927. Tolkien noted that his sons were highly amused by the Snergs, 'a race of people only slightly taller than the average table but broad in the shoulders and of great strength'.

Tolkien himself only found the time or the inclination to read a limited amount of fiction. In general he preferred the lighter contemporary novels. He liked the stories of John Buchan, and he also read some of Sinclair Lewis's work; certainly he knew *Babbitt*, the novel published in 1922 about a middle-aged American businessman whose well-ordered life gradually comes off the rails.

Odd ingredients go into literary melting-pots, and both the *Land of Snergs* and *Babbitt* played a small part in *The Hobbit*. Tolkien wrote to W. H. Auden that the former 'was probably an unconscious source-book: for the Hobbits, not of anything else', and he told an interviewer that the word *hobbit* 'might have been associated with Sinclair Lewis's Babbitt. Certainly not rabbit, as some people think. Babbitt has the same bourgeois smugness that hobbits do. His world is the same limited place.'

There is less mystery about the origins of another story that Tolkien wrote at some time during the nineteen-thirties, perhaps in part to amuse his children, but chiefly to please himself. This is *Farmer Giles of Ham*, whose territory, 'The Little Kingdom', is Oxfordshire and Buckinghamshire, and which clearly grew from the implications of the place-name Worminghall (meaning 'reptile-hall' or 'dragon-hall'), a village a few miles to the east of Oxford. The first version of the story, considerably shorter than that eventually published, is a plain tale that draws its humour from the events rather than from the narrative style. It too was offered to Tolkien's publishers as a possible successor to *The Hobbit*, and like its companions was considered excellent but not exactly what was wanted at that moment.

Some months later, early in 1938, Tolkien was due to read a paper to an undergraduate society at Worcester College on the subject of fairy-stories. But the paper had not been written, and as the day approached Tolkien decided to read *Farmer Giles* instead. When he reconsidered it, he decided that he could make some improvements, and in the rewriting that followed he turned it into a longer story with sophisticated humour. A few nights later he read it at Worcester College. 'I was very much surprised at the result,' he recorded afterwards. 'The audience was apparently not bored – indeed they were generally convulsed with mirth.' When it became apparent that the sequel to *The Hobbit* would not be ready for some considerable time, he offered the revised *Farmer Giles* to his publishers, and it was accepted with enthusiasm; but wartime delays and Tolkien's dissatisfaction with the original choice of illustrator meant that the book did not appear until 1949, with pictures by a young artist named Pauline Diana Baynes. Her mock-medieval drawings delighted Tolkien, and he wrote of them: 'They are more than illustrations, they are a collateral theme.' Miss Baynes's success with *Farmer Giles* led to her being chosen as illustrator for C. S. Lewis's Narnia stories, and she later drew the pictures for Tolkien's anthology of poems and for *Smith of Wootton Major*; she and her husband became friends with the Tolkiens in later years.

Farmer Giles did not attract much notice at the time of its publication, and it was not until the success of *The Lord of the Rings* had reflected upon the sales of Tolkien's other books that it reached a wide public. At one time Tolkien considered writing a sequel to it, and he sketched the plot in some detail; it was to concern Giles's son George Worming and a page-boy named Suet, as well as re-introducing Chrysophylax the dragon, and it was to be set in the same countryside as its predecessor. But by 1945 the war had scarred the Oxfordshire landscape that Tolkien loved so much, and he wrote to his publishers: 'The sequel (to *Farmer Giles*) is plotted but unwritten, and likely to remain so. The heart has gone out of the Little Kingdom, and the woods and plains are aerodromes and bomb-practice targets.'

Though sometimes touching on deep feelings, the short stories that Tolkien wrote for his children in the nineteen-twenties and thirties were really *jeux d'esprit*. His real commitment was to grander themes, both in verse and prose.

He continued to work on his long poem 'The Gest of Beren and Lúthien' and on the alliterative verses telling the story of Túrin and the dragon. In 1926 he sent these and other poems to R. W. Reynolds, who had taught him English literature at King Edward's School, and asked for his criticism. Reynolds approved of the various shorter pieces that Tolkien sent, but only gave lukewarm praise to the major mythological poems. Undeterred, and encouraged by C. S. Lewis's approval of the Beren and Lúthien poem, Tolkien continued to work at them both. But though the Túrin verses reached more than two thousand lines and the 'Gest' more than four thousand, neither poem was completed; and by the time Tolkien came to revise *The Silmarillion* (after he had written *The Lord of the Rings*) he had perhaps abandoned any intention of incorporating them into the published text of the cycle. Nevertheless both poems were important in the development of the legends, particularly the 'Gest', which contains the fullest version of the Beren and Lúthien story.

The poems were also important for Tolkien's technical development as a writer. The rhyming couplets of the early stanzas of the 'Gest' are occasionally monotonous in rhythm or banal in rhyme, but as Tolkien became more experienced in the metre the poem grew much surer, and it has many fine passages. The Túrin verses are in an alliterative measure, a modern version of the Anglo-Saxon verse form; and in them Tolkien displays great skill. This passage describes Túrin's childhood and adolescence in the elven kingdom of Doriath:

> Much lore be learned, and loved wisdom,
> but fortune followed him in few desires;
> oft wrong and awry what he wrought turnéd;
> what he loved he lost, what he longed for he won not;
> and full friendship he found not easily,
> nor was lightly loved for his looks were sad.
> He was gloomy-hearted, and glad seldom
> for the sundering sorrow that seared his youth.
> On manhood's threshold he was mighty holden
> in the wielding of weapons; and in weaving song
> he had a minstrel's mastery; but mirth was not in it.

In adapting and modernising this ancient poetic style for his own purposes Tolkien was achieving something quite unusual and remarkably powerful. It is a pity that he wrote – or at least published – so little alliterative verse, for it suited his imagination far more than did modern rhyme-schemes.

He wrote other poems of some length during the nineteen-thirties, by no means all of them directly connected with his own mythology. One, inspired by the Celtic legends of Brittany, was 'Aotrou and Itroun' (Breton for 'Lord and Lady'), of which the earliest manuscript is dated September 1930. The poem tells the story of a childless lord who obtains a potion from an enchantress or 'Corrigan' (the generic Breton term for a person of fairy race). As a result of the philtre, twins are born to the lord's wife, but the Corrigan demands in payment that the lord should wed her, and his refusal has tragic consequences. 'Aotrou and Itroun' was published some years later by Tolkien's friend and fellow philologist Gwyn Jones, in the *Welsh Review*. It is in alliterative verse, and also incorporates a rhyme-scheme.

Another major poem from this period has alliteration but no rhyme. This is 'The Fall of Arthur', Tolkien's only imaginative incursion into the Arthurian cycle, whose legends had pleased him since childhood, but which he found 'too lavish, and fantastical, incoherent and repetitive'. Arthurian stories were also unsatisfactory to him as myth in that they explicitly contained the Christian religion. In his own Arthurian poem he did not touch on the Grail but began an individual rendering of the Morte d'Arthur, in which the king and Gawain go to war in 'Saxon lands' but are summoned home by news of Mordred's treachery. The poem was never finished, but it was read and approved by E. V. Gordon, and by R. W. Chambers, Professor of English at London University, who considered it to be 'great stuff – really heroic, quite apart from its value as showing how the *Beowulf* metre can be used in modern English'. It is also interesting in that it is one of the few pieces of writing in which Tolkien deals explicitly with sexual passion, describing Mordred's unsated lust for Guinever (which is how Tolkien chooses to spell her name):

> His bed was barren; there black phantoms
> of desire unsated and savage fury
> in his brain had brooded till bleak morning.

But Tolkien's Guinever is not the tragic heroine beloved by most Arthurian writers; instead she is described as

> lady ruthless,
> fair as fay-woman and fell-mindéd,
> in the world walking for the woe of men.

Although 'The Fall of Arthur' was abandoned in the mid nineteen-thirties, Tolkien wrote as late as 1955 that he still hoped to complete it; but in the event it remained unfinished.

Once or twice he decided to move away from the mythical, legendary, and fantastic, and wrote a conventional short story for adults, in a modern setting. The results were unremarkable, showing that his imagination needed myth and legend in order to realise its full potential. And indeed the greater part of his attention was still occupied by *The Silmarillion*. He made numerous revisions and recastings of the principal stories in the cycle, deciding to abandon the original sea-voyager 'Eriol' to whom the stories were told, and instead renaming him 'Ælfwine' or 'elf-friend'. He also spent much time (probably more than he devoted to the actual stories) to working on the elvish languages and alphabets; he had now invented a new alphabet which he first called 'Quenyatic' and then 'Fëanorian', and after 1926 he wrote his diary in it. He also frequently turned his attention to geography and other subsidiary topics within the cycle of legends.

By the late nineteen-thirties all this work on *The Silmarillion* had resulted in a large body of manuscript, much of it in an exquisite hand. But as yet there was no move on Tolkien's part to publish any of it. Indeed few people knew of its existence. Outside the Tolkien family the only person acquainted with it was C. S. Lewis. Within the family the most frequent listener to the stories was Tolkien's third son, Christopher. The boy, wrote Tolkien in his diary, had grown into 'a nervy, irritable, cross-grained, self-tormenting, cheeky person. Yet there is something intensely loveable about him, to me at any rate, from the very similarity between us.' On many evenings in the early nineteen-thirties Christopher, huddled for warmth by the study stove, would listen motionless while his father told him (in impromptu fashion, rather than reading aloud) about the elvish wars against the black power, and of how Beren and Lúthien made their perilous journey to the very heart of Morgoth's iron stronghold. These were not mere stories: they were legends that came alive as his father spoke, vivid accounts of a grim world where foul orcs and a sinister Necromancer guarded the way, and a dreadful red-eyed wolf tore the elvish companions of Beren to pieces one by one; but a world also where the three great elvish jewels, the Silmarilli, shone with a strange and powerful light, a world where against all odds the quest could be victorious.

Tolkien's feelings towards his third son were perhaps one of the factors that made him begin a new book. More explicitly it owed its origins to C. S. Lewis who (Tolkien reported) one day said: ' "Tollers, there is too little of what we really like in stories. I am afraid we shall have to try and write some ourselves." We agreed' (said Tolkien) 'that he should try "space-travel", and I should try "time-travel".' They also decided that each story should lead to the discovery of Myth.

Lewis's story was *Out of the Silent Planet*, which proved to be the first book of his 'Ransom' trilogy.[1] Tolkien's answer to the challenge was a story called 'The Lost Road', in which two time-travellers, father and son, find themselves discovering the mythology of *The Silmarillion*, as they journey back to the land of Númenor.

Tolkien's legend of Númenor, the great island in the West that is given to the men who aided the Elves in the wars against Morgoth, was probably composed some time before the writing of 'The Lost Road', perhaps in the late nineteen-twenties or early thirties. It had one of its origins in the nightmare that had disturbed him since childhood, his 'Atlantis-haunting' in which he 'had the dreadful dream of the ineluctable Wave, either coming up out of a quiet sea, or coming in towering over the green inlands'. When the inhabitants of Númenor are beguiled by Sauron (the lieutenant of Morgoth who had already appeared in the long poem about Beren and Lúthien) into breaking a divine commandment and sailing West towards the forbidden lands, a great storm rises, a huge wave crashes on Númenor, and the entire island is cast into the abyss. Atlantis has sunk.

The Númenor story combines the Platonic legend of Atlantis

---

[1] This and the subsequent books were read to the Inklings by Lewis as they were written. The first two books gained Tolkien's almost wholehearted approval (though he did not admire all of Lewis's invented names), and it was partly due to his support that *Out of the Silent Planet*, which had been rejected by two publishers, was accepted by The Bodley Head and published in 1938. He liked *Perelandra* even more than the first story, but when Lewis began to read *That Hideous Strength* to the Inklings, Tolkien recorded of it: 'Tripish, I fear'; and a better acquaintance with the book did not make him change his mind. He regarded it as spoiled by the influence of Charles Williams's Arthurian-Byzantine mythology.

Tolkien recognised that the character of Ransom, the philologist hero of Lewis's stories, was perhaps modelled in part on himself. He wrote to his son Christopher in 1944: 'As a philologist I may have some part in him, and recognize some of my opinions and ideas Lewisified in him.'

with the imaginative qualities of *The Silmarillion*. At the end, Tolkien tells how with the sinking of Númenor the shape of the world is changed, and the Western lands are 'removed for ever from the circles of the world'. The world itself is bent, yet the Straight Road to the Ancient West still remains for those who can find it. This is the 'Lost Road' that gave the title to the new story.

'The Lost Road' itself (as opposed to the Númenor tale it was designed to introduce) is clearly a kind of idealised autobiography. Its protagonists are a father and son. The father, a professor of history named Alboin (the Lombardic form of 'Ælfwine'), invents languages, or rather he finds that words are transmitted to him, words that seem to be fragments of ancient and forgotten languages. Many of these words refer to the downfall of Númenor, and the story breaks off, unfinished, with Alboin and his son setting off on their journey through time towards Númenor itself. The story is rather cloying in its portrayal of the father-son relationship as Tolkien would have liked it to be; and it is notable that neither Alboin nor his own father (who appears at the beginning of the story) is encumbered with a wife, both men having been widowed at an early age. The story was probably read to the Inklings; certainly Lewis listened to the Númenor legend, for he refers to it in *That Hideous Strength*, mis-spelling it 'Numinor'. (He also borrowed from Tolkien when he gave his hero Ransom the first name 'Elwin', which is a version of 'Ælfwine'; and again when he named his Adam and Eve in *Perelandra* 'Tor and Tinidril', which Tolkien considered to be 'certainly an echo' of Tuor and Idril in 'The Fall of Gondolin'.)

'The Lost Road' was abandoned ('owing to my slowness and uncertainty,' said Tolkien) shortly after the time-travellers in the story reached Númenor. But Tolkien returned to the time-travelling theme as a way of introducing the Númenor legend when, at the end of 1945, he began to write 'The Notion Club Papers'. This uses the Inklings themselves (in thin disguise) as a setting, and this time it is two Oxford dons, members of the informal literary club that provides the title, who set off on the time-journey. But like its predecessor the story breaks off at the end of the introductory narrative, before the actual time-travelling has been more than superficially described. 'The Notion Club Papers' captures much of the spirit of the Inklings, though Tolkien scarcely attempts any portraits of his friends. One part of the story did reach print, a

171

poem about the medieval voyage of St Brendan, a legend that Tolkien adapted to fit his own mythology. Under the title 'Imram' (Gaelic for 'voyage') the poem appeared in *Time & Tide* in 1955. On its own it is a little bare, a forlorn memorial to an unfinished and promising story.

So it was that during the nineteen-twenties and thirties Tolkien's imagination was running along two distinct courses that did not meet. On one side were the stories composed for mere amusement, often specifically for the entertainment of his children. On the other were the grander themes, sometimes Arthurian or Celtic, but usually associated with his own legends. Meanwhile nothing was reaching print, beyond a few poems in the *Oxford Magazine* which indicated to his colleagues that Tolkien was amused by dragons' hoards and funny little men with names like Tom Bombadil: a harmless pastime, they felt, if a little childish.

Something was lacking, something that would bind the two sides of his imagination together and produce a story that was at once heroic and mythical and at the same time tuned to the popular imagination. He was not aware of this lack, of course; nor did it seem particularly significant to him when suddenly the missing piece fell into place.

It was on a summer's day, and he was sitting by the window in the study at Northmoor Road, laboriously marking School Certificate exam papers. Years later he recalled: 'One of the candidates had mercifully left one of the pages with no writing on it (which is the best thing that can possibly happen to an examiner) and I wrote on it: *"In a hole in the ground there lived a hobbit"*. Names always generate a story in my mind. Eventually I thought I'd better find out what hobbits were like. But that's only the beginning.'

V

1925–1949(ii) : The Third Age

1
Enter Mr Baggins

Really that missing piece had been there all the time. It was the Suffield side of his own personality.

His deep feeling that his real home was in the West Midland countryside of England had, since his undergraduate days, defined the nature of his scholarly work. The same motives that had led him to study *Beowulf, Gawain,* and the *Ancrene Wisse* now created a character that embodied everything he loved about the West Midlands: Mr Bilbo Baggins, the hobbit.

We can see certain superficial precedents for this invention: the Snergs, the name Babbitt, and in Tolkien's own stories the original four-foot Tom Bombadil and the tiny Timothy Titus. But this does not tell us very much. The personal element is far more revealing. In the story, Bilbo Baggins, son of the lively Belladonna Took, herself one of the three remarkable daughters of the Old Took, descended also from the respectable and solid Bagginses, is middle aged and unadventurous, dresses in sensible clothes but likes bright colours, and has a taste for plain food; but there is something strange in his character that wakes up when the adventure begins. John Ronald Reuel Tolkien, son of the enterprising Mabel Suffield, herself one of the three remarkable daughters of old John Suffield (who lived to be nearly a hundred), descended also from the respectable and solid Tolkiens, was middle aged and inclined to pessimism, dressed in sensible clothes but liked coloured waistcoats when he could afford them, and had a taste for plain food. But there was something unusual in his character that had already manifested itself in the creation of a mythology, and it now led him to begin this new story.

Tolkien himself was well aware of the similarity between creator and creation. 'I am in fact a hobbit,' he once wrote, 'in all but size. I like gardens, trees, and unmechanized farmlands; I smoke a pipe, and like good plain food (unrefrigerated), but detest French cooking; I like, and even dare to wear in these dull days, ornamental waistcoats. I am fond of mushrooms (out of a field); have a very simple sense of humour (which even my appreciative critics find tiresome); I go to bed late and get up late (when possible). I do not travel much.' And as if to emphasise the personal parallel, Tolkien chose for the hobbit's house the name 'Bag End', which was what the local people called his Aunt Jane's Worcestershire farm. Worcestershire, the county from which the Suffields had come, and in which his brother Hilary was at that time cultivating the land, is of all West Midland counties The Shire from which the hobbits come; Tolkien wrote of it: 'Any corner of that county (however fair or squalid) is in an indefinable way "home" to me, as no other part of the world is.' But the village of Hobbiton itself with its mill and river is to be found not in Worcestershire but in Warwickshire, now half hidden in the red-brick skirt of Birmingham but still identifiable as the Sarehole where Ronald Tolkien spent four formative years.

The hobbits do not owe their origins merely to personal parallels. Tolkien once told an interviewer: 'The Hobbits are just rustic English people, made small in size because it reflects the generally small reach of their imagination – not the small reach of their courage or latent power.' To put it another way, the hobbits represent the combination of small imagination with great courage which (as Tolkien had seen in the trenches during the First World War) often led to survival against all chances. 'I've always been impressed,' he once said, 'that we are here, surviving, because of the indomitable courage of quite small people against impossible odds.'

In some ways it is wrong to talk of hobbits as the 'missing piece' that was needed before the two sides of Tolkien's imagination during the nineteen-twenties and thirties could meet and fuse; at least chronologically wrong, because Tolkien probably began to write *The Hobbit* quite early in this period. It would be more accurate to say that not until the book was finished and published – indeed not until he began to write the sequel – did he realise the significance of hobbits, and see that they had a crucial role to play in his mythology. In itself *The Hobbit* began as merely another story for amusement. Moreover it nearly suffered the fate of so many others and remained unfinished.

While we can see quite clearly why Tolkien began to write the story, it proves impossible to say exactly when. The manuscript gives no indication of date, and Tolkien himself was unable to remember the precise origins of the book. In one account he said: 'I am not sure but I think the Unexpected Party (the first chapter) was hastily written before 1935 but certainly after 1930 when I moved to 20 Northmoor Road.' Elsewhere he wrote: 'On a blank leaf I scrawled "In a hole in the ground there lived a hobbit". I did not and do not know why. I did nothing about it, for a long time, and for some years I got no further than the production of Thror's Map. But it became *The Hobbit* in the early nineteen-thirties.' This recollection that there was a hiatus between the original idea and the composition of the main body of the story is confirmed by a note that Tolkien scribbled on a surviving page of the original Chapter One: 'Only page preserved of the first scrawled copy of *The Hobbit* which did not reach beyond the first chapter.' In 1937, shortly after the book was published, Christopher Tolkien recorded (in his letter to Father Christmas) this account of the book's origins: 'Daddy wrote it ages ago, and read it to John, Michael and me in our Winter "Reads" after tea in the evening; but the ending chapters were rather roughly done, and not typed out at all; he finished it about a year ago.' And writing to his publishers during the same year, Tolkien declared: 'My eldest boy was thirteen when he heard the serial. It did not appeal to the younger ones who had to grow up to it successively.'

These statements lead to the conclusion that the book was begun in 1930 or 1931 (when John, the eldest boy, was thirteen); certainly there was a completed typescript in existence (lacking only the final chapters) in time for it to be shown to C. S. Lewis late in 1932. However John and Michael Tolkien do not believe this to be the entire picture, for they have a clear memory of certain elements in the story being told to them in the study at *22* Northmoor Road, that is, before 1930. They are not certain that what they were listening to at that time was necessarily a *written* story: they believe that it may well have been a number of impromptu tales which were later absorbed into *The Hobbit* proper.

The manuscript of *The Hobbit* suggests that the actual writing of the main part of the story was done over a comparatively short period of time: the ink, paper, and handwriting style are consistent, the pages are numbered consecutively, and there are almost no chapter divisions. It would also appear that Tolkien wrote the story fluently and with little hesitation, for there are comparatively few erasures or revisions. Originally the dragon was called 'Pryftan', the name 'Gandalf' was given to the chief dwarf, and the wizard was called 'Bladorthin'. The dragon's name was soon changed to 'Smaug', from the Germanic verb *smugan* meaning 'to squeeze through a hole'; Tolkien called this 'a low philological jest'. But the name 'Bladorthin' was retained for some time, and it was not until the draft was well advanced that the chief dwarf was renamed 'Thorin Oakenshield' and the name 'Gandalf' (taken, like all the dwarf-names, from the Elder Edda) was given to the wizard, for whom it was eminently suitable on account of its Icelandic meaning of 'sorcerer-elf' and hence 'wizard'.

The story began, then, merely for personal amusement. Certainly Tolkien had at first no intention that the bourgeois comfortable world of Bilbo Baggins would be related in any way to the vast mythological landscape of *The Silmarillion*. Gradually, however, elements from his mythology began to creep in. Inevitably the dwarves suggested a connection, for 'dwarves' (spelt in that fashion) had played a part in the earlier work; and when in the first chapter of *The Hobbit* the wizard mentioned 'the Necromancer' there was a reference to the legend of Beren and Lúthien. Soon it was apparent that the journey of Bilbo Baggins and his companions lay across a corner of that Middle-earth which had its earlier history chronicled in *The Silmarillion*. In Tolkien's words this was 'the world into which Mr Baggins strayed'. And if the events of the new story were clearly set long after those of *The Silmarillion*, then, since the earlier chronicles recorded the history of the First and Second Ages of Middle-earth, it appeared that *The Hobbit* was to be a tale of the Third Age.

'One writes such a story,' said Tolkien, 'out of the leaf-mould of the mind'; and while we can still detect the shape of a few of the leaves – the Alpine trek of 1911, the goblins of the 'Curdie' books of George Macdonald, an episode in *Beowulf* when a cup is stolen from a sleeping dragon – this is not the essential point of Tolkien's metaphor. One learns little by raking through a compost heap to see what dead plants originally went into it. Far better to observe its effect on the new and growing plants that it is enriching. And in *The Hobbit* the leaf-mould of Tolkien's mind nurtured a rich growth with which only a few other books in children's literature can compare.

For it *is* a children's story. Despite the fact that it had been drawn into his mythology, Tolkien did not allow it to become overwhelmingly serious or even adult in tone, but stuck to his original intention of amusing his own and perhaps other people's children. Indeed he did this too consciously and deliberately at times in the first draft, which contains a large number of 'asides' to juvenile readers, remarks such as 'Now you know quite enough to go on with' and 'As we shall see in the end'. He later removed many of these, but some remain in the published text – to his regret, for he came to dislike them, and even to believe that any deliberate talking down to children is a great mistake in a story. 'Never mind about the young!' he once wrote. 'I am not interested in the "child" as such, modern or otherwise, and certainly have no intention of meeting him/her half way, or a quarter of the way. It is a mistaken thing to do anyway, either useless (when applied to the stupid) or pernicious (when inflicted on the gifted).' But when he wrote *The Hobbit* he was still suffering from what he later called 'the contemporary delusions about "fairy-stories" and children' – delusions that not long afterwards he made a conscious decision to renounce.

The writing of the story progressed fluently until the passage not far from the end where the dragon Smaug is about to die. Here Tolkien hesitated, and tried out the narrative in rough notes – something he was often to do in *The Lord of the Rings* but seems to have done only rarely in *The Hobbit*. These notes suggest that Bilbo Baggins might creep into the dragon's lair and stab him. 'Bilbo plunges in his little magic knife,' he wrote. 'Throes of dragon. Smashes walls and entrance to tunnel.' But this idea, which scarcely suited the character of the hobbit or provided a grand enough death for Smaug, was rejected in favour of the published version where the dragon is slain by the archer Bard. And then, shortly after he had described the death of the dragon, Tolkien abandoned the story.

Or to be more accurate, he did not write any more of it down. For the benefit of his children he had narrated an impromptu conclusion to the story, but, as Christopher Tolkien expressed it, 'the ending chapters were rather roughly done, and not typed out at all'. Indeed they were not even written in manuscript. The typescript of the nearly finished story, made in the small neat typeface of the Hammond machine, with italics for the songs, was occasionally shown to favoured friends, together with its accompanying maps (and perhaps already a few illustrations). But it did not often leave Tolkien's study, where it sat, incomplete and now likely to remain so. The boys were growing up and no longer asked for 'Winter Reads', so there was no reason why *The Hobbit* should ever be finished.

One of the few people to be shown the typescript of *The Hobbit* was a graduate named Elaine Griffiths, who had been a pupil of Tolkien's and had become a family friend. Upon his recommendation she was engaged by the London publishers George Allen & Unwin to revise Clark Hall's translation of *Beowulf*, a popular under-graduate 'crib'. One day in 1936 (some time after *The Hobbit* had been abandoned) a member of Allen & Unwin's staff came down to Oxford to see Elaine Griffiths about the project. This was Susan Dagnall, who had read English at Oxford at the same time as Elaine Griffiths and indeed knew her well. From her she learnt of the existence of the unfinished but remarkable children's story that Professor Tolkien had written. Elaine Griffiths suggested that Susan Dagnall should go to Northmoor Road and try to borrow the typescript. Susan Dagnall went, met Tolkien, asked for the typescript, and was given it. She took it back to London, read it, and decided that it was certainly worthy of consideration by Allen & Unwin. But it stopped short just after the death of the dragon. She sent the typescript back to Tolkien, asking him if he would finish it, and preferably soon, so that the book could be considered for publication in the following year.

Tolkien got down to work. On 10 August 1936 he wrote: '*The Hobbit* is now nearly finished, and the publishers clamouring for it.' He engaged his son Michael, who had cut his right hand badly on a school window, to help with the typing, using his left hand. The whole labour was finished by the first week in October, and the typescript was sent to Allen & Unwin's offices near the British Museum, bearing the title *The Hobbit, or There and Back Again*.

The firm's chairman, Stanley Unwin, believed that the best judges of children's books were children, so he handed *The Hobbit* to his ten-year-old son Rayner, who read it and wrote this report:

Bilbo Baggins was a hobbit who lived in his hobbit-hole and

never went for adventures, at last Gandalf the wizard and his dwarves perswaded him to go. He had a very exiting time fighting goblins and wargs. at last they got to the lonley mountain; Smaug, the dragon who gawreds it is killed and after a terrific battle with the goblins he returned home – rich! This book, with the help of maps, does not need any illustrations it is good and should appeal to all children between the ages of 5 and 9.

The boy earned a shilling for the report, and the book was accepted for publication.

Despite what Rayner Unwin had written, it was decided that *The Hobbit* did need illustrations. Tolkien was modest about his talents as an artist, and when at the publishers' suggestion he submitted a number of drawings which he had made for the story he commented: 'The pictures seem to me mostly only to prove that the author cannot draw.' But Allen & Unwin did not agree, and they gladly accepted eight of his black and white illustrations.

Although Tolkien had some idea of the processes involved in the production of books, he was surprised by the number of difficulties and disappointments during the following months; indeed the machinations and occasionally the downright incompetence of publishers and printers continued to amaze him until the end of his life. *The Hobbit* maps had to be redrawn by him because his originals had incorporated too many colours, and even then his scheme of having the general map as an endpaper and Thror's map placed within the text of Chapter One was not followed. The publishers had decided that both maps should be used as endpapers, and in consequence his plan for 'invisible lettering', which would appear when Thror's map was held up to the light, had to be abandoned. He also had to spend a good deal of time on the proofs – though this was entirely his fault. When the page-proofs arrived at Northmoor Road in February 1937 he decided that he ought to make substantial revisions to several parts of the book, for he had let the manuscript go without checking it with his usual thoroughness, and he was now unhappy about a number of passages in the story; in particular he did not like many of the patronising 'asides' to juvenile readers, and he also saw that there were many inconsistencies in the description of the topography, details which only the most acute and painstaking reader would notice, but which he himself with his passion for perfection could not allow to pass. In a few days he had covered the proofs with a host of alterations. With typical consideration for the printers he ensured that his revisions occupied an identical area of type to the original wording – though here he was wasting his time, for the printers decided to reset the entire sections that he had revised.

The Hobbit was published on 21 September 1937. Tolkien was a little nervous of Oxford reaction, especially as he was currently holding a Leverhulme Research Fellowship, and he remarked: 'I shall now find it very hard to make people believe that this is not the major fruits of "research" 1936–7.' He need not have worried: at first Oxford paid almost no attention.

A few days after publication the book received an accolade in the columns of *The Times*. 'All who love that kind of children's book which can be read and re-read by adults', wrote the reviewer, 'should take note that a new star has appeared in this constellation. To the trained eye some characters will seem almost mythopoeic.' The eye in question was that of C. S. Lewis, at that time a regular reviewer for *The Times Literary Supplement*, who had managed to get this notice of his friend's book into the parent journal. Naturally, he also reviewed the book in glowing terms in the *Supplement* itself. There was an equally enthusiastic reaction from many other critics, although some took a delight in pointing out the ineptness of the publisher's 'blurb' that compared the book to *Alice in Wonderland* simply because both were the work of Oxford dons; and there were a few dissenting voices, among them that of the reviewer who wrote (somewhat puzzlingly) in *Junior Bookshelf*: 'The courageous freedom of real adventure doesn't appear.'

The first edition of *The Hobbit* had sold out by Christmas. A reprint was hurried through, and four of the five coloured illustrations that Tolkien had drawn for the book were now included in it; he had apparently never offered them to Allen & Unwin, and it was not until they passed through the publisher's office on the way to Houghton Mifflin, who were to publish the book in America, that their existence was discovered. When the American edition was issued a few months later it too received approbation from most critics, and it was awarded the *New York Herald Tribune* prize for the best juvenile book of the season. Stanley Unwin realised that he had a children's best-seller in his list. He wrote to Tolkien: 'A large public will be clamouring next year to hear more from you about Hobbits!'

2

'The new Hobbit'

A few weeks after *The Hobbit* had been published Tolkien went to London and had lunch with Stanley Unwin to discuss a possible successor to the book. He found that the publisher, small, bright-eyed, and bearded, looked 'exactly like one of my dwarves, only I don't think he smokes'. Unwin certainly did not smoke, nor did he drink alcohol (he came from a strict Nonconformist family), and each man found the other rather strange. Unwin learnt that Tolkien had a large mythological work called *The Silmarillion* that he now wanted to publish, though Tolkien admitted that it was not very suitable as a successor to the adventures of Bilbo Baggins; he also said that he had several short stories for children, 'Mr Bliss', 'Farmer Giles of Ham', and 'Roverandom'; and there was an unfinished novel called 'The Lost Road'. Unwin asked Tolkien to send all of these manuscripts to his office in Museum Street.

They were sent, and they were read. The children's stories were all enjoyed, but none of them was about hobbits, and Stanley Unwin was certain that this was what the people who had enjoyed the first book wanted. As for 'The Lost Road', it was obviously unsuitable for a juvenile audience. But *The Silmarillion* presented a more complex problem.

The manuscript of this lengthy work – or rather, the bundle of manuscripts – had arrived in a somewhat disordered state, and the only clearly continuous section seemed to be the long poem 'The Gest of Beren and Lúthien'. So this poem was passed to a publisher's reader. The reader did not think much of it; in fact in his report he was very rude about the rhyming couplets. But he hastened to say that he found the prose version of the Beren and

Lúthien story enthralling – Tolkien had presumably attached it to the poem for the purpose of completing the story, for the poem itself was unfinished. 'The tale here proceeds at a stinging pace,' the reader reported to Stanley Unwin, and continued enthusiastically (albeit in rather nonsensical terms of praise): 'It is told with a picturesque brevity and dignity that holds the reader's interest in spite of its eye-splitting Celtic names. It has something of that mad, bright-eyed beauty that perplexes all Anglo-Saxons in face of Celtic art.'

There is no evidence that any other part of *The Silmarillion* was read by Allen & Unwin at this juncture. Nevertheless Stanley Unwin wrote to Tolkien on 15 December 1937:

> *The Silmarillion* contains plenty of wonderful material; in fact it is a mine to be explored in writing further books like *The Hobbit* rather than a book in itself. I think this was partly your own view, was it not? What we badly need is another book with which to follow up our success with *The Hobbit* and alas! neither of these manuscripts (the poem and *The Silmarillion* itself) quite fits the bill. I still hope that you will be inspired to write another book about the Hobbit.

In his letter Unwin also passed on to Tolkien the reader's enthusiastic if misguided compliments about the section of *The Silmarillion* that he had seen.

Tolkien replied (on 16 December 1937):

> My chief joy comes from learning that *The Silmarillion* is not rejected with scorn. I have suffered a sense of fear and bereavement, quite ridiculous, since I let this private and beloved nonsense out; and I think if it had seemed to you to be nonsense I should have felt really crushed. But I shall certainly now hope one day to be able, or to be able to afford, to publish *The Silmarillion*! Your reader's comments afford me delight. I am sorry the names split his eyes – personally I believe (and here I believe I am a good judge) they are good, and a large part of the effect. They are coherent and consistent and made upon two related linguistic formulae, so that they achieve a reality not fully achieved by other name-inventors (say Swift or Dunsany!). Needless to say they are not Celtic! Neither are the tales.

I did not think any of the stuff I dropped on you filled the bill. But I did want to know whether any of the stuff had any exterior or non-personal value. I think it is plain that quite apart from it, a sequel or successor to *The Hobbit* is called for. I promise to give this thought and attention. But I am sure you will sympathize when I say that the construction of elaborate and consistent mythology (and two languages) rather occupies the mind, and the Silmarils are in my heart. So that goodness knows what will happen. Mr Baggins began as a comic tale among conventional and inconsistent Grimm's fairy-tale dwarves, and got drawn into the edge of it – so that even Sauron the terrible peeped over the edge. And what more can hobbits do? They can be comic, but their comedy is suburban unless it is set against things more elemental. But the real fun about orcs and dragons (to my mind) was before their time. Perhaps a new (if similar) line?

Stanley Unwin probably did not understand much of this letter; but in any case Tolkien was really thinking aloud and beginning to plan, for a mere three days later, on 19 December 1937, he wrote to Charles Furth, one of the editorial staff at Allen & Unwin: 'I have written the first chapter of a new story about Hobbits– "A long expected party".'

The new story began rather like the first hobbit tale. Mr Bilbo Baggins of Hobbiton gives a party to celebrate his birthday, and after making a speech to his guests he slips on the magic ring that he acquired in *The Hobbit*, and vanishes. The reason for his disappearance, as given in this first draft, is that Bilbo 'had not got any money or jewels left' and was going off in search of more dragon-gold. At this point the first version of the opening chapter breaks off, unfinished.

Tolkien had as yet no clear idea of what the new story was going to be about. At the end of *The Hobbit* he had stated that Bilbo 'remained very happy to the end of his days, and those were extraordinarily long'. So how could the hobbit have any new adventures worth the name without this being contradicted? And had he not explored most of the possibilities in Bilbo's character? He decided to introduce a new hobbit, Bilbo's son – and to give him the name of a family of toy koala bears owned by his children, 'The Bingos'. So he crossed out 'Bilbo' in the first draft and above it

185

wrote 'Bingo'. Then another idea occurred to him, and he wrote it down in memorandum form (as he was often to do during the invention of this new story): 'Make *return of ring* a motive.'

The ring, after all, was both a link with the earlier book and one of the few elements in it that had not been fully developed. Bilbo had acquired it accidentally from the slimy Gollum beneath the Misty Mountains. Its power of making the wearer invisible had been exploited fully in *The Hobbit*, but it might be supposed to have other properties. Tolkien made some further notes: 'The Ring: whence its origin? Necromancer? Not very dangerous, when used for good purpose. But it exacts its penalty. You must either lose it, or *yourself*.' Then he rewrote the opening chapter, calling the hero 'Bingo Bolger-Baggins' and making him Bilbo's nephew rather than his son. He typed it out, and at the beginning of February 1938 he sent it to Allen & Unwin, asking if Stanley Unwin's son Rayner, who had written the original report on *The Hobbit*, would care to let him have an opinion on it.

Stanley Unwin wrote on 11 February that Rayner had read it and was delighted with it, and he told Tolkien: 'Go right ahead.'

Tolkien was encouraged, but he replied: 'I find it only too easy to write opening chapters – and at the moment the story is not unfolding. I squandered so much on the original "Hobbit" (which was not meant to have a sequel) that it is difficult to find anything new in that world.' Nevertheless he set to work again, and wrote a second chapter which he called 'Three's Company'. It told how Bingo with his cousins Odo and Frodo set off to make a journey across the countryside under the stars.

'Stories tend to get out of hand,' Tolkien wrote to his publisher a few weeks later, 'and this has taken an unpremeditated turn.' He was referring to the appearance, unplanned by him, of a sinister 'Black Rider' who is clearly searching for the hobbits. It was indeed the first of several unpremeditated turns that the story was to take. Unconsciously, and usually without forethought, Tolkien was bending his tale away from the jolly style of *The Hobbit* towards something darker and grander, and closer in concept to *The Silmarillion*.

A third chapter was written, untitled but in essence the same chapter that was eventually published as 'A Short Cut to Mushrooms'. Tolkien then typed out everything he had written (and rewritten), and once again sent it to Rayner Unwin for comment.

Again the boy approved of it, though he said that there was 'too much hobbit talk', and asked what the book would be called.

What indeed? And, much more important, Tolkien still did not have a clear idea what it was all about. Nor did he have much time to devote to it. Besides the usual calls on his attention – lecturing, examining, administration, research – there was the additional worry of a mysterious heart condition that had been diagnosed in his son Christopher; the boy, who had recently followed his brothers to a Catholic boarding-school in Berkshire, was ordered to stay at home for many months and kept lying on his back, and his father devoted much time and care to him. Not for many weeks was the new story again considered. Tolkien had made a note at the end of the three chapters that he had already written: 'Bingo is going to do something about the Necromancer who is planning an attack on the Shire. They have to find Gollum, and find where he got the ring, for 3 are wanted.' But promising as this may have seemed at first, it did not immediately produce results, and on 24 July 1938 he wrote to Charles Furth at Allen & Unwin: 'The sequel to *The Hobbit* has remained where it stopped. It has lost my favour, and I have no idea what to do with it.'

Shortly afterwards news came of E. V. Gordon's death in hospital, and this blow contributed further to delay with the new story. Yet at about this time Tolkien began to organise his thoughts on the central matter of the Ring, and began to write some dialogue between Bingo and the elf Gildor, explaining the nature of it. It is, says the elf, one of a number of rings that were made by the Necromancer, and it seems that *he* is looking for it. The Black Riders, explains the elf, are 'Ring-wraiths' who have been made permanently invisible by other rings. Now at last ideas began to flow, and Tolkien wrote a passage of dialogue between Bingo and the wizard Gandalf in which it is determined that the Ring must be taken many hundreds of miles to the dark land of Mordor, and there cast into 'one of the Cracks of Earth' where a great fire burns. This was basis enough for the story to be continued, taking the hobbits to the house of Tom Bombadil. When this was done, on 31 August 1938, Tolkien wrote to Allen & Unwin that the book was 'flowing along, and getting quite out of hand. It had reached about Chapter VII and progresses towards quite unforseen goals.' Then he went off with the family, including Christopher who was now in much better health, for a holiday at Sidmouth.

There he did a good deal of work on the story, bringing the hobbits to a village inn at 'Bree' where they meet a strange character, another unpremeditated element in the narrative. In the first drafts Tolkien described this person as 'a queer-looking brown-faced hobbit', and named him 'Trotter'. Later he was to be recast as a man of heroic stature, the king whose return to power gives the third volume of the book its title; but as yet Tolkien had no more idea than the hobbits who he was. The writing continued, bringing Bingo to Rivendell; and at about this time Tolkien scribbled on a spare sheet: 'Too many hobbits. Also Bingo Bolger-Baggins a bad name. Let Bingo = Frodo.' But below this he wrote: 'No – I am now too used to Bingo.' There was also the problem of why the Ring seemed so important to everyone – this had not yet been established clearly. Suddenly an idea occurred to him, and he wrote: 'Bilbo's ring proved to be the *one ruling Ring* – all others had come back to Mordor: but this one had been lost.'

The one ruling ring that controlled all the others; the ring that was the source and instrument of the power of Sauron, the Dark Lord of Mordor; the ring that must be carried to its destruction by the hobbits, or else the whole world will come under Sauron's domination. Now everything fell into place, and the story was lifted from the 'juvenile' level of *The Hobbit* into the sphere of grand and heroic romance. There was even a name for it: when next he wrote about it to Allen & Unwin, Tolkien referred to it as 'The Lord of the Rings'.

What had happened was almost inevitable. Tolkien had not really wanted to write any more stories like *The Hobbit*; he had wanted to get on with the serious business of his mythology. And that was what he could now do. The new story had attached itself firmly to *The Silmarillion*, and was to acquire the dignity of purpose and the high style of the earlier book. True, the hobbits were still hobbits, small people with fur on their feet and funny names like Baggins and Gamgee (the family joke about 'Gaffer Gamgee' had led to the inclusion of a character of that name, and, more important, to the invention of his son 'Sam', who was to play a major part in the story). In a sense the hobbits had only been acquired by accident from the earlier book. But now, for the first time, Tolkien realised the significance of hobbits in Middle-earth. The theme of his new story was large, but it was to have its centre in the courage of these small people; and the heart of the book was to be found in the inns and gardens of The Shire, Tolkien's representation of all that he loved best about England.

Now that the full nature of the story had become apparent, there were fewer false starts or reconsiderations. Home from the Sidmouth holiday, Tolkien spent many hours during the autumn of 1938 continuing the tale, so that by the end of the year it was well into what eventually became Book II. Usually he worked at night, as was his habit, warmed by the idiosyncratic stove in his study grate at Northmoor Road, and writing with his dip-pen on the backs of old examination answers – so that much of *The Lord of the Rings* is interspersed with fragments of long-forgotten essays by undergraduates. Each chapter would begin with a scribbled and often illegible draft; then would come a rewriting in a fairer hand; and finally a typescript done on the Hammond machine. The only major change still to be made was in the matter of the hero's name. After a brief period in the summer of 1939 when he considered changing everything he had done so far and starting all over again with Bilbo as the hero – presumably on the principle that the hero of the first book ought to be the hero of the second – Tolkien went back to his intention of using the 'Bingo' character; but as the name 'Bingo' had now become quite unbearable to him in view of the serious nature the story had taken on, he changed it to 'Frodo', a name that already belonged to a minor character. And 'Frodo' it remained.

At about the time that Tolkien decided to call the book *The Lord of the Rings*, Chamberlain signed the Munich agreement with Hitler. Tolkien, like many others at the time, was suspicious not so much of German intentions as of those of Soviet Russia; he wrote that he had 'a loathing of being on any side that includes Russia,' and added: 'One fancies that Russia is probably ultimately far more responsible for the present crisis and choice of moment than Hitler.' However this does not mean that the placing of Mordor (the seat of evil in *The Lord of the Rings*) in the East is an allegorical reference to contemporary world politics, for as Tolkien himself affirmed it was a 'simple narrative and geographical necessity'. Elsewhere he made a careful distinction between allegory and applicability: 'I cordially dislike allegory in all its manifestations, and always have done so since I grew old and wary enough to detect its presence. I much prefer history, true or feigned, with its varied applicability to the thought and experience of readers. I think that many confuse "applicability" with "allegory"; but the one resides in the freedom of the reader, and the other in the purposed domination of the author.' As C. S. Lewis wrote of *The Lord of the Rings*: 'These things were not devised to reflect any particular situation in the real world. It was the other way round; real events began, horribly, to conform to the pattern he had freely invented.'

Tolkien hoped to continue work on the book in the early months of 1939, but there were endless distractions, among them his commitment to deliver the Andrew Lang Lecture at the University of St Andrews at the beginning of March. For his subject he had chosen the topic originally promised to the undergraduate society at Worcester College a year previously: fairy-stories. It was appropriate to the occasion, being a subject that had much concerned Lang himself, and it was also much in Tolkien's mind while he was writing his new story. *The Hobbit* was clearly designed for children and *The Silmarillion* for adults, but he was aware that *The Lord of the Rings* was less easy to categorise. In October 1938 he wrote to Stanley Unwin that it was 'forgetting "children" and becoming more terrifying than *The Hobbit*'. And he added: 'It may prove quite unsuitable.' But he felt strongly that fairy-stories are not necessarily for children, and he decided to devote much of his lecture to the proof of this belief.

He had touched on the crucial point in the poem 'Mythopoeia' that he had written for C. S. Lewis many years before, and he decided to quote from it in the lecture:

> The heart of man is not compound of lies,
> but draws some wisdom from the only Wise,
> and still recalls Him. Though now long estranged,
> Man is not wholly lost nor wholly changed.
> Dis-graced he may be, yet is not de-throned,
> and keeps the rags of lordship once he owned:
> Man, Sub-creator, the refracted light
> through whom is splintered from a single White
> to many hues, and endlessly combined
> in living shapes that move from mind to mind.
> Though all the crannies of the world we filled
> with Elves and Goblins, though we dared to build
> Gods and their houses out of dark and light,

and sowed the seed of dragons – 'twas our right
(used or misused). That right has not decayed:
we make still by the law in which we're made.

'Man, Sub-creator' was in one sense a new way of expressing what
is often called 'the willing suspension of disbelief', and Tolkien
made it the central argument of the lecture.

'What really happens', he wrote, 'is that the story-maker proves
a successful "sub-creator". He makes a Secondary World which
your mind can enter. Inside it, what he relates is "true": it accords
with the laws of that world. You therefore believe it, while you
are, as it were, inside. The moment disbelief arises, the spell is
broken; the magic, or rather art, has failed. You are then out in the
Primary World again, looking at the little abortive Secondary
World from outside.'

He made a good many points in the lecture, perhaps too many
for an entirely cogent argument. But at the end he asserted in
powerful terms that there is no higher function for man than the
'sub-creation' of a Secondary World such as he was already making
in *The Lord of the Rings*, and he gave expression to his hope that
in one sense this story and the whole of his related mythology
might be found to be 'true'. 'Every writer making a secondary
world', he declared, 'wishes in some measure to be a real maker,
or hopes that he is drawing on reality: hopes that the peculiar
quality of this secondary world (if not all the details) are derived
from Reality, or are flowing into it.' Indeed he went so far as to say
that it was a specifically Christian venture to write such a story as
he was now engaged upon. 'The Christian,' he said, 'may now
perceive that all his bents and faculties have a purpose, which can
be redeemed. So great is the bounty with which he has been
treated that he may now, perhaps, fairly dare to guess that in
Fantasy he may actually assist in the effoliation and multiple
enrichment of creation.'

The lecture was delivered at St Andrews on 8 March 1939 (the
date has been variously and erroneously given as 1938 and 1940);
and afterwards Tolkien returned with a new enthusiasm to the
story whose purpose he had justified. That story had been begun
as a mere 'sequel' to *The Hobbit*, at the instigation of his publisher,
but now, especially after the declaration of high purpose that he
had made in the lecture, the Ring was as important to him as the

Silmarils. In fact it was now clear that *The Lord of the Rings* was not so much a sequel to *The Hobbit* as a sequel to *The Silmarillion*. Every aspect of the earlier work was playing a part in the new story: the mythology itself, which provided both a historical setting and a sense of depth, the elvish languages that he had developed so painstakingly and thoroughly over more than twenty-five years, even the Fëanorian alphabet in which he had kept his diary from 1926 to 1933, and which he now used for elvish inscriptions in the story. Yet to his friends, Tolkien still referred to the story in modest terms as 'the new Hobbit' or 'the Hobbit sequel'.

Under this title it was read chapter by chapter to the Inklings, and was received with much enthusiasm; although not everyone who listened to the story was delighted by the 'high style' of prose that had begun to predominate in the book. Tolkien had moved from the comparatively colloquial approach of the opening chapters into a manner that was more and more archaic and solemn as he progressed. He was well aware of this; indeed it was entirely deliberate, and it was discussed by him at the time in print – just as the intentions of the book had been discussed in the St Andrews lecture. This time the context was his introduction to the revised Clark Hall translation of *Beowulf*. Elaine Griffiths had found herself unable to complete the revision, and after failing to find the time to get it done himself Tolkien had handed the task over to his colleague Charles Wrenn, who was then at the University of London. Wrenn completed the work speedily, but Allen & Unwin had to wait for many months before Tolkien could be persuaded to marshal his thoughts sufficiently to write the introduction that he had promised for the volume. When he did write it, this introduction proved to be a lengthy discussion of the principles of translation, and in particular an argument in favour of the adoption of a 'high style' when dealing with heroic matters. Consciously or unconsciously, he was really discussing *The Lord of the Rings*, which had at that time (the beginning of 1940) reached the middle of what was to become Book II.

In the introduction Tolkien declared, in justification of a high style: 'We are being at once wisely aware of our own frivolity if we avoid *hitting* and *whacking* and prefer "striking" and "smiting"; *talk* and *chat* and prefer "speech" and "discourse"; *well-bred, brilliant*, or *polite noblemen* (visions of snobbery columns in the Press, and fat men on the Riviera) and prefer the "worthy, brave and courteous men" of long ago.' From this time onwards he put these stylistic precepts more and more into practice in *The Lord of the Rings*. This was almost inevitable, for as the story grew grander in scale and purpose it adopted the style of *The Silmarillion*; yet Tolkien did not make any stylistic revision of the first chapters, which had been written in a much lighter vein; and he himself noted when reading the book again twenty-five years later: 'The first volume is really very different to the rest.'

The outbreak of war in September 1939 did not have any immediate major effect on Tolkien's life; but during this time, to his inevitable sorrow, family life changed as the boys left home. John, the eldest, who had read English at his father's old college, Exeter, was training for the Catholic priesthood in Rome, and was later evacuated with his fellow-students to Lancashire. Michael spent a year at Trinity College and then became an anti-aircraft gunner. Christopher, recovered from his illness, returned to school for a brief period before following his brother to Trinity. Only Priscilla, the youngest of the family, was still living at home. There was some disruption of the regular pattern of life at Northmoor Road: domestic help became scarce, evacuees and lodgers were sometimes accommodated, hens were installed in the garden to increase the supply of eggs, and Tolkien took turns of duty as an air raid warden, sleeping in the damp little hut that served as the local headquarters. There were, however, no German air attacks on Oxford; nor was Tolkien required, as were a number of dons, to undertake work for the War Office or other government departments.

As the war progressed, the character of the University changed greatly, for large numbers of service cadets were drafted to Oxford for 'short courses' before they took up their duties as officers; Tolkien organised a syllabus for naval cadets in the English School, and modified many of his lectures to suit the less specialist audiences. But in general terms his life was much as it had been before the war, and his distress at the continuation of hostilities was almost as much for ideological as for personal reasons. 'People in this land', he wrote in 1941, 'seem not even yet to realize that in the Germans we have enemies whose virtues (and they are virtues) of obedience and patriotism are greater than ours in the mass. I have in this War a burning private grudge against that ruddy little ignoramus Adolf Hitler for ruining, perverting, misapplying, and making for ever accursed, that noble northern spirit, a supreme contribution to Europe, which I have ever loved, and tried to present in its true light.'

Many years later, Tolkien recalled that the writing of *The Lord of the Rings* halted for almost a year late in 1940, when it had reached the point at which the Company discovers Balin's tomb in Moria. If this is true – and other evidence would seem to confirm that there was a hiatus at about this time – it was only the first of several major delays or hesitations in the writing, none of them ascribable to any specific external cause.

When work was resumed, Tolkien drew up outlines for the end of the story – which he did not imagine was more than a few chapters away – and began to sketch the episode where two of the hobbits encounter Treebeard, the being who was the ultimate expression of Tolkien's love and respect for trees. When eventually he came to write this chapter (so he told Nevill Coghill) he modelled Treebeard's way of speaking, *'Hrum, Hroom',* on the booming voice of C. S. Lewis.

Allen & Unwin had originally hoped that the new story would be ready for publication a mere couple of years after they had issued *The Hobbit.* That hope had faded, and in 1942 even the original *Hobbit* had to go out of print when the warehouse stock of copies was burnt in the London blitz. But Stanley Unwin continued to take an interest in the progress of the 'new Hobbit', and in December 1942 he received a letter from Tolkien which reported: 'It is now approaching completion. I hope to get a little free time this vacation, and might hope to finish it off early next year. It has reached Chapter XXXI and will require at least six more to finish (these are already sketched).'

Yet Chapter XXXI (the original number of 'Flotsam and Jetsam') was only at the end of what became Book III; and in the event there were to be not six but thirty-one more chapters before the book was complete. Tolkien tried to tackle the story in the months that followed, and he wrote a little more of it. But by the summer of 1943 he had to admit that he was 'dead stuck'.

One cause of the difficulty was his perfectionism. Not content with writing a large and complex book, he felt he must ensure that every single detail fitted satisfactorily into the total pattern. Geography, chronology, and nomenclature all had to be entirely consistent. He had been given some assistance with the geography, for his son

Christopher helped him by drawing an elaborate map of the terrain covered by the story. Tolkien himself had been making rough sketch-maps since beginning work on the book; he once said: 'If you're going to have a complicated story you must work to a map; otherwise you'll never make a map of it afterwards.' But the map in itself was not enough, and he made endless calculations of time and distance, drawing up elaborate charts concerning events in the story, showing dates, the days of the week, the hours, and sometimes even the direction of the wind and the phase of the moon. This was partly his habitual insistence on perfection, partly sheer revelling in the fun of 'sub-creation', but most of all a concern to provide a totally convincing picture. Long afterwards he said: 'I wanted people simply to get inside this story and take it (in a sense) as actual history.'

Name-making also involved much of his attention, as was inevitable, for the invented languages from which the names were constructed were both the mainspring of his mythology and in themselves a central activity of his intellect. Once again, the elvish languages Quenya and Sindarin, now more sophisticated than they had been when he began *The Silmarillion* twenty-five years earlier, played a principal role in name-making, and were used in the composition of elvish poems and songs. The story also called for the invention of at least the rudiments of several other languages, and all this took time and energy. Moreover he had reached a point where the story divided into several independent and in themselves complicated chains of events, and while he believed that it would only take him two or three chapters to get Frodo and Sam Gamgee to Mordor he could not yet face unravelling the complexities of the simultaneous events in Gondor and Rohan. It had taken him nearly six years to bring the story this far; how could he ever find the time and energy to finish it, let alone to complete and revise *The Silmarillion*, which still clamoured for attention? He was fifty-one, tired, and fearful that in the end he would achieve nothing. He had already gained a reputation for almost indefinite procrastination in his philological work, and this sometimes amused him, though it was often saddening to him; but as to never finishing his mythology, that was a dreadful and numbing thought.

One day at about this time Lady Agnew, who lived opposite in Northmoor Road, told him that she was nervous about a large poplar tree in the road; she said that it cut off the sun from her garden, and she feared for her house if it fell in a gale. Tolkien thought that this was ridiculous. 'Any wind that could have uprooted it and hurled it on her house', he said, 'would have demolished her and her house without any assistance from the tree.' But the poplar had already been lopped and mutilated, and though he managed to save it now, Tolkien began to think about it. He was after all 'anxious about my own internal Tree', his mythology; and there seemed to be some analogy.

One morning he woke up with a short story in his head, and scribbled it down. It was the tale of a painter named Niggle, a man who, like Tolkien, 'niggled' over details: 'He used to spend a long time on a single leaf, trying to catch its shape, and its sheen, and the glistening of dewdrops on its edges. Yet he wanted to paint a huge tree. There was one picture in particular which bothered him. It had begun with a leaf caught in the wind, and it became a tree; and the tree grew, sending out innumerable branches, and thrusting out the most fantastic roots. Strange birds came and settled on the twigs and had to be attended to. Then all round the tree, and behind it, through the gaps in the leaves and boughs, a country began to open out.'

In the story, which he called *Leaf by Niggle*, Tolkien expressed his worst fears for his mythological Tree. Like Niggle he sensed that he would be snatched away from his work long before it was finished – if indeed it could ever be finished in this world. For it is in another and brighter place that Niggle finds his Tree finished, and learns that it is indeed a real tree, a true part of creation.

The story was not published for many months, but the actual business of writing it helped to exorcise some of Tolkien's fear, and to get him to work again on *The Lord of the Rings*; though the immediate impulse came from C. S. Lewis.

By the beginning of 1944 *The Lord of the Rings* had lain untouched for many months, and Tolkien wrote: 'I do not seem to have any mental energy or invention.' But Lewis had noticed what had happened, and he urged Tolkien to get going again and finish the story. 'I needed some pressure,' said Tolkien, 'and shall probably respond.' At the beginning of April he resumed work, beginning to write what eventually became Book IV, which takes Frodo and Sam Gamgee across the marshes towards Mordor where they hope to destroy the Ring by hurling it into the Cracks of Doom.

Christopher Tolkien had now been called up into the R.A.F.,

and had been sent to South Africa to train as a pilot (much to the regret of his father, who believed that aerial warfare was both immoral and excessively dangerous). Tolkien was already writing long letters to Christopher, and now these letters carried a detailed account of progress on the book, and of reading it to the Lewis brothers and Charles Williams in the White Horse, a pub they favoured at the time. Here are a few extracts from the letters:

Wednesday 5 April 1944: 'I have seriously embarked on an effort to finish my book, and have been sitting up rather late: a lot of re-reading and research required. And it is a painful tricky business getting into swing again. A few pages for a lot of sweat; but at the moment they are just meeting Gollum on a precipice.'

Saturday 8 April: 'Spent part of day (and night) struggling with chapter. Gollum is playing up well on his return. A beautiful night with high moon. About 2 a.m. I was in the warm silver-lit garden, wishing we two could go for a walk. Then went to bed.'

Thursday 13 April: 'I miss you hourly, and am lonely without you. I have friends, of course, but can seldom see them. I did see C.S.L. and Charles Williams yesterday for almost two hours. I read my recent chapter; it received approbation. I have begun another. Shall have spare copies typed, if possible, and sent out to you. Now I will return to Frodo and Gollum for a brief spell.'

Friday 14 April: 'I managed to get an hour or two's writing, and have brought Frodo nearly to the gates of Mordor. Afternoon lawnmowing. Term begins next week, and proofs of Wales papers have come. Still I am going to continue "Ring" in every salvable moment.'

Tuesday 18 April: 'I hope to see C.S.L. and Charles W. tomorrow morning and read my next chapter—on the passage of the Dead Marshes and the approach to the Gates of Mordor, which I have now practically finished. Term has almost begun: I tutored Miss Salu for an hour. The afternoon was squandered on plumbing (stopping overflow) and cleaning out fowls. They are laying generously (9 again yesterday). Leaves are out: the white-grey of the quince, the grey-green of young apples, the full green of hawthorn, the tassels of flower even on the sluggard poplars.'

Sunday 23 April: 'I read my second chapter, Passage of the Dead Marshes, to Lewis and Williams on Wed. morning. It was approved. I have now nearly done a third: Gates of the Land of

Shadow. But this story takes me in charge, and I have already taken three chapters over what was meant to be one! And I have neglected too many things to do it. I am just enmeshed in it now, and have to wrench my mind away to tackle exam-paper proofs, and lectures.'

Tuesday 25 April: 'Gave a poor lecture, saw the Lewises and C.W. (White Horse) for ½ hour; mowed three lawns, and wrote letter to John, and struggled with recalcitrant passage in "The Ring". At this point I require to know how much later the moon gets up each night when nearing full, and how to stew a rabbit!'

Thursday 4 May: 'A new character has come on the scene (I am sure I did not invent him, I did not even want him, though I like him, but there he came walking into the woods of Ithilien): Faramir, the brother of Boromir – and he is holding up the "catastrophe" by a lot of stuff about the history of Gondor and Rohan. If he goes on much more a lot of him will have to be removed to the appendices – where already some fascinating material on the hobbit Tobacco industry and the Languages of the West have gone.'

Sunday 14 May: 'I did a certain amount of writing yesterday, but was hindered by two things: the need to clear up the study (which had got into the chaos that always indicates literary or philological preoccupation) and attend to business; and trouble with the moon. By which I mean that I found my moons in the crucial days between Frodo's flight and the present situation (arrival at Minas Morgul) were doing impossible things, rising in one part of the country and setting simultaneously in another. Rewriting bits of back chapters took all afternoon!'

Sunday 21 May: 'I have taken advantage of a bitter cold grey week (in which the lawns have not grown in spite of a little rain) to write: but struck a sticky patch. All that I had sketched or written before proved of little use, as times, motives, etc., have all changed. However at last with v. great labour, and some neglect of other duties, I have now written or nearly written all the matter up to the capture of Frodo in the high pass on the very brink of Mordor. Now I must go back to the other folk and try to bring things to the final crash with some speed. Do you think *Shelob* is a good name for a monstrous spider creature? It is of course only "She + lob" (= spider), but written as one, it seems to be quite noisome.'

Wednesday 31 May: 'I have done no serious writing since Monday. Until midday today I was sweating at Section Papers: and took my MSS. to the Press at 2 p.m. today – the last possible day. Yesterday: lecture – puncture, after fetching fish, so I had to foot it to town and back, and as bike-repairs are impossible I had to squander afternoon in a grimy struggle, which ended at last in my getting tyre off, mending one puncture in inner tube, and gash in outer, and getting thing on again. Io! triumphum!

'The Inklings meeting [held the previous Thursday night] was very enjoyable. Hugo was there: rather tired-looking, but reasonably noisy. The chief entertainment was provided by a chapter of Warnie Lewis's book on the times of Louis XIV (very good I thought it); and some excerpts from C.S.L.'s "Who Goes Home" – a book on Hell, which I suggested should have been called rather "Hugo's Home".[1] I did not get back till after midnight. The rest of my time, barring chores in and out door, has been occupied by the desperate attempt to bring "The Ring" to a suitable pause, the capture of Frodo by Orcs in the passes of Mordor, before I am obliged to break off by examining. By sitting up all hours, I managed it: and read the last 2 chapters ('Shelob's Lair' and 'The Choices of Master Samwise') to C.S.L. on Monday morning. He approved with unusual fervour, and was actually affected to tears by the last chapter, so it seems to be keeping up.'

Book IV of *The Lord of the Rings* was typed and sent out to Christopher in South Africa. By this time Tolkien was mentally exhausted by his feverish burst of writing. 'When my weariness has passed,' he told Christopher, 'I shall get on with my story.' But for the time being he achieved nothing. 'I am absolutely dry of any inspiration for the Ring,' he wrote in August, and by the end of the year he had done nothing new except draft a synopsis for the remainder of the story. He meditated rewriting and completing 'The Lost Road', the unfinished story of time-travel that he had begun many years before, and he discussed with Lewis the idea of their collaborating on a book about the nature, function, and origin of Language. But nothing was done about either of these projects, and Lewis, referring some time later to the non-appearance of the book on Language, described Tolkien as 'that great

---

[1] 'Who Goes Home' was eventually published under the title *The Great Divorce*.

but dilatory and unmethodical man'. 'Dilatory' was not altogether fair, but 'unmethodical' was often true.

Tolkien made little if any progress on *The Lord of the Rings* during 1945. On 9 May the war in Europe came to an end. The next day Charles Williams was taken ill. He underwent an operation at an Oxford hospital, but died on 15 May. Even if Williams and Tolkien had not inhabited the same plane of thought, the two men had been good friends, and the loss of Williams was a bitter thing, a symbol that peace would not bring an end to all troubles – something that Tolkien knew only too well. During the war he had said to Christopher: 'We are attempting to conquer Sauron with the Ring', and now he wrote: 'The War is not over (and the one that is, or the part of it, has largely been lost). But it is of course wrong to fall into such a mood, for Wars are always lost, and The War always goes on; and it is no good growing faint.'

In the autumn of 1945 he became Merton Professor of English Language and Literature, and hence a Fellow of Merton College, an institution that he found 'agreeably informal' after Pembroke. A few months later the retirement of David Nichol Smith raised the question of whom to appoint to the Merton Professorship of English Literature. Tolkien was one of the electors, and he wrote: 'It ought to be C. S. Lewis, or perhaps Lord David Cecil, but one never knows.' And in the event both these men were passed over, and the chair was offered to and accepted by F. P. Wilson. Though there is no reason to suppose that Tolkien did not support Lewis in the election, the gap between the two friends widened a little after this; or to be more accurate there was a gradual cooling on Tolkien's part. It is impossible to say precisely why. Lewis himself probably did not notice it at first, and when he did he was disturbed and saddened by it. Tolkien continued to attend gatherings of the Inklings, as did his son Christopher (who after the war resumed his undergraduate studies at Trinity College); Christopher was first invited to the Inklings to read aloud from *The Lord of the Rings*, as Lewis alleged he read better than his father, and later he became an Inkling in his own right. But though Tolkien could regularly be seen in the 'Bird and Baby' on Tuesday mornings and at Magdalen on Thursday nights, there was not the same intimacy as of old between him and Lewis.

In part the friendship's decay may have been hastened by Lewis's sometimes stringent criticisms of details in *The Lord of the*

Rings, particularly his comments on the poems, which (with the notable exception of the alliterative verses) he tended to dislike. Tolkien was often hurt by Lewis's comments, and he generally ignored them, so that Lewis later remarked of him: 'No one ever influenced Tolkien – you might as well try to influence a bandersnatch.' In part the increasing coolness on Tolkien's side was probably also due to his dislike of Lewis's 'Narnia' stories for children. In 1949 Lewis began to read the first of them, *The Lion, the Witch and the Wardrobe*, aloud to Tolkien. It was received with a snort of contempt. 'It really won't do!' Tolkien told Roger Lancelyn Green. 'I mean to say: "Nymphs and their Ways, The Love-Life of a Faun"!' Nevertheless Lewis completed it, and when it and its successors were published in their turn, 'Narnia' found as wide and enthusiastic an audience as that which had enjoyed *The Hobbit*. Yet Tolkien could not find it in his heart to reverse his original judgement. 'It is sad', he wrote in 1964, 'that "Narnia" and all that part of C.S.L.'s work should remain outside the range of my sympathy, as much of my work was outside his.' Undoubtedly he felt that Lewis had in some ways drawn on Tolkien ideas and stories in the books; and just as he resented Lewis's progress from convert to popular theologian he was perhaps irritated by the fact that the friend and critic who had listened to the tales of Middle-earth had as it were got up from his armchair, gone to the desk, picked up a pen, and 'had a go' himself. Moreover the sheer number of Lewis's books for children and the almost indecent haste with which they were produced undoubtedly annoyed him. The seven 'Narnia' stories were written and published in a mere seven years, less than half the period in which *The Lord of the Rings* gestated. It was another wedge between the two friends, and after 1954 when Lewis was elected to a new chair of Medieval and Renaissance Literature at Cambridge, and was obliged to spend much of his time away from Oxford, he and Tolkien only met on comparatively rare occasions.

With the end of the war *The Hobbit* was reprinted, and arrangements were made to publish *Farmer Giles of Ham*. In the summer of 1946 Tolkien told Allen & Unwin that he had made a very great effort to finish *The Lord of the Rings*, but had failed; the truth was that he had scarcely touched it since the late spring of 1944. He declared: 'I really do hope to have it done before the autumn,' and he did manage to resume work on it in the following weeks. By the end of the year he told his publishers that he was 'on the last chapters'. But then he moved house.

The house in Northmoor Road was too big for the family such as it now was, and was too expensive to maintain. So Tolkien put his name down for a Merton College house, and when one became available in Manor Road near the centre of Oxford he made arrangements to rent it. He, Edith, Christopher, and Priscilla moved in during March 1947; John was by now working as a priest in the Midlands, and Michael, married with an infant son, was a schoolmaster.

Almost immediately Tolkien realised that the new home was unbearably cramped. 3 Manor Road was an ugly brick house, and it was very small. He had no proper study, merely a 'bed-sitter' in the attic. It was agreed that as soon as Merton could provide a better house, the family would move again. But for the time being it would have to do.

Rayner Unwin, the son of Tolkien's publisher, who as a child had written the report that secured the publication of *The Hobbit*, was now an undergraduate at Oxford, and had made the acquaintance of Tolkien. In the summer of 1947 Tolkien decided that *The Lord of the Rings* was sufficiently near completion for him to be shown a typescript of the greater part of the story. After reading it, Rayner reported to his father at Allen & Unwin that it was 'a weird book' but nevertheless 'a brilliant and gripping story'. He remarked that the struggle between darkness and light made him suspect allegory, and commented: 'Quite honestly I don't know who is expected to read it: children will miss something of it, but if grown ups will not feel infra dig to read it many will undoubtedly enjoy themselves.' He had no doubt at all that the book deserved publication by his father's firm, and he suggested that it would have to be divided into sections, commenting that in this respect Frodo's ring resembled that of the Nibelungs.

Stanley Unwin passed these comments to Tolkien. The comparison of his Ring with the *Nibelungenlied* and Wagner always annoyed Tolkien; he once said: 'Both rings were round, and there the resemblance ceased.' Nor, of course, was he pleased by the suggestion of allegory; he replied: 'Do not let Rayner suspect "Allegory". There is a "moral", I suppose, in any tale worth telling. But that is not the same thing. Even the struggle between darkness and light (as he calls it, not me) is for me just a particular phase of history, one example of its pattern, perhaps, but not The Pattern; and the actors are individuals – they each, of course, contain universals, or they would not live at all, but they never represent them as such.' However he was on the whole very pleased by Rayner's enthusiasm for the book, and he concluded by saying: 'The thing is to finish the thing as devised, and then let it be judged.'

Yet even now he did not finish. He revised, niggled, and corrected earlier chapters, spending so much time at it that his colleagues came to regard him as lost to philology. But the final full stop was something he could not yet achieve.

During the summer of 1947 he drafted a revision to *The Hobbit* which would provide a more satisfactory explanation of Gollum's attitude to the Ring; or rather, an explanation that fitted better with the sequel. When this was written he sent it to Stanley Unwin asking for an opinion on it. Unwin mistakenly assumed that it was intended for inclusion in the next reprint of *The Hobbit* without any further discussion on the matter, and he passed it directly to his production department. Many months later, Tolkien was astonished to see the revised chapter in print when the page-proofs of the new impression were sent to him.

In the following months *The Lord of the Rings* at last reached its conclusion. Tolkien recalled that he 'actually wept' when writing the account of the heroes' welcome that is given to the hobbits on the Field of Cormallen. Long ago he had resolved to take the chief protagonists across the sea towards the West at the end of the book, and with the writing of the chapter that describes the setting sail from the Grey Havens the huge manuscript was nearly complete. Nearly, but not quite. 'I like tying up loose ends,' Tolkien once said, and he wished to make sure that there were no loose ends in his great story. So he wrote an Epilogue in which Sam Gamgee told his children what happened to each of the principal characters who did not sail West. It ended with Sam listening to 'the sigh and murmur of the Sea upon the shores of Middle-earth'.

And that *was* the end; but now Tolkien had to revise, again and again, until he was completely satisfied with the entire text, and this took many months. He once said of the book: 'I don't suppose there are many sentences that have not been niggled over.' Then he typed out a fair copy, balancing his typewriter on his attic bed because there was no room on his desk, and using two fingers because he had never learned to type with ten. Not until the autumn of 1949 was it all finished.

Tolkien lent the completed typescript to C. S. Lewis, who replied after reading it:

My dear Tollers,

Uton herian holbytlas indeed. I have drained the rich cup and satisfied a long thirst. Once it really gets under weigh the steady upward slope of grandeur and terror (not unrelieved by green dells, without which it would indeed be intolerable) is almost unequalled in the whole range of narrative art known to me. In two virtues I think it excels: sheer sub-creation – Bombadil, Barrow Wights, Elves, Ents – as if from inexhaustible resources, and construction. Also in *gravitas*. No romance can repel the charge of 'escapism' with such confidence. If it errs, it errs in precisely the opposite direction: all victories of hope deferred and the merciless piling up of odds against the heroes are near to being too painful. And the long *coda* after the eucatastrophe, whether you intended it or no, has the effect of reminding us that victory is as transitory as conflict, that (as Byron says) 'there's no sterner moralist than pleasure', and so leaving a final impression of profound melancholy.

Of course this is not the whole story. There are many passages I could wish you had written otherwise or omitted altogether. If I include none of my adverse criticisms in this letter that is because you have heard and rejected most of them already (*rejected* is perhaps too mild a word for your reaction on at least one occasion!). And even if all my objections were just (which is of course unlikely) the faults I think I find could only delay and impair appreciation: the substantial splendour of the tale can carry them all. *Ubi plura nitent in carmine non ego paucis offendi maculis.*

I congratulate you. All the long years you have spent on it are justified.

Yours,
Jack Lewis

Tolkien himself did not think it was flawless. But he told Stanley Unwin: 'It is written in my life-blood, such as that is, thick or thin; and I can no other.'

VI

1949–1966 : Success

1

Slamming the gates

It had taken twelve years to write *The Lord of the Rings*. By the time that he had finished it, Tolkien was not far from his sixtieth birthday.

Now of course he wanted to see the huge book in print. But he was not sure that he wanted Allen & Unwin to publish it, even though he had discussed it with them while it was being written, and they had encouraged him and shown approval of the manuscript. For he believed that he had now found someone who would publish it together with *The Silmarillion*.

Over the years he had become angry with Allen & Unwin for rejecting *The Silmarillion* in 1937 – though in truth they had not really rejected it at all; Stanley Unwin had merely said that it was not suitable as a sequel to *The Hobbit*. And Tolkien had come to believe that it was a case of 'once rejected, always rejected'. Which was a pity, he thought, because he wanted to publish *The Silmaril-lion*. It was possible to say that *The Lord of the Rings* stood up as an independent story, but since it included obscure references to the earlier mythology it would be much better if the two books could be published together. But most of all he wanted to find an audience for the earlier book, and this seemed the ideal, perhaps the only, opportunity. So when Milton Waldman from the publishing house of Collins showed an interest in publishing both works, Tolkien was strongly inclined to abandon Allen & Unwin and join forces with him.

Waldman, a Catholic, had been introduced to Tolkien by Gervase Mathew, a scholar and Dominican priest who often attended meetings of the Inklings. When Waldman learnt that

Tolkien had completed a lengthy sequel to that very successful book *The Hobbit* he expressed interest, and late in 1949 Tolkien sent him a bulky manuscript. But it was not *The Lord of the Rings*; it was *The Silmarillion*. The earlier mythological work, begun in 1917 as 'The Book of Lost Tales', was still incomplete, but Tolkien had begun work on it again while he was finishing *The Lord of the Rings*, and it was in a sufficiently ordered state for Waldman to read it. It was like nothing else Waldman had ever seen: a strange archaically-worded tale of elves, evil powers, and heroism. Some of it was typed, but much was in finely-lettered manuscript. Waldman told Tolkien that he thought it was remarkable, and he said that he wanted to publish it – providing Tolkien could finish it. Tolkien was delighted. Waldman had passed the first test: he had (provisionally) accepted *The Silmarillion*. He was invited down to Oxford by Tolkien, and was handed the manuscript of *The Lord of the Rings*. He took it on holiday and began to read it.

By the beginning of January 1950 he had almost finished it, and again he told Tolkien that he was delighted. 'It is a real work of creation,' he wrote, although he added that the length of the book worried him. But he was very hopeful that Collins would be able to put it into print. Indeed they were in a good position to do so. Most publishers, including Allen & Unwin, had been desperately short of paper since the war; however, Collins were not simply publishers but were also stationers, diary manufacturers, and printers, so they had a far greater allowance of paper than most firms. And as to the commercial viability of Tolkien's lengthy mythological stories, the company's chairman William Collins had already told Waldman that he would be happy to publish any fiction by the author of *The Hobbit*. In fact it was really the lucrative *Hobbit* that Collins wanted to acquire; while Tolkien, unhappy with the first post-war reprint of *The Hobbit* which had (for economy reasons) been shorn of its coloured plates, told Waldman that he would be happy to see it bought from Allen & Unwin and reissued according to his original intentions. He was also cross with Allen & Unwin for what he considered to be inadequate publicity for *Farmer Giles of Ham*, and he believed that Collins would be better at selling his books. So all seemed set fair for a working partnership between Tolkien and Collins.

There was, however, one point which Waldman wished to clear up. 'I take it,' he wrote to Tolkien, 'that you have no commitment either moral or legal to Allen & Unwin.' Tolkien replied: 'I believe myself to have no *legal* obligation. There was a clause in the contract for *The Hobbit* providing for a two months' consideration of my next book. That has been satisfied by (a) Stanley Unwin's subsequent rejection of *The Silmarillion* and (b) by *Farmer Giles*. But I have had friendly personal relations with Stanley U. and especially with his second son Rayner. If all this constitutes a *moral* obligation, then I am under one. However, I shall certainly try to extricate myself, or at least *The Silmarillion* and all its kin, from the dilatory coils of A. and U. if I can – in a friendly fashion if possible.'

Tolkien had in fact worked himself into a state of mind in which he considered Allen & Unwin to be if not an enemy, then at least a very unreliable ally, while Collins seemed to represent all that he hoped for. The real position was much more complex, as events were to prove.

In February 1950 Tolkien wrote to Allen & Unwin to say that *The Lord of the Rings* was finished. But he did not exactly encourage them to show an interest. 'My work has escaped from my control,' he told them, 'and I have produced a monster: an immensely long, complex, rather bitter, and rather terrifying romance, quite unfit for children (if fit for anybody); and it is not really a sequel to *The Hobbit*, but to *The Silmarillion*. Ridiculous and tiresome as you may think me, I want to publish them both – *The Silmarillion* and *The Lord of the Rings*. That is what I should like. Or I will let it all be. I cannot contemplate any drastic re-writing or compression. But I shall not have any just grievance (nor shall I be dreadfully surprised) if you decline so obviously unprofitable a proposition.' Almost as a footnote he added that the two books together added up to the vast size of (in his estimate) more than a million words.

Stanley Unwin replied, admitting that the size of the books set a problem, but asking whether they could not be split into 'three or four to some extent self-contained volumes?' No, answered Tolkien, they could not; the only natural division was between the two works themselves. And he went even further in deliberately discouraging Unwin from showing any more interest. 'I now wonder', he wrote, 'whether many beyond my friends, not all of whom have endured to the end, would read anything so long. Please do not think I shall feel I have a just grievance if you decline to become involved.' ('I profoundly hope that he will let go without demanding the MS.,' he wrote to Waldman.)

But Sir Stanley Unwin (who had received a knighthood just after the war) was not to be deterred so easily. He wrote to his son Rayner, who was studying at Harvard, and asked for his advice. Rayner replied: '*The Lord of the Rings* is a very great book in its own curious way and deserves to be produced somehow. *I* never felt the lack of a *Silmarillion* when reading it. But although he claims not to contemplate any drastic rewriting, etc., surely this is a case for an editor who would incorporate any *really* relevant material from *The Silmarillion* into *The Lord of the Rings* without increasing the already enormous bulk of the latter and, if feasible, even cutting it. Tolkien wouldn't do it, but someone whom he would trust and who had sympathy (one of his sons?) might possibly do it. If this is not workable I would say publish *The Lord of the Rings* as a prestige book, and after having a second look at it, drop *The Silmarillion*.' Unwisely, Stanley Unwin sent a copy of this letter to Tolkien.

Tolkien was furious. He wrote to Unwin in April 1950 that Rayner's letter confirmed his worst suspicions, 'i.e. that you may be willing to take *The Lord*, but that is more than enough, and you do not want any trimmings; certainly not *The Silmarillion* which you have no intention of genuinely reconsidering. A rejection is after all a rejection, and remains valid. But the question of "dropping" *The Silmarillion*, after a discreet feint, and taking *The Lord* (edited) just does not arise. I have not offered, am not offering *The Lord of the Rings* to you, or anyone else, on such conditions – as surely I made plain before. I want a decision, yes or no: to the proposal I made: and not to any imagined possibility.'

Stanley Unwin replied on 17 April: 'I am more sorry than I can say that you should feel it necessary to present me with an ultimatum, particularly one in connection with a manuscript which I have never seen in its final and complete form. As you demand an *immediate* "yes" or "no" the answer is "no"; but it might well have been yes given time and the sight of the typescript. With sorrow, I must perforce leave it at that.'

Tolkien had achieved his objective. Now he was free to publish with Collins. In the meantime he was moving house once again: Merton College had offered him 99 Holywell, an old house of much character with a large number of rooms, and he, Edith, and Priscilla moved there from Manor Road (which was only a few hundred yards away) in the early spring of 1950. Priscilla was now an undergraduate at Lady Margaret Hall, while Christopher, no longer living at home, was working as a freelance tutor in the English Faculty and completing a B.Litt.

Milton Waldman of Collins was quite certain in his own mind that his firm would publish Tolkien's books. He arranged for Tolkien to come to the Collins offices in London, where he met William Collins and discussed the books with the production department. All seemed ready for an agreement to be signed and *The Lord of the Rings* to be put into print, likewise *The Silmarillion*, when it was finished, although Tolkien would still have to do a good deal of work on the latter book before it was in a publishable state. There was just one matter that remained to be settled: in May 1950 Waldman came to Oxford and told Tolkien that *The Lord of the Rings* 'urgently wanted cutting'. Tolkien was dismayed. He told Waldman that he had 'cut often and hard already', but he would try again as soon as he found the time. Waldman in his turn was taken aback to learn that in Tolkien's estimate *The Silmarillion* would, when completed, be almost as long as *The Lord of the Rings*; taken aback because the manuscript that he had read was nothing like so lengthy.

Tolkien's estimate was in fact wildly inaccurate. The total length of *The Silmarillion* as then planned for publication would perhaps have been as much as one hundred and twenty-five thousand words, maybe less, but certainly nothing like as long as the half-million or so words of *The Lord of the Rings*. But Tolkien, who considered that *The Silmarillion* was as important as the later book, had come to believe that in consequence it was as long. Nor did he help matters at this juncture by handing Waldman several additional chapters from *The Silmarillion* without explaining how they fitted into the story. Waldman was a little puzzled by them. 'They leave me rather bewildered,' he said. Altogether, negotiations which should have been clear and simple were becoming confused.

At this point Waldman left for Italy, where he generally spent much of the year, only visiting London during the spring and autumn. His absence did not help. William Collins knew little about Tolkien's books and had left the whole business in Waldman's hands. Then Waldman became ill and his autumn trip to London was delayed. The consequence was that by the end of 1950, a year after the completion of *The Lord of the Rings*, Tolkien found that he was no nearer to publishing it. Word of this percolated through to Stanley Unwin, who wrote to say that he still hoped 'to have the privilege of being connected with its publication'. But Tolkien was not to be wooed back to Allen & Unwin so easily. His reply was friendly, but he made no reference to the book.

Much of Tolkien's time was occupied by academic and administrative duties in Oxford, and by visits to Belgium (for philological work) and to Ireland (as an examiner); and soon another year had passed with nothing further achieved towards publication. Late in 1951 he wrote a long letter to Milton Waldman, outlining in about ten thousand words the structure of his entire mythology, and hoping by this to convince Waldman that the books were interdependent and indivisible. But by March 1952 he had still not signed an agreement with Collins, and *The Silmarillion* was still not ready for publication. William Collins was in South Africa, Waldman was in Italy, and the price of paper had soared. Tolkien (who had really been as much responsible for the delay as anyone) wrote to Collins saying that his time had been wasted. Either they must publish *The Lord of the Rings* immediately, or he would send the manuscript back to Allen & Unwin. The result was inevitable, for William Collins did not like ultimata any more than did Stanley Unwin. He came back from South Africa, read Tolkien's letter, and replied on 18 April 1952: 'I am afraid we are frightened by the very great length of the book which, with the present cost of paper, does mean a very big outlay'; and he told Tolkien that it did indeed seem best for him to send the manuscript back to Allen & Unwin.

But would Allen & Unwin have him back?

On 22 June 1952 Tolkien wrote to Rayner Unwin, now returned to England and working for his father's firm: 'As for *The Lord of the Rings* and *The Silmarillion*, they are where they were. The one finished, the other still unfinished (or unrevised), and both gathering dust. I have rather modified my views. Better something than nothing! Although to me all are one, and *The Lord of the Rings* would be better far (and eased) as part of the whole, I would gladly consider the publication of any part of the stuff. Years are becoming precious. What about *The Lord of the Rings*? Can anything be done about that, to unlock gates I slammed myself?'

2

A big risk

Rayner Unwin did not need to be asked twice. He suggested that Tolkien should send the manuscript of *The Lord of the Rings* to Allen & Unwin at once, by registered post. But Tolkien had only one typescript of the book in its final and revised form, and he did not want to consign that to the post. He wanted to hand it over in person – and, as it happened, that was not possible for some weeks. During August he was on holiday in Ireland, and in the same month he visited George Sayer, a friend of C. S. Lewis, who taught at Malvern College and who often visited the Inklings. While Tolkien was staying with Sayer in Worcestershire, his host recorded him reading and singing from *The Hobbit* and from the typescript of *The Lord of the Rings*, which he had brought with him. When he listened to these recordings, Tolkien was 'much surprised to discover their effectiveness as recitations, and (if I may say so) my own effectiveness as a narrator'. Many years later, after Tolkien's death, the tapes made on this occasion were issued on long-playing gramophone records.

Tolkien had never before encountered a tape-recorder at close quarters – he pretended to regard Sayer's machine with great suspicion, pronouncing the Lord's Prayer in Gothic into the microphone to cast out any devils that might be lurking within. But after the recording sessions at Malvern he was so impressed with the device that he acquired a machine to use at home, and began to amuse himself by making further tapes of his work. Some years previously he had written what proved to be a very effective 'radio play'. Entitled *The Homecoming of Beorhtnoth, Beorhthelm's Son*, it is in effect a 'sequel' to the Anglo-Saxon poem *The Battle of Maldon*, for it recounts an imaginary episode after that battle when two servants of the duke Beorhtnoth come in the darkness to retrieve their master's corpse from the battlefield. Written in a modern equivalent of Anglo-Saxon alliterative verse, it marks the passing of the heroic age, whose characteristics are exemplified and contrasted in the youthful romantic Torhthelm and the practical old farmer Tídwald. *The Homecoming of Beorhtnoth* was in existence by 1945, but it was not published until 1953, in which year it appeared in *Essays and Studies*. It was never performed on a stage, but a year after publication it was transmitted on the BBC Third Programme. Tolkien was deeply irritated by this radio production, which ignored the alliterative metre and delivered the verse as if it were iambic pentameters. He himself recorded a version that was much more to his own satisfaction on the tape-recorder in his study at home, in which he not only played both parts but improvised some dextrous sound-effects. Although made purely for personal amusement, this recording is a fine demonstration of Tolkien's not inconsiderable talents as an actor. He had shown these talents before the war, when in 1938 and 1939 he had impersonated Chaucer in the 'Summer Diversions' arranged in Oxford by Nevill Coghill and John Masefield. On these occasions he had recited from memory the *Nun's Priest's Tale* and (the next year) *The Reeve's Tale*. He was not enthusiastic about drama as an art-form, considering it to be tiresomely anthropocentric and therefore restricting. But he did not extend this dislike to the dramatic recitation of verse, in which category he presumably placed his own *Beorhtnoth*.

On 19 September 1952 Rayner Unwin came to Oxford and collected the typescript of *The Lord of the Rings*. His father, Sir Stanley Unwin, was in Japan, so it was up to Rayner himself to make the next moves. He decided not to delay by rereading the bulky typescript, for he had seen virtually all of it five years earlier, and he still had a vivid impression of the story. Instead he began immediately to obtain an estimate of production costs, for he was concerned to keep the price of the book within the limit to which the ordinary buyer (and the circulating libraries in particular) would go. After calculations and discussions in the Allen & Unwin offices, it seemed that the best thing would be to divide the book into three volumes, which could be sold (with only a small profit margin) at twenty-one shillings each. This was still a lot of money, rather more than the top price for a novel, but it was the best that could be done. Rayner sent a telegram to his father to ask whether they could publish the book, admitting that it was 'a big risk', and warning that the firm could lose up to a thousand pounds through the project. But he concluded that in his opinion it was a work of genius. Sir Stanley replied by cable, telling him to publish it.

On 10 November 1952 Rayner Unwin wrote to Tolkien to say that the firm would like to publish *The Lord of the Rings* under a profit-sharing agreement. This meant that Tolkien would not receive conventional royalty payments on a percentage basis. Instead he would be paid 'half profits'; that is, he would receive nothing until the sales of the book had been sufficient to cover its costs, but thenceforward he would share equally with the publisher in any profits that might accrue. This method, which had once been common practice but was by this time little used by other firms, was still favoured by Sir Stanley Unwin for all potentially uneconomical books. It helped to keep down the price of such books, since there was no need to include an additional sum in the costing to cover the author's royalties. On the other hand if the book sold unexpectedly well, the author would benefit more substantially than under a royalty agreement. Not that Allen & Unwin expected *The Lord of the Rings* to sell more than a few thousand copies, for it was bulky, unconventional, and did not appeal to any one 'market', being neither a children's book nor an adult novel.

The news soon spread among Tolkien's friends that the book had at last been accepted for publication. C. S. Lewis wrote to congratulate him, remarking: 'I think the prolonged pregnancy has drained a little vitality from you: there'll be a new ripeness and freedom when the book's out.' At that particular moment Tolkien felt anything but free. He wanted to read the typescript of the book once more before it went to the printers, and to iron out any remaining inconsistencies. (Fortunately Rayner Unwin had not asked him to make any cuts, such as Milton Waldman had suggested.) There was also the tricky matter of the appendices to the book, which he had planned for some time; they were to contain information that was relevant to the story but which could not be fitted into the narrative. As yet these appendices existed only in the form of rough drafts and scattered notes, and he could see that it would take a great deal of time to organise them. He was also worried about the necessity of making a clear and accurate map to accompany the book, for a number of topographical and narrative changes had rendered the working map (drawn by Christopher many years before) inaccurate and inadequate. Besides all this, he had a backlog of many years' academic work on hand which he could no longer ignore. And he had decided to move house yet again.

The house in Holywell Street, where the Tolkiens had lived since 1950, was a building of much character, but it was made almost unbearable by the stream of motor traffic that roared past it all day and much of the night. 'This charming house', Tolkien wrote, 'has become uninhabitable: unsleepable-in, unworkable-in, rocked, racked with noise, and drenched with fumes. Such is modern life. Mordor in our midst.' He and Edith were now on their own, Priscilla having left Oxford to work in Bristol; and Edith had become very lame from rheumatism and arthritis, so that she found the many stairs in the house troublesome. By the spring of 1953 Tolkien had found and bought a house in Headington, a quiet Oxford suburb to the east of the city. He and Edith moved there in March.

Despite the dislocation caused by the move, Tolkien managed to complete his final revision for what was to be the first volume of *The Lord of the Rings* by mid-April, and he sent it to Allen & Unwin for typesetting to begin. Soon afterwards he delivered the text of the second volume. He had already discussed with Rayner Unwin the question of independent titles for the three volumes, which Unwin considered preferable to an overall title with volume numbers. Although the book was one continuous story and not a trilogy – a point that Tolkien was always concerned to emphasise – it was felt that it would be best if it appeared volume by volume under different titles, thus earning three sets of reviews rather than one, and perhaps disguising the sheer size of the book. Tolkien was never entirely happy about the division, and he insisted on retaining *The Lord of the Rings* as the overall title. But after a good deal of discussion he and Rayner eventually agreed upon *The Fellowship of the Ring, The Two Towers,* and *The Return of the King* for the volume titles, though Tolkien really preferred 'The War of the Ring' for the third volume, as it gave away less of the story.

The 'production' problems that Tolkien now encountered were similar to those he had met with in *The Hobbit*. He cared very much that his beloved book should be published as he had intended, but once again many of his designs were modified, frequently through considerations of cost. Among items that were declared to be too expensive were red ink for the 'fire-letters' which appear on the Ring, and the halftone colour process that would be necessary to reproduce the facsimile Tolkien had made of 'The Book of Mazarbul', a burnt and tattered volume that (in the story) is found in the Mines of Moria. He was much saddened by this, for he had spent many hours making this facsimile, copying out the pages in runes and elvish writing, and then deliberately damaging them, burning the edges and smearing the paper with substances that looked like dried blood. All this work was now wasted.[1] He was also infuriated by his first sight of the proofs, for he found that the printers had changed several of his spellings, altering *dwarves* to *dwarfs, elvish* to *elfish, further* to *farther,* and ('worst of all' said Tolkien) *elven* to *elfin.* The printers were reproved; they said in self-defence that they had merely followed the dictionary spellings. (Similar 'corrections' to Tolkien's spelling were made in 1961 when Puffin Books issued *The Hobbit* as a paperback, and this time to Tolkien's distress the mistake was not discovered until the book had reached the shops.) Another worry was the matter of the map, still not dealt with; or rather the maps, for an additional plan of the Shire was now thought to be necessary. 'I am stumped,' Tolkien wrote in October 1953. 'Indeed in a panic. They are essential; and urgent; but I just cannot get them done.' In the end he handed over the job to his original map-maker, Christopher, who somehow managed to interpret his father's overlaid, altered, and often contradictory rough sketches, and to produce from them a readable and neatly lettered general map and smaller plan of the Shire.

The first volume of *The Lord of the Rings* was to be published in the summer of 1954, and the remaining two volumes were to follow one by one after short intervals. There was only a modest print order: three and a half thousand copies of the first volume and slightly fewer of the other two, for the publishers considered that this should be enough to cater for the moderate interest the book was expected to attract. As to publicity, Rayner Unwin had panicked at the thought of writing a 'blurb' for the dust-jacket of the book, for it defied conventional description. So he and his father solicited the help of three authors who were likely to have

---

[1]Pages from 'The Book of Mazarbul' were eventually reproduced in the 'Tolkien Calendar' for 1977.

something worth saying about it: Naomi Mitchison, who was a devotee of *The Hobbit*, Richard Hughes, who had long ago praised the first book, and C. S. Lewis. All three responded with fluent words of commendation, Mrs Mitchison comparing *The Lord of the Rings* with science-fiction and Malory, and Lewis drawing a parallel with Ariosto. ('I don't know Ariosto,' Tolkien once said, 'and I'd loathe him if I did.')

Publication day for the first volume approached. It was more than sixteen years since Tolkien had begun to write the book. 'I am dreading the publication,' he told his friend Father Robert Murray, 'for it will be impossible not to mind what is said. I have exposed my heart to be shot at.'

3

Cash or kudos

'This book is like lightning from a clear sky. To say that in it heroic romance, gorgeous, eloquent, and unashamed, has suddenly returned at a period almost pathological in its anti-romanticism, is inadequate. To us, who live in that odd period, the return – and the sheer relief of it – is doubtless the important thing. But in the history of Romance itself – a history which stretches back to the *Odyssey* and beyond – it makes not a return but an advance or revolution: the conquest of new territory.' This review of *The Fellowship of the Ring* (the first volume of *The Lord of the Rings*) appeared in *Time & Tide* on 14 August 1954, a few days after the book had been published. Its author was C. S. Lewis.

Perhaps it was a little excessive for Lewis to contribute to the publisher's 'blurb' and also to review the book, but he wanted to do everything in his power to help Tolkien; though before sending his contribution for the 'blurb' to Rayner Unwin he had warned Tolkien: 'Even if he and you approve my words, think twice before using them: I am certainly a much, and perhaps an increasingly, hated man whose name might do you more harm than good.' Prophetic words, for more than one critic reviewing the book in August 1954 displayed an extraordinary personal animosity to Lewis, and used (or wasted) a good deal of space in mocking Lewis's comparison of Tolkien to Ariosto. Edwin Muir wrote in the *Observer*: 'Nothing but a great masterpiece could survive the bombardment of praise directed at it from the blurb,' and although Muir admitted enjoying the book he declared that he was disappointed with the 'lack of the human discrimination and depth which the subject demanded. Mr Tolkien', continued Muir, 'describes a tremendous conflict between good and evil, on which hangs the future of life on earth. But his good people are consistently good, his evil figures immutably evil; and he has no room in his world for a Satan both evil and tragic.' (Mr Muir had evidently forgotten Gollum, evil, tragic, and very nearly redeemed.) Several critics carped at Tolkien's prose style, among them Peter Green in the *Daily Telegraph* who wrote that it 'veers from pre-Raphaelite to Boy's Own Paper', while J. W. Lambert in the *Sunday Times* declared that the story has two odd characteristics: 'no religious spirit of any kind, and to all intents and purposes no women' (neither statement was entirely fair, but both were reflected in later writings by other critics). Yet for all these harsh judgements there were many who were enthusiastic, and even among the mockers there were some who were drawn to commendation. Green in the *Telegraph* had to admit that the book 'has an undeniable fascination', while Lambert in the *Sunday Times* wrote: 'Whimsical drivel with a message? No; it sweeps along with a narrative and pictorial force which lifts it above that level.' Perhaps the wisest remark came from the *Oxford Times* reviewer who declared: 'The severely practical will have no time for it. Those who have imagination to kindle will find themselves completely carried along, becoming part of the eventful quest and regretting that there are only two more books to come.'

The reviews were good enough to promote sales, and it soon became clear that the three and a half thousand copies that had been printed of the first volume would be insufficient to meet the demand. Six weeks after publication, a reprint was ordered. Tolkien himself wrote: 'As for the reviews, they were a good deal better than I feared.' In July he had visited Dublin to receive an honorary Doctorate of Letters from the Catholic University of Ireland. He went overseas again in October to be given another honorary degree, at Liège, and these and other calls on his time delayed his work on the appendices for *The Lord of the Rings*. The printers had already set up the type for the text of the third volume, from which Tolkien had now decided to omit the somewhat sentimental epilogue that dealt with Sam and his family. But the third volume could not be printed until the appendices arrived, as well as the enlarged map of Gondor and Mordor that Tolkien now felt to be required, and the index of names that he had promised in the preface to the first volume.

The second volume, *The Two Towers*, was published in mid-November. Reviews were similar in tone to those of the first volume. The third volume was now eagerly awaited by the supporting faction, for the story had broken off with Frodo imprisoned in the Tower of Cirith Ungol, and as the reviewer in the *Illustrated London News* declared, 'The suspense is cruel.' Meanwhile the deadline that Allen & Unwin had set for the delivery of the appendices passed without any manuscript arriving at their office. 'I am dreadfully sorry,' Tolkien wrote. 'I have been trying hard.' And he did manage to send some of the material to the publishers shortly afterwards; some, but not all.

In America, Houghton Mifflin had published *The Fellowship of the Ring* in October; *The Two Towers* followed shortly after. American reviews of the first two volumes were on the whole cautious. But enthusiastic articles by W. H. Auden in the *New York Times* – 'No fiction I have read in the last five years has given me more joy,' wrote Auden – helped to boost sales, and during the following year a large number of copies were bought by American readers.

By January 1955, two months after the publication of the second volume, Tolkien had still not completed the appendices that were required so urgently. He had abandoned any hope of making an index of names, having found that the job would take too long. Freed of this burden, he completed more material during January and February, but he found the task maddeningly difficult. He had at one time planned to fill an entire 'specialist volume' with details of the history and linguistics of his mythological peoples, and he had amassed a great deal of notes on these topics. But now he had to compress everything, for the publishers could only give him a short space at the end of the book. However, he pressed on, spurred by the letters he was already receiving from readers who took the book almost as history, and demanded more information on many topics. This attitude to his story flattered him, for it was the type of response that he had hoped to arouse, yet he remarked: 'I am not at all sure that the tendency to treat this whole thing as a kind of vast game is really good – certainly not for me, who find that kind of thing only too fatally attractive.' Nevertheless it was encouraging to know that the material he was so laboriously preparing on the Shire Calendars, the Rulers of Gondor, and the Tengwar of Fëanor would be read voraciously by a large number of people.

The appendices were still unfinished by March, and strongly-worded letters began to arrive at the offices of Allen & Unwin, complaining about the non-appearance of the third volume. It was clear to the publishers that the book was arousing more than the usual interest for fiction. Rayner Unwin pleaded with Tolkien to get the work done, but it was not until 20 May that the final copy for the appendices reached the printers. The last map, prepared by Christopher, who had worked for twenty-four hours non-stop to finish it, had been sent some weeks before; so now there should be no more delays. But there were. First the chart of runes was printed wrongly, and Tolkien had to make corrections. Then other queries were raised by the printers and forwarded to Tolkien to be answered; but by this time he had gone on holiday to Italy.

He made the journey by boat and train with Priscilla, while Edith went on a Mediterranean cruise with three friends. He kept a diary, and recorded his feeling of having 'come to the heart of Christendom: an exile from the borders and far provinces returning home, or at least to the home of his fathers'. In Venice among the canals he found himself 'almost free of the cursed disease of the internal combustion engine of which all the world is dying'; and he wrote afterwards: 'Venice seemed incredibly, elvishly lovely – to me like a dream of Old Gondor, or Pelargir of the Númenorean Ships, before the return of the Shadow.' He and Priscilla travelled on to Assisi, where the queries from the printers reached him, but he could not deal with them until he was reunited with his notes on his return to Oxford. So it was not until 20 October, almost a year after the publication of *The Two Towers*, that *The Return of the King* reached the bookshops. A note on the last page apologised for the absence of the promised index.

Now that all three volumes had appeared, the critics were able to make a full assessment of *The Lord of the Rings*. C. S. Lewis paid another tribute in *Time & Tide*: 'The book is too original and too opulent for any final judgment on a first reading. But we know at once that it has done things to us. We are not quite the same men.' A new voice was added to the chorus of praise when Bernard Levin wrote in *Truth* that he believed it to be 'one of the most remarkable works of literature in our, or any, time. It is comforting, in this troubled day, to be once more assured that the meek shall inherit the earth.' But there were further criticisms of the style. John Metcalf wrote in the *Sunday Times*: 'Far too often Mr Tolkien strides away into a kind of Brewers' Biblical, enwreathed with inversions, encrusted with archaisms'; and Edwin Muir returned to the attack in a review in the *Observer* headed 'A Boy's World'. 'The astonishing thing', he wrote, 'is that all the characters are boys masquerading as adult heroes. The hobbits, or halflings, are ordinary boys; the fully human heroes have reached the fifth form; but hardly one of them knows anything about women, except by hearsay. Even the elves and the dwarfs and the ents are boys, irretrievably, and will never come to puberty.'

'Blast Edwin Muir and his delayed adolescence,' snorted Tolkien. 'He is old enough to know better. If he had an M.A. I should nominate him for the professorship of poetry – sweet revenge.'

By now, opinions were firmly polarised. The book had acquired its champions and its enemies, and as W. H. Auden wrote: 'Nobody seems to have a moderate opinion; either, like myself, people find it a masterpiece of its genre, or they cannot abide it.' And this was how it was to remain for the rest of Tolkien's life: extreme praise from one faction, total contempt from the other. On the whole Tolkien himself did not mind this very much; indeed it amused him. He wrote of it:

> *The Lord of the Rings*
> is one of those things:
> if you like you do:
> if you don't, then you boo!

Oxford University did not exactly boo. It was too polite to do that. But, as Tolkien himself reported, his colleagues said to him: 'Now we know what you have been doing all these years! Why the edition of this, and the commentary on that, and the grammars and glossaries, have all remained "promised" but unfinished. You have had your fun and you must now do some *work*.' The first fruit of this demand was a lecture, already overdue by many months, in a series on the Celtic element in the English language. Tolkien delivered it under the title 'English and Welsh' on 21 October 1955, the day after the publication of *The Return of the King*. It was a long and rather diffuse examination of the relationship between the two languages, but it was intended (as Tolkien explained) as little more than a curtain-raiser for the series. Certainly it contains much of value in the way of autobiographical comment by Tolkien on the history of his own interest in languages. At the beginning of the lecture Tolkien apologised for its tardiness, adding in mitigation that among the many tasks which had hindered him was 'the long-delayed appearance of a large "work", if it can be called that, which contains, in the way of presentation that I find most natural, much of what I personally have received from the study of things Celtic'.

By now it had become clear that *The Lord of the Rings* was not going to lose a thousand pounds for Allen & Unwin. Sales of the book increased steadily, if not yet remarkably. They were boosted by a radio dramatisation of the book, which inevitably did not meet with Tolkien's approval, for if he had reservations about drama in general he was even more strongly opposed to the 'adaptation' of stories, believing that this process invariably reduced them to their merely human and thus most trivial level. However the radio broadcasts contributed to the book's popularity, and early in 1956 Tolkien received his first payment from Allen & Unwin under the 'half profits' agreement, a cheque for more than three and a half thousand pounds. This was considerably more than his annual salary from the university, and though he was of course delighted he also realised that income tax was going to be a very serious problem. Sales rose even more during 1956, and the cheque that he received a year later was substantially larger. In consequence of this unexpected income he wished that he had opted for retirement from his professorship at sixty-five instead of agreeing (as he had) to continue until sixty-seven, the usual Oxford retiring age. Worries about tax, which soon proved to be justified, also meant that when in 1957 Marquette University, a Catholic institution in the Middle West of America, offered to buy the manuscripts of his principal published stories, he accepted with alacrity. The sum of £1,250 (which was then the equivalent of five thousand dollars) was paid, and in the spring of 1958 the originals of *The Hobbit, The Lord of the Rings,* and *Farmer Giles of Ham,* together with the still unpublished *Mr Bliss,* made their way across the Atlantic.

Besides money, *The Lord of the Rings* was bringing Tolkien a large number of fan-letters. Those who wrote included a real Sam Gamgee, who had not read *The Lord of the Rings* but had heard that his name appeared in the story. Tolkien was delighted, explained how he had come by the name, and sent Mr Gamgee a signed copy of all three volumes. Later he said: 'For some time I lived in fear of receiving a letter signed "S. Gollum". That would have been more difficult to deal with.'

Allen & Unwin had begun to negotiate for translations of *The Lord of the Rings* into foreign languages. The first result of this was the Dutch edition, published in 1956, after Tolkien had made stringent criticisms of the translator's first attempts to render the complex series of names in the story into his own language. In the end Tolkien was satisfied with the Dutch version, but he was much less pleased with a Swedish translation of the book that appeared three years later. Not only did he disapprove of much of the actual translation (he had a working knowledge of Swedish) but he was also angered by a foreword to the book inserted by the translator. Tolkien called this foreword 'five pages of impertinent nonsense'. In it, the translator interpreted *The Lord of the Rings* as an allegory of contemporary world politics, referred to Tolkien telling the story to 'a host of grandchildren', and described the scenery of the very ordinary Oxford suburb of Headington where Tolkien was now living (which stands on a slight eminence known as Headington Hill) as 'the leafy orchard-landscape . . . with the Barrowdowns or Headington Hills in the rear'. After Tolkien had registered a strong protest, this foreword was withdrawn by the Swedish publishers from further editions of the book.

In the following years *The Lord of the Rings* was translated into all the major European languages, and many others, with the consequence that Tolkien received a number of invitations to travel abroad and be fêted. He accepted only one such invitation, to go to Holland in the spring of 1958, and this expedition proved a great success. He was assured of a warm welcome, for he had been friends for several years with Professor Piet Harting of Amsterdam University, who met him on his arrival and entertained him regally. The main event was a 'Hobbit Dinner' organised by a Rotterdam bookseller, at which Tolkien made a lively speech in English interspersed with Dutch and Elvish. It was in part a parody of Bilbo's party speech at the beginning of *The Lord of the Rings*, and it concluded with Tolkien recalling 'that it is now exactly twenty years since I began in earnest to complete the history of our revered hobbit-ancestors of the Third Age. I look East, West, North, South, and I do not see Sauron; but I see that Saruman has many descendants. We Hobbits have against them no magic weapons. Yet, my gentlehobbits, I give you this toast: To the Hobbits. May they outlast the Sarumans and see spring again in the trees.'

By this time it was clear that *The Lord of the Rings* was something of an international 'hot property'. Stanley Unwin warned Tolkien that offers would soon be forthcoming for the film rights, and the two men agreed upon their policy: either a respectable 'treatment' of the book, or else a good deal of money. As Sir Stanley put it, the choice was between 'cash or kudos'. The first overtures from the film world came at the end of 1957 when Tolkien was approached by three American businessmen who showed him drawings for a proposed animated motion-picture of *The Lord of the Rings*. These gentlemen (Mr Forrest J. Ackerman, Mr Morton Grady Zimmerman, and Mr Al Brodax) also delivered to him a scenario or 'Story Line' for the proposed film. Reading this, Tolkien discovered that it did not exactly treat the book with respect. A number of names were consistently mis-spelt (Boromir was rendered 'Borimor'), virtually all walking was dispensed with in the story and the Company of the Ring were transported everywhere on the backs of eagles, and the elvish waybread *lembas* was described as a 'food concentrate'. There did not seem to be much prospect of kudos in this, and as there was not much cash either, negotiations were not continued. But it was an indication of things to come. In the meanwhile Tolkien's income from his books remained high. 'I am afraid', he said, 'I cannot help feeling there is a lot to be said for "the grosser forms of literary success" as a sneering critic recently called it.'

Sales of *The Hobbit* and *The Lord of the Rings* continued to rise steadily, but there was no drastic change in the pattern until 1965. Early in that year it was learnt that an American publisher who appeared not to suffer from an excess of scruples was planning to issue an unauthorised paperback edition of *The Lord of the Rings*, almost certainly without paying royalties to Tolkien. Because of the confused state of American copyright at that time, the publisher doubtless thought that he could do this with impunity; and he also realised that such an edition would probably sell widely, especially among American students, who were already showing an interest in the book. The only way to save the situation was for Tolkien's authorised American publishers, Houghton Mifflin, to issue their own paperback as quickly as possible, and this they planned to do, in collaboration with Ballantine Books. But in order to register this new edition as copyright, they would have to make a number of textual changes so that the book was technically 'new'. Rayner Unwin came to Oxford to explain all this to Tolkien, and to ask him to make some hasty revisions of *The Lord of the Rings*, and of *The Hobbit*, so that the latter book could be protected as well. Tolkien agreed, and Unwin returned, satisfied, to London.

Normally the very mention of the word 'revision' set Tolkien to work. But on this occasion he did nothing about it for the time being. He was quite used to missing deadlines and failing to meet urgent demands for manuscripts, and now he continued to polish his new story *Smith of Wootton Major* (which he had just written), and to work also on his translation of *Gawain*, and on some notes on the Elvish poem *Namárië* which the composer Donald Swann wanted to set to music as part of a Tolkien song-cycle. By the time he had finished all these tasks it was June, and what Tolkien and others regarded as an American 'pirate' edition of *The Lord of the Rings* had been issued.

The publishers were Ace Books, who (when challenged) alleged there was nothing illegal in their paperback, even though it was printed entirely without the permission of Tolkien or his authorised publishers, and even though no royalty payment had been offered to the author. Indeed the Ace edition had also been manufactured with some care, so that it was quite a bargain at seventy-five cents for each volume. There were a number of errors in the typesetting, but on the whole the printers had reproduced Tolkien's text accurately; ludicrously so, since they had included both the promise in the foreword of the index of names and the note at the end apologising for its absence. Ace were already well known as publishers of science fiction, and clearly a lot of people were going to buy their edition until an authorised paperback could be issued. An urgent request was sent to Tolkien to complete the revisions (which it was assumed he had been working on assiduously for the last six months) as soon as possible.

So Tolkien began, though he turned not to *The Lord of the Rings* for which revision was urgent, but to *The Hobbit* for which it was not. He spent many hours searching for some revision notes that he had already made, but he could not find them. Instead he found a typescript of 'The New Shadow', a sequel to *The Lord of the Rings* which he had begun a long time ago but had abandoned after a few pages. It was about the return of evil to Middle-earth. He sat up till four a.m. reading it and thinking about it. When the next day he did get down to *The Hobbit* he found a good deal of it 'very poor' and had to restrain himself from rewriting the entire book. The business of making revisions took some time, and when he turned at last to *The Lord of the Rings* the summer was well advanced. He decided on a number of changes that would correct remaining inaccuracies, and checked through the index which had now been prepared for him, but it was not until August that he was able to send the revised text to America.

Meanwhile the authorised paperback publishers, Ballantine Books, had decided that they could not wait any longer. In order to get at least one Tolkien book into the shops they published *The Hobbit* in the original text without waiting for Tolkien's revisions, which they planned to include in a later edition. They sent him a copy, and he was astonished by the picture on the cover. Ace Books for all their moral 'piracy' had employed a cover artist who knew something about the story, but Ballantine's cover picture seemed to have no relevance whatever to *The Hobbit*, for it showed a hill, two emus, and a curious tree bearing bulbous fruit. Tolkien exploded: 'What has it got to do with the story? Where is this place? Why emus? And what is the thing in the foreground with pink bulbs?' When the reply came that the artist hadn't time to read the book, and that the object with pink bulbs was 'meant to suggest a Christmas tree', Tolkien could only answer: 'I begin to feel that I am shut up in a madhouse.'

In October 1965 the 'authorised' paperback of *The Lord of the Rings* was published in America in three volumes, with Tolkien's revisions incorporated, and with the emus and the Christmas tree on the cover of the first volume, though this picture was later removed and one of Tolkien's own drawings was substituted; two more of his pictures were used for the second and third volumes. Each copy carried a message from Tolkien: 'This paperback edition and no other has been published with my consent and co-operation. Those who approve of courtesy (at least) to living authors will purchase it and no other.'

But this did not immediately produce the desired result. The

Ballantine edition (because it paid a royalty) cost twenty cents per volume more than the Ace edition, and the American student buyers did not at first show a preference for it. Clearly something more would have to be done. Curiously Tolkien himself played a prominent and efficient part in the campaign that now began; curiously, because he was no businessman, and ironically, because the unbusinesslike habits of his recent years were now turned to good advantage. He had been accustomed to 'waste' many hours that ought to have been spent on completing work for publication by writing innumerable replies to fan-letters, but this did mean that he had already built up an affectionate following of many dozens of enthusiastic correspondents, especially in America, and they were now only too glad to spring to his defence. On his own initiative he began to include a note in all his replies to American readers, informing them that the Ace edition was unauthorised, and asking them to tell their friends. This soon had a remarkable effect. American readers not only began to refuse to buy the Ace edition but demanded, often in forcible terms, that booksellers remove it from their shelves. A fan-club, 'The Tolkien Society of America', which had recently been formed, now joined in the battle. By the end of the year the sales of Ace copies began to fall sharply; and when the cause was taken up by the Science Fiction Writers of America, an influential body that now applied considerable pressure to Ace, the result was that Ace wrote to Tolkien offering to pay him a royalty for every copy they had sold, and stating that they would not reprint after their present stocks had been exhausted. So a treaty was signed, and 'The War over Middle-earth', as one journalist had dubbed it, came to an end.

But the most important consequence was yet to come. The dispute had attracted considerable publicity, and as a result Tolkien's name and the titles of his books were now very widely known in America. Approximately one hundred thousand copies of the Ace edition of *The Lord of the Rings* had been sold during 1965, but this figure was soon passed by the 'authorised' paperback, which quickly reached the one million mark. Ace had unwittingly done a service to Tolkien, for they had helped to lift his book from the 'respectable' hard-cover status in which it had languished for some years and had put it at the top of the popular best-sellers. And by now a 'campus cult' had begun.

Clearly there was much in Tolkien's writing that appealed to

American students. Its implied emphasis on the protection of natural scenery against the ravages of an industrial society harmonised with the growing ecological movement, and it was easy to see *The Lord of the Rings* as a tract for the times. But its chief appeal lay, as Lewis had seen long ago, in its unabashed return to heroic romance. The harsher critics might call it escapism, while the harsher still might compare it to the sinister influence of the hallucinatory drugs that were then fashionable in some student circles, but, whatever the reason, to hundreds of thousands of young Americans the story of Frodo's journey with the Ring now became The Book, surpassing all previous best-sellers. At the end of 1966 a newspaper reported: 'At Yale the trilogy is selling faster than William Golding's *Lord of the Flies* at its crest. At Harvard it is outpacing J. D. Salinger's *The Catcher in the Rye*.' Lapel badges began to appear bearing slogans such as 'Frodo Lives', 'Gandalf for President', and 'Come to Middle-earth'. Branches of the Tolkien Society mushroomed along the West Coast and in New York State, and eventually grew into the 'Mythpoeic Society', devoted also to studying the works of C. S. Lewis and Charles Williams. Members of fan-clubs held 'hobbit picnics' at which they ate mushrooms and drank cider, and dressed up as characters from the stories. Eventually, Tolkien's writings began to achieve respectability in American academic circles, and were the subject of theses with such titles as 'A Parametric Analysis of Antithetical Conflict and Irony in J. R. R. Tolkien's *The Lord of the Rings*', Volumes of Tolkien criticism began to appear in campus bookshops. A President's daughter, an astronaut, and a film star wrote to express their enthusiasm for Tolkien's writings. Among the graffiti that could be seen on American walls was: 'J. R. R. Tolkien is Hobbit-forming'.

The wildfire of this American enthusiasm spread to other countries. At festivities in Saigon a Vietnamese dancer was seen bearing the lidless eye of Sauron on his shield, and in North Borneo a 'Frodo Society' was formed. At about the same time, interest in Tolkien's books showed a marked increase in Britain, partly because those who had first read them as children were now reaching adulthood and were communicating their enthusiasm to their friends, and partly as a reflection of the cult that had grown up in America. British sales of the books rose sharply, a Tolkien Society began to meet in London and elsewhere in the country, students at Warwick University renamed the Ring Road around their campus 'Tolkien Road', and a 'psychedelic magazine' entitled *Gandalf's Garden* was issued with the avowed objective 'to bring beautiful people together'. Its first issue explained that Gandalf 'is fast becoming absorbed in the youthful world spirit as the mythological hero of the age'.

As for Tolkien himself, writing to his colleague Norman Davis he referred to the widespread enthusiasm for his books as 'my deplorable cultus'; and to a reporter who asked him if he was pleased by the enthusiasm of the young Americans he replied: 'Art moves them and they don't know what they've been moved by and they get quite drunk on it. Many young Americans are involved in the stories in a way that I'm not.'

Sales of the books continued to increase, and though it is impossible to give an accurate figure it would appear that by the end of 1968 approximately three million copies of *The Lord of the Rings* had been sold around the world. Numerous translations appeared in a variety of languages.[1]

Press reporters began to seek Tolkien out in increasing numbers, and although in principle he disliked giving interviews, his natural courtesy made it difficult for him to turn them away; eventually he selected several for whom he had a particular liking and insisted on communicating with them alone. Visitors of all kinds arrived on business connected with his books, and again, though he wished to remain undisturbed, he usually agreed to see them. In general he tended to like people when he first met them, and then to find them irritating within a short time; eventually, perhaps with this in mind, he installed an alarm-clock which he set to ring a few minutes after the visitor had arrived, whereupon he would imply that he had some other matter to attend to and would show the caller out.

Americans who were enthusiastic about his books began to make pilgrimages to see him. Dick Plotz, founder member of the Tolkien Society of America, called to interview him for a fan-magazine. Professor Clyde S. Kilby from Illinois arrived showing much interest in *The Silmarillion*, for which the Tolkien enthusiasts were now waiting impatiently; Tolkien showed Kilby some of the *Silmarillion* manuscripts, and was glad of his appreciative remarks. Another academic from the Middle West, William Ready, visited

[1]For a full list of translations see Appendix C.

Tolkien and later published a book about him which Tolkien found 'insulting and offensive'; and from then onwards he was more careful about visitors. Early in 1968 the BBC made a film about him, which they called 'Tolkien in Oxford'; he performed unselfconsciously to the camera, and enjoyed himself in a mild way. Yet on the whole this kind of thing did not please him. He wrote to a reader: 'Being a cult figure in one's own lifetime I am afraid is not at all pleasant. However I do not find that it tends to puff one up; in my case at any rate it makes me feel extremely small and inadequate. But even the nose of a very modest idol cannot remain entirely untickled by the sweet smell of incense.'

VII

1959–1973 : Last years

1

Headington

Fame puzzled him. It was not something that he had ever expected or felt to be appropriate. Certainly let his readers be enthusiastic about the stories, but why should they make a fuss of him? And they were indeed making a fuss. He was having to deal with a huge mound of correspondence from fans, and many readers did not merely send him letters. They enclosed gifts of every kind: paintings, sculptures, drinking-goblets, photographs of themselves dressed as characters from the books, tape-recordings, food, drink, tobacco, and tapestries. 76 Sandfield Road, where the Tolkiens were now living, was already filled to bursting with books and papers, and now it began to overflow with gifts. Tolkien spent day after day writing letters of thanks. When Allen & Unwin offered to assist with the answering of his fan-mail he accepted with gratitude. But since his private address had received some publicity and his telephone number could be found in the Oxford directory, he was troubled in another way. Callers began to arrive without appointment, asking him to autograph books or to give them money. Usually they were polite, occasionally mad or threatening. The telephone would ring in the middle of the night: an unknown American was on the line, wishing to speak to Tolkien in person, and quite unaware of the time difference. Worst of all, people began to take photographs through the windows. It was not the kind of thing that should happen in an ordered world, a scoured Shire.

As Tolkien grew older, many of his characteristics became more deeply marked. The hasty way of talking, the bad articulation and the parenthetic sentences, grew to be more pronounced. Attitudes

235

long held, such as his dislike of French cooking, became absurd caricatures of themselves. What he once wrote of prejudices held by C. S. Lewis could have been said of himself in old age: 'He had several, some ineradicable, being based on ignorance but impenetrable by information.' At the same time he had nothing like so many prejudices as Lewis; nor is 'prejudice' exactly the right word, for it implies that his actions were based upon these opinions, whereas in truth his stranger beliefs rarely had any bearing on his behaviour. It was not so much a matter of prejudice as the habit (and it is not an uncommon Oxford habit) of making dogmatic assertions about things of which he knew very little.

In some ways he found old age deeply distressing, while in other respects it brought out the best in him. He was saddened by the consciousness of waning powers, and wrote in 1965: 'I find it difficult to work – beginning to feel old and the fire dying down.' Occasionally this plunged him into despair, and in his later years he was particularly prone to the gloom that had always characterised his life; the very sense of retirement and withdrawal was sufficient to bring out this side in his nature. But the other side of his personality, the capacity for high spirits and good fellowship, remained just as strong, and if anything it too increased to balance the growing gloom. The approach of old age suited him physically, and as the angularity of his long thin face softened into wrinkles and folds, and there was a suggestion of increased girth behind the coloured waistcoat which he now almost invariably wore, friends noted that the ripening of age was distinctly becoming. Certainly his capacity for enjoying the company of others seemed to increase as the years passed; while the twinkling eyes, the enthusiastic way of talking, the explosive laugh, the easy friendliness, and the expansiveness over the dinner-table or in a bar, made him the most congenial of companions.

'He was a man of "cronies",' wrote C. S. Lewis in the obituary of Tolkien, 'and was always best in some small circle of intimates where the tone was at once Bohemian, literary, and Christian.' Yet when Tolkien retired from the Merton Professorship in the summer of 1959 he placed himself almost deliberately out of reach of such cronies, away from the society of those whom (apart from his own family) he loved best; and as a result he experienced a measure of unhappiness. In these later years he still saw a little of Lewis, making occasional visits to the 'Bird and Baby' and to the Kilns,

Lewis's house on the other side of Headington; and he and Lewis might conceivably have preserved something of their old friendship had not Tolkien been puzzled and even angered by Lewis's marriage to Joy Davidman, which lasted from 1957 until her death in 1960. Some of his feelings may be explained by the fact that she had been divorced from her first husband before she married Lewis, some by resentment of Lewis's expectation that his friends should pay court to his new wife – whereas in the thirties Lewis, very much the bachelor, had liked to ignore the fact that his friends had wives to go home to. But there was more to it than that. It was almost as if Tolkien felt betrayed by the marriage, resented the intrusion of a woman into his friendship with Lewis – just as Edith had resented Lewis's intrusion into her marriage. Ironically it was Edith who became friends with Joy Davidman.

The cessation in the mid nineteen-fifties of Tolkien's regular meetings with Lewis marked the closing of the 'clubbable' chapter in his life, a chapter that had begun with the T.C.B.S. and had culminated in the Inklings. From this time onwards he was essentially a solitary man who led most of his life at home. This was chiefly through necessity, for he was greatly concerned for Edith's health and well-being; and as she was becoming increasingly lame with every year, besides suffering from constant digestive trouble, he felt it his duty to be with her as much of the time as was possible. But this change in his life was also to some extent a deliberate withdrawal from the society in which he had lived, worked, and talked for forty years; for Oxford itself was changing, and his generation was making way for a different breed of men, less discursive, less sociable in the old way, and certainly less Christian.

In his Valedictory Address, given to a packed audience in Merton College Hall at the end of his final summer term, Tolkien touched on some of the changes that were taking place in Oxford. He directed some barbed remarks towards the increasing emphasis on post-graduate research, which he described as 'the degeneration of real curiosity and enthusiasm into a "planned economy", under which so much research time is stuffed into more or less standard skins and turned out in sausages of a size and shape approved by our own little printed cookery book'. Yet he ended not with any discussion of academic matters, but by quoting from his own Elvish song of farewell, 'Namárië'. At last, after four decades of university service, he was looking forward to devoting all his time to his legends, and especially to the completion of *The Silmarillion*, which Allen & Unwin were now extremely keen to publish, and for which they had already been waiting for several years.

Sandfield Road was not the best place for retirement. Tolkien had already lived there for six years and was aware of the limitations that it would impose; yet even so he was perhaps not fully expecting the sense of isolation that began when he no longer had to make the daily journey into college. The Sandfield Road house was two miles from the centre of Oxford, and the nearest bus-stop was some distance away, further than Edith was able to walk with ease. Consequently any journey into Oxford or to the Headington shops involved the hiring of a taxi. Nor did friends call with such frequency as they had when the Tolkiens lived in the centre of the city. As to the family, Christopher and his wife Faith often paid visits; Faith, a sculptor, had made a bust of her father-in-law which the English Faculty presented to Tolkien on his retirement; later Tolkien had it cast in bronze at his own expense, and the bronze was placed in the Faculty library. But Christopher, who was now a lecturer, later a Fellow, at New College, was much engaged with his own work. John was now in charge of his own parish in Staffordshire, while Michael was teaching in the Midlands and could only come for occasional visits with his family (a son and two daughters). Priscilla was now back in Oxford, working as a probation officer, and she saw a good deal of her parents; but she lived on the further side of the city and she too had her own concerns.

Tolkien's contacts with academic life were now restricted to occasional visits from Alistair Campbell, the Anglo-Saxon scholar who had succeeded Charles Wrenn as professor, and to lunches with his former pupil Norman Davis, the new Merton Professor of English Language and Literature. Davis and his wife soon realised that these meals were an important feature of life for the Tolkiens, offering a release from the confined domestic routine at Sandfield Road. Once every week or so the Davises would call to take them to whichever country hotel was the current favourite – and none remained in favour with the Tolkiens for long, due to some defect in the cooking, the size of the bill, or the fact that the route to it involved the use of a new road which had spoiled the scenery. At the hotel they would have a round of drinks – Edith found that a large brandy agreed with her digestion – and then a good lunch with no lack of wine. During the meal Lena Davis would talk to Edith, of whom she was very fond, freeing the two men for their own conversation. But besides this and family events there was little else in Tolkien's social life.

Exeter College elected him to an Honorary Fellowship in 1963, Merton following suit with an Emeritus Fellowship. But though he was always welcome in both colleges and was sent frequent invitations, he rarely attended a college dinner; and when he did so he ate little, suspecting the worst of the cooking. Nor would he dine away from home unless Priscilla or a friend was able to keep Edith company for the evening. Concern for her well-being always took precedence with him.

Immediately after his retirement there was a good deal to occupy him in the matter of domestic arrangements. He had to move all his books out of his college room and find space for them at home, and since his upstairs study-bedroom at Sandfield Road was already crammed, he decided to convert the garage (unoccupied, since there was no car) into a library-cum-office. The shifting of books took many months, and it did no good to the lumbago of which he now complained. But at last everything was in place and he could begin the major task of revising and completing *The Silmarillion*.

Inevitably, given his habit of drastic rewriting, he had decided that the whole work needed to be reconstructed, and he began this great labour. He was helped by his part-time secretary Elisabeth Lumsden, who like two of her successors, Naomi Collyer and Phyllis Jenkinson, became friends with him and Edith. But no sooner had he begun to make progress than he was interrupted by the arrival of the proofs of his *Ancrene Wisse* edition, delayed by a printing strike. Reluctantly he abandoned his mythology and turned to the labour of correcting two hundred and twenty-two pages of Middle English with detailed footnotes. Once the *Ancrene Wisse* was out of the way, he began to turn back to what he called his 'real work', but he felt that before continuing with *The Silmarillion* he ought to complete the revision of his *Gawain* and *Pearl* translations, and to write the introduction that the publishers required for them. Nor did he manage to finish any of this before turning to another task for Allen & Unwin, the revision of his lecture on Fairy-Stories which they wished to reprint together with *Leaf by Niggle*. Thus there was a perpetual discontinuity, a breaking of threads in his work which delayed achievement and frustrated him more and more.

A lot of his time was also spent simply in answering letters. Readers wrote to him by the score, praising, criticising, and asking for more information about elements in the stories. Tolkien took every letter seriously, especially if it came from a child or an elderly person. Sometimes he would make two or three drafts of his reply – and then be dissatisfied with the result, or so undecided as to what he should say that he never sent anything. Or he would lose a letter after writing it, and spend hours turning out the garage or his study-bedroom until he had found it. The search might reveal other forgotten things, an unanswered letter or an unfinished story, and he would abandon what he had set out to do, and sit down and read (or rewrite) whatever he had discovered. Many days passed in this fashion.

He was always glad to deal with requests from readers who wanted to name their house or their pet or even their child after a place or a character in his books; indeed he considered it only proper that they *should* ask him, and he was angered when a hydro-foil was given the name 'Shadowfax' (the horse ridden by Gandalf) without his permission. Those who did write on such matters were often rewarded in unexpected ways; a breeder of Jersey cattle ask-ing if he could use 'Rivendell' as a herd-name received a letter from Tolkien to the effect that the Elvish word for 'bull' was *mundo*, and suggesting a number of names for individual bulls that might be derived from it. (When he had posted this letter, Tolkien sat down to work out how it was that *mundo* came to mean 'bull', something that he had not previously considered.) With these and similar matters occupying him more and more, he spent little time work-ing on *The Silmarillion*.

Nevertheless he continued to attend to it, and he might have succeeded in preparing it for publication at this time if he had been able to discipline himself into adopting regular working methods. But much of his time was spent simply in playing Patience, often far into the night. It was a habit of many years' standing, and he had invented a large number of games of his own, which he would pass on gleefully to other Patience players. Certainly he did a good deal of thinking while apparently frittering away the time over cards; but he would usually be filled with remorse at hours spent in this fashion. Often he would pass much of the day drawing marvellously intricate patterns on the backs of old newspapers, while solving the crossword. Inevitably these patterns were caught up in his stories, and became Elvish heraldic devices, Númenórean carpet designs, or drawings of exotic plants with names in Quenya or Sindarin. At first he would be delighted with them. But then he would feel ashamed at his dilatory ways, and would try to get down to work; then the telephone would ring, or Edith would call him to come shopping or have tea with a friend, and he would have to abandon work for the day.

He himself was thus partly to blame for the fact that he did not get much done. And this in itself depressed him, and made him even less capable of achieving much, while he was also saddened by what often seemed to him a monotonous and restricting way of life. 'The days seem blank,' he wrote, 'and I cannot concentrate on anything. I find life such a *bore* in this imprisonment.'

In particular he felt lonely at the lack of male company. His old friend and doctor, R. E. Havard of the Inklings, was a near neighbour and (being a Catholic) often sat next to him at mass on Sundays. Their conversation on the way home after church was an important part of Tolkien's week, but it often only made him nostalgic.

C. S. Lewis died on 22 November 1963, aged sixty-four. A few days later, Tolkien wrote to his daughter Priscilla: 'So far I have felt the normal feelings of a man of my age – like an old tree that is losing all its leaves one by one: this feels like an axe-blow near the roots.'

He refused a request to write an obituary of Lewis, and he turned down an invitation to contribute to the memorial volume. But he spent many hours pondering over Lewis's last book, *Letters to Malcolm, Chiefly on Prayer.*

Soon after Lewis's death, he began to keep a diary, which was something he had not done for many years. In part it was an excuse for using another alphabet that he had invented; he called it his 'New English Alphabet', and noted that it was intended as an improvement on what he called 'the ridiculous alphabet propounded by persons competing for the money of that absurd man Shaw'. It used some conventional letters (though giving them different sound-values), some international phonetic signs, and some symbols from his own Fëanorian alphabet. He employed it in his diary when he wanted to write about private matters. Like all his diaries, this was more often a record of sorrows than of joys, and it does not provide an entirely balanced picture of his life at Sandfield Road. It does however indicate the appalling depths of gloom to which he could sink, albeit only for short periods. 'Life is grey and grim,' he wrote at one such moment. 'I can get nothing done, between staleness and boredom (confined to quarters), and anxiety and distraction. What am I going to do? Be sucked down into residence in a hotel or old-people's home or club, without books or contacts or talk with men? God help me!'

Not untypically, Tolkien turned this particular depression to good effect. Just as his despair over his failure to finish *The Lord of the Rings* had given birth to *Leaf by Niggle*, so anxiety over the future and his growing grief at the approach of old age led him to write *Smith of Wootton Major*.

This story arose in an odd way. An American publisher had asked Tolkien to write a preface for a new edition of George Macdonald's *The Golden Key*. He usually refused invitations of this sort, but this time, for no apparent reason, he accepted. He set to work at the end of January 1965, a time when his spirits were particularly low. He found Macdonald's book far less to his taste than he had recalled, and noted that it was 'illwritten, incoherent, and bad, in spite of a few memorable passages'. (Indeed Tolkien had none of C. S. Lewis's passionate devotion to Macdonald; he liked the Curdie books, but found much of Macdonald's writing spoilt for him by its moral allegorical content.) But despite this reaction to the story, and again uncharacteristically, he pressed on with the task, as if he had to get something finished to prove that he was not incapable of work. He began to explain, to the young readers for whom the edition was intended, the meaning of the term 'Fairy'. He wrote:

> *Fairy* is very powerful. Even the bad author cannot escape it. He probably makes up his tale out of bits of older tales, or things he half remembers, and they may be too strong for him to spoil or disenchant. Someone may meet them for the first time in his silly tale, and catch a glimpse of Fairy, and go on to better things. This could be put into a short story like this. There was once a cook, and he thought of making a cake for a children's party. His chief notion was that it must be very sweet . . .

The story was meant to last only for a few paragraphs. But it went on and on, until Tolkien stopped, realising that it had a life of its own and should be completed as something separate. In the first draft it was called 'The Great Cake', but he soon adopted the title *Smith of Wootton Major*. (The Macdonald preface was never finished.)

Smith was unusual in two ways: it was composed on the typewriter – something Tolkien did not normally do – and it was related closely and even consciously to himself. He called it 'an old man's story, filled with the presage of bereavement', and elsewhere he said that it was 'written with deep emotion, partly drawn from the experience of the bereavement of "retirement" and of advancing age'. Like Smith, the village lad who swallows a magic star and so obtains a passport to Faery, Tolkien had, in his imagination, wandered for a long while through mysterious lands; but now he felt the approach of the end, and knew that he would soon have to surrender his own star, his imagination. It was indeed the last story that he ever wrote.

Not long after it was completed, Tolkien showed it to Rayner Unwin, who was delighted with it, but felt that it needed the company of other stories to make up a sufficiently substantial volume. However, Allen & Unwin eventually decided to issue the story on its own, and it was published in Britain and America during 1967, with illustrations by Pauline Baynes. *Smith of Wootton Major* was generally well received by the critics, though none of them perceived its personal content nor remarked that it was uncharacteristic of its author in containing an element of allegory. Tolkien wrote of this: 'There is *no* allegory in the Faery, which is conceived as having a real extramental existence. There is some trace of allegory in the Human part, which seems to me obvious though no reader or critic has yet averted to it. As usual there is no "religion" in the story; but plainly enough the Master Cook and the Great Hall, etc., are a (somewhat satirical) allegory of the village-church, and village parson: its functions steadily decaying and losing all touch with the "arts", into mere eating and drinking – the last trace of anything "other" being left in the children.'

During this period Tolkien completed two other books for publication. His revision of the lecture *On Fairy-Stories* was published in 1964 together with *Leaf by Niggle* under the overall title *Tree and Leaf*; and when in 1961 his aunt Jane Neave, then eighty-nine, wrote to ask him 'if you wouldn't get out a small book with Tom Bombadil at the heart of it, the sort of size of book that we old 'uns can afford to buy for Christmas presents', the result was *The Adventures of Tom Bombadil*. The verses that Tolkien selected for this book had been written by him mostly during the nineteen-twenties and thirties, the exceptions being 'Bombadil Goes A-Boating', which was composed especially for the book, and 'Cat', written in 1956 to amuse Tolkien's granddaughter Joan Anne. The book, again illustrated by Pauline Baynes, was issued just in time to delight Jane Neave, who died a few months later.

If life in retirement sometimes seemed 'grey and grim', it also had many elements that Tolkien enjoyed. For the first time he had enough money. As early as 1962, before the amazing increase in American sales, he wrote of his income: 'It is an astonishing situation, and I hope I am sufficiently grateful to God. Only a little while ago I was wondering if we should be able to go on living here, on my inadequate pension. But saving universal catastrophe, I am not likely to be hard up again in my time.'

Tax took a large proportion of his earnings, but on the whole he bore this philosophically; though on one occasion he crossed a cheque for a large sum payable to the tax authorities with the words 'Not a penny for Concorde'. Near the end of his life he made a financial settlement that passed on most of his assets to his four children.

He was generous with his new-found wealth, giving a substantial sum (anonymously) to his parish church in Headington during his last years. In particular he was always glad to provide for the needs of members of his family. He bought a house for one of his children, a car for another, gave a cello to a grandson, and paid the school fees for a granddaughter. But despite his affluence, the habit of watching every penny – a habit acquired during years of heavy expense and a small income – could not be broken easily; and his diary, besides including a daily record of the weather, invariably contained a detailed account of even the smallest amounts of cash spent: 'Airmail 1s 3d, Gillette Blades 2s 11d, postage 7½d, Steradent 6s 2d.' He never spent money carelessly; he and Edith did not install any electrical gadgets in the home, for they had never been accustomed to them and did not imagine that they needed them now. Not only was there no television in the house, but no washing-machine or dish-washer either.

Yet the fact that he now had plenty of money did give Tolkien much pleasure. He indulged in selected extravagances which were entirely to his taste: a good lunch with wine at a restaurant after a morning's shopping in Oxford, a black corduroy jacket and a new waistcoat from Hall's the tailor, and new clothes for Edith.

He and Edith were still very different people with widely differing interests, and even after fifty years of marriage they were not always ideal company for each other. Occasionally there were moments of irritation between them, just as there had been throughout their lives. But there was still, as there had always been, great love and affection, perhaps even more now that the strain of bringing up a family had passed. Now they had time simply to sit and talk; and they often did this, especially on summer evenings after supper, on a bench in the front porch at Sandfield Road, or in the garden among their roses, he with his pipe and she smoking a cigarette, a habit that she had taken up late in life. Inevitably much of their talk would be about the family, an endless source of interest to them both. The *concept* of the family, something that they had scarcely known themselves as children, had always mattered to them, and they now found the role of grandparents entirely to their liking, delighting in the visits of grandchildren. Their Golden Wedding, celebrated in 1966 with much ceremony, gave them great pleasure. Among the events to mark it was a performance at their party in Merton College of Donald Swann's Tolkien song-cycle, *The Road Goes Ever On*, with the composer at the piano and the songs sung by William Elvin – 'A name of good omen!' said Tolkien.

The domestic arrangements at Sandfield Road were by no means ideal, and the situation deteriorated as over the years Edith's health became worse. Despite her increasing lameness from arthritis she managed to do all the cooking, most of the housework, and some of the gardening; but as the nineteen-sixties advanced and she came closer to her eightieth birthday it was clear that she could not manage for much longer. A daily help generally came in for a few hours, but it was not a small house and there was much to be done, while at the same time it was not big enough for a resident housekeeper to be accommodated with convenience, even supposing that a suitable person could have been found. Tolkien himself did what he could to help, and since he was good with his hands he could mend broken furniture or repair fuses; but he too was becoming increasingly stiff, and by the beginning of 1968, when he was seventy-six and Edith seventy-nine, they had decided to move to a more convenient house. A move would also have the advantage of making it possible to keep his whereabouts secret, and so of avoiding the now almost intolerable stream of fan-mail, gifts, telephone calls, and visitors. As to where they should move to, he and Edith considered several possibilities in the Oxford area. But eventually they settled on Bournemouth.

2

Bournemouth

Even by the standard of English seaside towns, Bournemouth is a peculiarly unlovable place, an urban sprawl that owes most of its architecture to the late nineteenth and early twentieth centuries, an anaemic English equivalent of the French Riviera. Like the majority of south-coast resorts, it attracts the elderly in large numbers. They come to spend their last years in bungalows and villas, or as residents in faded hotels where they are welcomed in winter but where the weekly rates rise sharply during the summer season. They take the air along the sea-front at East Cliff or West Cliff; they patronise the public library, the Winter Gardens, and the golf course; they stroll among the conifers of Boscombe and Branksome Chine; and eventually they die.

Yet Bournemouth serves its purpose. It provides a setting in which elderly people of some affluence can be comfortable, and can spend their time with others of their age and class. Edith Tolkien had come to like it very much; and not without reason, for in Bournemouth for the first time in her life she had made a large number of friends.

Some years previously she had begun to take holidays at the Miramar Hotel on the sea-front in the west of the town, an expensive but comfortable and friendly establishment chiefly patronised by people like herself. After Tolkien had retired and had given up his examination visits to Ireland, he had begun to accompany her on these Bournemouth holidays, and he soon realised that on the whole she was far happier there than she was at home in Oxford. This was scarcely surprising, for the social setting of the Miramar was very close to what she had known in the Jessop household at

Cheltenham between 1910 and 1913: upper middle-class, affluent, unintellectual, and with an easy friendliness towards its own kind. At the Miramar she felt entirely at home, back in her own milieu, as she had never been in Oxford or at any other time during her married life. True, many of the other guests at the hotel were titled, rich, and self-assured. Yet they were all essentially of the same breed: conservative, glad to talk about their own children and grandchildren and about mutual acquaintances, happy to pass most of the day in the residents' lounge with occasional interruptions for walks by the sea, content to sit over their post-prandial coffee and watch the nine o'clock news in the television room before going to bed. Nor did Edith feel any sense of inferiority, for she was now as well off financially as any of them; and as to titles, her status as the wife of an internationally famous author cancelled out any feeling she might have of inadequacy.

On a more practical basis, the Miramar became increasingly the ideal answer to the Tolkiens' domestic problems. When the strain of keeping house became too much for Edith, it was easy to book their usual rooms and to arrange for their regular hire-car driver to take them down to Bournemouth. At the Miramar, Edith would soon recover much of her strength, not to say her good spirits; while Tolkien himself was often glad to initiate visits to Bournemouth simply to escape from the confines of Sandfield Road and from the despair caused by his own inability to get his work done.

He himself was not particularly happy at the Miramar. He shared little of Edith's delight in the type of person (as C. S. Lewis expressed it) 'whose general conversation is almost wholly narrative', and though he found an occasional articulate fellow male among the guests he was sometimes reduced to silent and impotent rage by the feeling of imprisonment. But in other respects the Bournemouth holidays suited him very well. He could work in his hotel room just as much (or just as little) as at Sandfield Road – providing he remembered to bring all the relevant papers with him, which was not always the case – and he enjoyed the comfort and the cooking. He and Edith had discovered a local doctor who proved unfailingly friendly and helpful if either of them should be unwell; there was a Catholic church reasonably near at hand; the hotel was close to the sea which he loved so much (albeit a rather more timid sea than he might have preferred); and above all he could see that Edith was happy. So the visits to Bournemouth continued, and when the Tolkiens decided to leave Sandfield Road and find another house it was not altogether surprising that they resolved to look for something near the Miramar.

'He lives in a hideous house – I cannot tell you how hideous, with hideous pictures.' W. H. Auden said this at a meeting of the Tolkien Society in New York, and his words were reported in a London newspaper in January 1966. Tolkien read them, and remarked: 'Since it is some years since his sole visit, in which he only entered Edith's room and had tea, he must be confused in his memories (if he really said just this).' It was a calm reaction to an insulting remark, and after showing a little initial displeasure in a letter to Auden, Tolkien was soon writing cordially to him once more.

Auden's remark was silly, and it was not true. The Sandfield Road house (to which he was referring) was no uglier than any others in that nondescript but modest street, nor were the pictures that adorned the walls of Edith's drawing-room any different from those in the average middle-class house of the district. But of course this is precisely what Auden was trying to say. As a man of sophisticated tastes he was astonished by the apparent ordinariness of Tolkien's life-style, and by the conformity of the house in the suburban road. This life-style did not specifically reflect Tolkien's own tastes; on the other hand he did not exactly object to it – indeed there was an ascetic side to him which did not even notice it. It is important to grasp this before coming to any conclusions about the life that Tolkien led in Bournemouth from 1968 until the end of 1971.

He and Edith bought a bungalow a short taxi-ride away from the Miramar. What Auden would have thought of this plain modern house, 19 Lakeside Road, can be easily imagined, for in his terms it was quite as 'hideous' as the Headington house. But from the point of view of the Tolkiens – both of them – it was exactly what they wanted. It had a well-equipped kitchen in which Edith could manage to cook with some ease despite her increasing disability; and besides a sitting-room, a dining-room, and a bedroom for each of them there was also a room that served as an indoor study for Tolkien, and he could use the double garage for a library-cum-office just as he had done at Sandfield Road. There was central heating – something they had never had before – and outside there was a verandah where they could sit and smoke in the evenings, a large garden with plenty of room for their roses and even a few vegetables, and at the bottom a private gate that led into the small wooded gorge known as Branksome Chine, and so down to the sea. There were Catholic neighbours who often took Tolkien to church in their car, regular domestic help, and the Miramar always near at hand for the accommodation of friends and members of the family who came down to see them – as well as for regular lunches, and even for sleeping overnight now and then when Edith needed a rest.

Inevitably the move to Bournemouth involved much sacrifice on Tolkien's part. He had little wish to leave Oxford, and he knew that he was cutting himself off from all but a limited contact with his family and close friends. And again, as with his retirement to Headington, he found the reality a little harsher than he had expected. 'I feel quite well,' he wrote to Christopher a year after moving to Bournemouth. 'And yet; and yet. I see no men of my own kind. I miss Norman. And above all I miss you.'

But the sacrifice had a purpose to it, and that purpose was achieved. Edith was happy at Lakeside Road, as happy as she had been during the holidays at the Miramar, and consistently happier than she had ever been before in their married life. Besides the comfort of the new house and the benefit she derived from the absence of stairs to be negotiated, there was also her continuing pleasure at visits to the Miramar and at the friendships she made there. She had ceased to be the shy, uncertain, sometimes troubled wife of an Oxford professor, and became herself once more, the sociable good-humoured Miss Bratt of the Cheltenham days. She was back in the setting where she really belonged.

And on the whole life was better for Tolkien himself. Edith's happiness was deeply gratifying to him, and was reflected in his own state of mind, so that the diary he kept for a brief time during these Bournemouth years shows very little of the despondency which often overtook him at Sandfield Road. The absence of what he called 'men of my own kind' was partly made up for by frequent visits from members of the family and friends, while the almost total lack of interruptions from fans (the address and telephone number, even the information that Tolkien was living on the south coast, were successfully kept secret) meant that a great deal more of his time was available for work. A certain amount of secretarial assistance was given by the doctor's wife, while Joy Hill, the member of Allen & Unwin's staff who dealt with his fan-mail, came down regularly to attend to letters. The move to Bournemouth was initially made more tiresome by a serious accident when Tolkien fell on the stairs at Sandfield Road and injured his leg badly, with the result that he had to spend some weeks in hospital and many more in plaster; but once he had recovered he was able, at least in theory, to begin to work with some thoroughness at *The Silmarillion*.

Yet it was difficult to decide exactly where to start. In one sense there was very little to be done. The story of *The Silmarillion* itself was complete, if the term 'story' could be used of a work beginning with an account of the creation of the world and dealing in the main with the struggle between the elves and the prime power of evil. To produce a continuous narrative Tolkien merely had to decide which version of each chapter he should use, for there were by now many versions, dating from his earliest work in 1917 to some passages written in the last few years. But this involved so many decisions that he did not know where to start. And even if he managed to complete this part of the work, he would then have to ensure that the whole book was consistent with itself. Over the years he had by his various alterations and rewritings produced a massive confusion of detail. Characters' names had been changed in one place and not in another. Topographical descriptions were disorganised and contradictory. Worst of all, the manuscripts themselves had proliferated, so that he was no longer certain which of them represented his latest thoughts on any particular passage. For security reasons he had in recent years made two copies of each typescript and had then kept each copy in a separate place. But he had never decided which was to be the working copy, and often he had amended each of them independently and in contradictory fashion. To produce a consistent and satisfactory text he would have to make a detailed collation of every manuscript, and the prospect of attempting this filled him with dismay.

Besides this, he was still uncertain how the whole work should be presented. He was inclined to abandon the original framework, the introductory device of the seafarer to whom the stories were told. But did it perhaps need some other device of this kind? Or was it enough simply to present it as the mythology that appeared in a shadowy form in *The Lord of the Rings*? And on the subject of that other book, he had made his task even more complicated by introducing into it several important characters, such as the elven-queen Galadriel and the treeish Ents, who had not appeared in the original *Silmarillion*, but who now required some mention in it. By this time he had managed to find satisfactory solutions to these problems, but he knew that he would have to ensure that *The Silmarillion* harmonised in every single detail with *The Lord of the Rings*, or else he would be bombarded with letters pointing out the inconsistencies. And even given these daunting technical challenges, he was still not beyond reconsidering some fundamental aspect of the whole story, the alteration of which would have meant a complete rewriting from the beginning.

By the summer of 1971, after three years at Bournemouth, he had begun to make progress, although as usual he was drawn aside to the consideration of detail rather than the planning of the whole. What form, he would wonder, should a particular name take? And then he would begin to contemplate a revision of some aspect of the elvish languages. Even when he did do some actual writing, it was not usually concerned with the revision of the narrative but with the huge mass of ancillary material that had now accumulated. Much of this material was in the form of essays on what might be called 'technical' aspects of the mythology, such as the relation between the ageing processes of elves and men, or the death of animals and plants in Middle-earth. He felt that every detail of his cosmos needed attention, whether or not the essays themselves would ever be published. Sub-creation had become a sufficiently rewarding pastime in itself, quite apart from the desire to see the work in print.

Sometimes he would put in long hours at his desk, but on other days he would soon turn to a game of Patience and abandon any pretence of working. Then there might be a good lunch at the Miramar with plenty of wine, and if he did not feel like doing any work after it, why should he? They could wait for the book. He would take his time!

Yet on other days he was distressed that time was leaking away so fast with the book still unfinished. And at the end of 1971 the Bournemouth episode came abruptly to a close. Edith, aged eighty-two, was taken ill in the middle of November with an inflamed gall-bladder. She was removed to hospital, and after a few days of severe illness she died, early on Monday 29 November.

3

Merton Street

After Tolkien had begun to recover from the first shock of Edith's death, there was no question of his remaining in Bournemouth. Clearly he would come back to live in Oxford, but at first there was uncertainty about what arrangement could be made. Then Merton College invited him to become a resident honorary Fellow, and offered him a set of rooms in a college house in Merton Street, where a scout and his wife could look after him. This was a most unusual honour and the perfect solution. Tolkien accepted with the greatest enthusiasm, and after spending the intervening weeks with members of his family he moved into 21 Merton Street at the beginning of March 1972, typically making friends with the three removal men and riding with them in their pantechnicon from Bournemouth to Oxford.

His flat in Merton Street consisted of a large sitting-room, a bedroom, and a bathroom. Charlie Carr, the college scout who acted as caretaker, lived in the basement with his wife. The Carrs showed much kindness to Tolkien, not only providing him with breakfast in his rooms (which was part of the official arrangement) but also cooking lunch or supper for him if he did not feel well or did not wish to dine in college. Another alternative to eating in Merton was to have a meal at the Eastgate Hotel next door, which had changed greatly since he had first dined there with Lewis in the thirties, and was no longer cheap; but he was now a rich man, and he could afford to eat there whenever he liked. Nevertheless a good many of his meals were taken in college, for he was entitled to free lunches and dinners, and was always made most welcome in the Senior Common Room.

Thus his way of life in 1972 and 1973 was on the whole entirely to his liking. He had suffered much distress at the loss of Edith, and he was essentially a lonely man now; yet he was free, as he had not been within memory, and he could live his life as he pleased. Just as Bournemouth had in some ways been a reward for Edith for all that she had faced in the early days of their marriage, so his almost bachelor existence in Merton Street seemed to be a reward for his patience at Bournemouth.

There was no question of his becoming inactive. He paid frequent visits to the village near Oxford where Christopher and his second wife Baillie lived; and, in the company of their small children Adam and Rachel, he would forget his lumbago and run about the lawn in some game, or would throw a matchbox into a high tree and then try to dislodge it with stones to amuse them. He went with Priscilla and his grandson Simon to Sidmouth for a holiday. He revisited his old T.C.B.S. friend Christopher Wiseman. He spent several weeks with John in his parish at Stoke-on-Trent, and with John he motored to visit his brother Hilary, still living on his fruit farm at Evesham.

Ronald and Hilary now resembled each other far more than they had ever done in their youth. Outside the window the plum-trees whose crop Hilary had picked patiently for more than four decades had grown old and bore little fruit. They should be cut down, and fresh saplings planted in their place. But Hilary was past tackling such work, and the trees had been left standing. The two old brothers watched cricket and tennis on the television, and drank whisky.

These two years of Tolkien's life were made happy by the honours that were conferred upon him. He received a number of invitations to visit American universities and receive doctorates, but he did not feel that he could face the journey. There were also many honours within his homeland. In June 1973 he visited Edinburgh to receive an honorary degree; and he was profoundly moved when, in the spring of the previous year, he went to Buckingham Palace to be presented with a C.B.E. by the Queen. But perhaps most gratifying of all was the award in June 1972 of an honorary Doctorate of Letters from his own University of Oxford; not, as was made clear, for *The Lord of the Rings*, but for his contribution to philology. Nevertheless at the degree ceremony the speech in his honour by the Public Orator (his old friend Colin Hardie) contained more than one reference to the chronicles of

Middle-earth, and it concluded with the hope 'that in such green leaf, as the Road goes ever on, he will produce from his store Silmarillion and scholarship'.

As to *The Silmarillion*, the months were again passing with little to show for them. There had been an inevitable delay while Tolkien reorganised his books and papers after the move from Bournemouth; and when at last he resumed work he found himself once more enmeshed in technical problems. Some years previously, he had decided that in the event of his dying before the book was finished, Christopher (who was of course well versed in the work) should complete it for publication. He and Christopher often discussed the book, contemplating the numerous problems that remained to be solved; but they made little progress.

Almost certainly he did not expect to die so soon. He told his former pupil Mary Salu that there was a tradition of longevity among his ancestors, and that he believed he would live for many years more. But late in 1972 there were warning signs. He began to suffer from severe indigestion, and, though an X-ray failed to reveal any cause more specific than 'dyspepsia', he was put on a diet and warned not to drink wine. And despite his unfinished work, it seemed that he did not relish the prospect of many more years living at Merton Street.

'I often feel very lonely,' he wrote to his old cousin Marjorie Incledon. 'After term (when the undergraduates depart) I am all alone in a large house with only the caretaker and his wife far below in the basement.'

True, there was a ceaseless stream of callers: his family, old friends, Joy Hill from Allen & Unwin to attend to fan-mail. There was constant business to be attended to with Rayner Unwin, and with Dick Williamson, his solicitor and adviser in many matters. There was also the regular Sunday morning drive by taxi to church in Headington, and then to Edith's grave in Wolvercote cemetery. But the loneliness did not cease.

As the summer of 1973 advanced, some of those close to him thought that he was more sad than usual, and seemed to be ageing faster. Yet the diet had apparently been successful, and in July he went to Cambridge for a dinner of the Ad Eundem, an inter-varsity dining club. On 25 August he wrote a belated note of thanks to his host, Professor Glyn Daniel:

Dear Daniel,

It is a long time since July 20th; but better (I hope) late than never to do what I should have done before being immersed in other matters: to thank you for your delightful dinner in St John's, and especially for your forbearance and great kindness to me personally. It proved a turning point! I suffered no ill effects whatever, and have since been able to dispense with most of the diet taboos I had to observe for some six months.

I look forward to the next A.E. dinner, and hope that you will be present.

Yours ever,
Ronald Tolkien.

Three days after writing this letter, on Tuesday 28 August, he travelled down to Bournemouth to stay with Denis and Jocelyn Tolhurst, the doctor and his wife who had looked after him and Edith when they had lived there.

The end was swift. On the Thursday he joined in celebrations to mark Mrs Tolhurst's birthday, but he did not feel well and would not eat much, though he drank a little champagne. During the night he was in pain, and next morning he was taken to a private hospital where an acute bleeding gastric ulcer was diagnosed. It so happened that Michael was on holiday in Switzerland and Christopher in France, and neither could have reached his bedside in time, but John and Priscilla were able to come down to Bournemouth to be with him. At first the reports on his condition were optimistic, but by Saturday a chest infection had developed, and early on the Sunday morning, 2 September 1973, he died, aged eighty-one.

VIII

The Tree

VIII
The Tree

Nowadays it is fashionable to regard the Inklings, the handful of men who met at Magdalen on Thursday nights in the nineteen-thirties and forties, as a homogeneous group of writers who exercised an influence over each other. Whether or not you subscribe to this view you may, if you are passing through Oxford, decide to visit the graves of the three best known Inklings, C. S. Lewis, Charles Williams, and J. R. R. Tolkien.

You will find Lewis's tomb in the churchyard of his own parish, Headington Quarry. A plain slab marks the grave, which is shared with his brother Major W. H. Lewis. It is adorned with a simple cross, and with the words *Men must endure their going hence.*

Williams lies beneath the shadow of St Cross Church in the centre of Oxford. His fellow Inkling Hugo Dyson is buried not far away, and the graveyard contains the tombs of many other University men of that generation.

Lewis and Williams were members of the Church of England, but there is now no Catholic burial-place in Oxford other than the corporation cemetery at Wolvercote, where a small area of ground is reserved for members of the Church of Rome. So if you are searching for the remaining grave you will have to travel far out from the centre of the city, beyond the shops and the ring-road, until you come to tall iron gates. Go through them and past the chapel, crossing the acres of other graves, until you come to a section where many of the tombstones are Polish; for this is the Catholic area, and the graves of emigrés predominate over English adherents to that faith. Several of the tombs bear glazed photographs of the deceased, and the inscriptions are florid. In consequence a grey slab of Cornish granite rather to the left of the group stands out clearly, as does its slightly curious wording: *Edith Mary Tolkien, Lúthien, 1889–1971. John Ronald Reuel Tolkien, Beren, 1892–1973.*

The grave stands in suburban surroundings, very different from the English countryside that Tolkien loved, but not dissimilar to the man-made places in which he spent most of his days. So, even at the end, at this plain grave in a public cemetery, we are reminded of the antithesis between the ordinary life he led and the extraordinary imagination that created his mythology.

Where did it come from, this imagination that peopled Middle-earth with elves, orcs, and hobbits? What was the source of the literary vision that changed the life of this obscure scholar? And why did that vision so strike the minds and harmonise with the aspirations of numberless readers around the world?

Tolkien would have thought that these were unanswerable questions, certainly unanswerable in a book of this sort. He disapproved of biography as an aid to literary appreciation; and perhaps he was right. His real biography is *The Hobbit, The Lord of the Rings,* and *The Silmarillion*; for the truth about him lies within their pages.

But at least he might allow an epitaph.

His requiem mass was held in Oxford four days after his death, in the plain modern church in Headington which he had attended so often. The prayers and readings were specially chosen by his son John, who said the mass with the assistance of Tolkien's old friend Fr. Robert Murray and his parish priest Mgr. Doran. There was no sermon or quotation from his writings. However, when a few weeks later a memorial service was held in California by some of his American admirers, his short story *Leaf by Niggle* was read to the congregation. He would perhaps have considered it not inappropriate:

Before him stood the Tree, his Tree, finished. If you could say that of a Tree that was alive, its leaves opening, its branches growing and bending in the wind that Niggle had so often felt and guessed, and had so often failed to catch. He gazed at the Tree, and slowly he lifted his arms and opened them wide.

'It's a gift!' he said.

THE END

Appendices

APPENDIX A

Simplified genealogical table of the ancestry of J. R. R. Tolkien

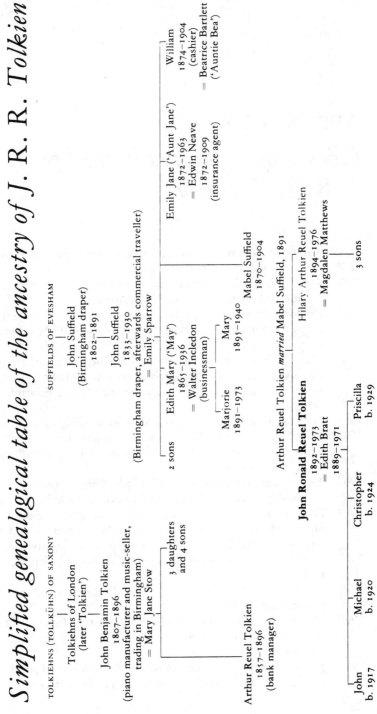

TOLKIEHNS (TOLKÜHN) OF SAXONY

Tolkiehns of London
(later 'Tolkien')

John Benjamin Tolkien
1807–1896
(piano manufacturer and music-seller,
trading in Birmingham)
= Mary Jane Stow

3 daughters
and 4 sons

Arthur Reuel Tolkien
1857–1896
(bank manager)

SUFFIELDS OF EVESHAM

John Suffield
(Birmingham draper)
1802–1891

John Suffield
1833–1930
(Birmingham draper, afterwards commercial traveller)
= Emily Sparrow

Edith Mary ('May')
1865–1936
= Walter Incledon
(businessman)

Marjorie
1891–1973

Mary
1895–1940

Emily Jane ('Aunt Jane')
1872–1963
= Edwin Neave
1872–1909
(insurance agent)

William
1874–1904
(cashier)
= Beatrice Bartlett
('Auntie Bea')

Mabel Suffield
1870–1904

Arthur Reuel Tolkien *married* Mabel Suffield, 1891

John Ronald Reuel Tolkien
1892–1973
= Edith Bratt
1889–1971

Hilary Arthur Reuel Tolkien
1894–1976
= Magdalen Matthews

3 sons

John
b. 1917

Michael
b. 1920

Christopher
b. 1924

Priscilla
b. 1929

APPENDIX B

Chronology of events in the life of J. R. R. Tolkien

1892   *3 January:* John Ronald Reuel Tolkien born at Bloemfontein.

1894   Birth of younger brother, Hilary.

1895   *Spring:* Mabel Tolkien takes the two boys back to England, Arthur Tolkien remaining in South Africa.

1896   *February:* Arthur Tolkien dies. *Summer:* Mabel Tolkien rents a cottage at Sarehole Mill, Birmingham. She and the boys remain there for four years.

1900   Mabel Tolkien is received into the Catholic Church. She and the boys move from Sarehole to a house in the Birmingham suburb of Moseley. Ronald begins to attend King Edward's School.

1901   Mabel and the boys move from Moseley to King's Heath.

1902   Mabel and the boys leave King's Heath and move to Oliver Road, Edgbaston. Ronald and Hilary are enrolled at St Philip's Grammar School.

1903   The boys are removed from St Philip's. Ronald obtains a scholarship to King Edward's and returns there in the autumn.

1904   Early in the year Mabel Tolkien is discovered to have diabetes. She spends some weeks in hospital. In the summer she and the boys stay at Rednal. In November she dies, aged thirty-four.

1905   The boys move into their Aunt Beatrice's house in Stirling Road.

1908   The boys move to Mrs Faulkner's house in Duchess Road. Ronald meets Edith Bratt.

1909   *Autumn:* Ronald's romance with Edith Bratt is discovered by Father Francis Morgan. Ronald fails to obtain a scholarship at Oxford.

1910   *January:* Ronald and Hilary move to new lodgings. Ronald continues to see Edith Bratt, but is then forbidden to communicate with her. *March:* Edith leaves Birmingham and moves to Cheltenham. *December:* Ronald wins an Exhibition at Exeter College, Oxford.

1911   Formation of 'The T.C.B.S.' *Summer:* Ronald leaves school. He visits Switzerland. *Autumn:* His first term at Oxford. *Christmas:* He takes part in a performance of *The Rivals* at King Edward's.

1913   *January:* Ronald's twenty-first birthday. He is reunited with Edith Bratt. *February:* He takes Honour Moderations and is awarded a Second Class. *Summer:* He begins to read for the Honours School of English Language and Literature. He visits France with a Mexican family.

1914   *January:* Edith is received into the Catholic Church. She and Ronald are formally betrothed. *Summer:* Ronald visits Cornwall. At the outbreak of war he determines to return to Oxford and complete his degree course.

1915   *Summer:* He is awarded First Class Honours in his final examination. After being commissioned in the Lancashire Fusiliers he begins training in Bedford and in Staffordshire.

1916   *22 March:* He and Edith are married. Edith moves to Great Haywood. *June:* Tolkien embarks for France. He travels to the Somme as a second lieutenant in the 11th Lancashire Fusiliers, and serves in action as Battalion Signalling Officer until the autumn. *November:* He returns to England suffering from 'trench fever'.

1917   *January and February:* While convalescing at Great Haywood he begins to write 'The Book of Lost Tales', which eventually becomes *The Silmarillion. Spring:* He is posted to Yorkshire, but spends much of the year in hospital. *November:* Birth of eldest son, John.

1918   Tolkien (now a full lieutenant) is posted to the Humber Garrison and to Staffordshire. In November, after the Armistice, he returns to Oxford with his family and joins the staff of the New English Dictionary.

1919   He begins work as a freelance tutor. He and Edith move to 1 Alfred Street.

1920   He is appointed Reader in English Language at Leeds University, and begins work there in the autumn. Birth of second son, Michael.

1921   Edith and the family join him in Leeds, eventually moving into 11 St Mark's Terrace.

1922   E. V. Gordon joins the staff at Leeds. He and Tolkien begin work on their edition of *Sir Gawain and the Green Knight.*

1924 Tolkien becomes Professor of English Language at Leeds University. He buys a house in Darnley Road. Birth of third son, Christopher.

1925 The edition of *Sir Gawain* is published. In the summer Tolkien is elected Rawlinson and Bosworth Professor of Anglo-Saxon at Oxford, and takes up the appointment in the autumn. He buys a house in Northmoor Road, and the family returns to Oxford early in the new year.

1926 Tolkien becomes friends with C. S. Lewis. Formation of 'The Coalbiters'.

1929 Birth of daughter, Priscilla.

1930 The family moves from 22 to 20 Northmoor Road. At about this time Tolkien begins to write *The Hobbit*. He abandons it before it is finished.

1936 He lectures on *Beowulf: the Monsters and the Critics*. The manuscript of *The Hobbit* is read by Susan Dagnall of Allen & Unwin, and at her suggestion Tolkien finishes the book. It is accepted for publication.

1937 *The Hobbit* is published in the autumn. At the suggestion of Stanley Unwin, Tolkien begins to write a sequel, which becomes *The Lord of the Rings*.

1939 Tolkien delivers his lecture *On Fairy-Stories* at St Andrews University. At the outbreak of war Charles Williams joins the Inklings.

1945 Tolkien is elected Merton Professor of English Language and Literature at Oxford.

1947 The Tolkiens move to Manor Road.

1949 Completion of *The Lord of the Rings*. Publication of *Farmer Giles of Ham*.

1950 Tolkien offers *The Lord of the Rings* to the publishing house of Collins. The family moves from Manor Road to Holywell Street.

1952 The manuscript of *The Lord of the Rings* is returned by Collins, and Tolkien passes it to Allen & Unwin.

1953 The Tolkiens move to Sandfield Road in the Oxford suburb of Headington.

1954 Publication of the first two volumes of *The Lord of the Rings*.

1955 Publication of the third volume.

1959 Tolkien retires from his professorship.

1962 Publication of *The Adventures of Tom Bombadil*.

1964 Publication of *Tree and Leaf*.

1965 Ace Books issue an unauthorised American edition of *The Lord of the Rings*. A 'campus cult' begins.

1967 Publication of *Smith of Wootton Major*.
1968 The Tolkiens move to Lakeside Road, Poole (adjacent to the town of Bournemouth).
1971 Edith Tolkien dies in November, aged eighty-two.
1972 Tolkien returns to Oxford, moving into rooms in Merton Street, He is awarded the C.B.E., and Oxford University confers an honorary Doctorate of Letters upon him.
1973 On 28 August he goes to Bournemouth to stay with friends. He is taken ill, and dies in a nursing-home in the early hours of Sunday 2 September, aged eighty-one.

APPENDIX C

The published writings of J. R. R. Tolkien

1911   Poem 'The Battle of the Eastern Fields' in *The King Edward's School Chronicle*, Volume XXVI No. 186, March 1911, pp. 22–7. (Birmingham, King Edward's School, 1911). [Tolkien also contributed reports on meetings of the school debating society to the magazine between November 1910 and June 1911, and editorials to the issues for June and July 1911.]

1913   Poem 'From the many-willow'd margin of the immemorial Thames' (unsigned) in *The Stapeldon Magazine*, Volume IV No. 20, December 1913, p. 11. (Published for Exeter College by B. H. Blackwell, Oxford).

1915   Poem 'Goblin Feet' in *Oxford Poetry, 1915*, edited by G.D.H.C[ole] and T.W.E[arp] (Oxford, B. H. Blackwell, 1915), pp. 64–5. [The poem was reprinted in *Oxford Poetry, 1914–1916* (Oxford, B. H. Blackwell, 1917), pp. 120–1; again in *The Book of Fairy Poetry*, edited by Dora Owen (London, Longmans, Green & Co., 1920), pp. 177–8; and again in *Fifty New Poems for Children* (Oxford, Basil Blackwell, 1922), pp. 26–7.]

1918   Introductory note (signed 'J. R. R. T.') in *A Spring Harvest*, poems by Geoffrey Bache Smith, late Lieutenant in the Lancashire Fusiliers (London, Erskine Macdonald Ltd, 1918). [Tolkien and C. L. Wiseman edited this collection of G. B. Smith's poetry and helped to arrange for its publication.]

1920   Poem 'The Happy Mariners' (signed 'J. R. R. T.') in *The Stapeldon Magazine*, Volume V No. 26, June 1920, pp. 69–70. (Published for Exeter College by B. H. Blackwell, Oxford).

1922   *A Middle English Vocabulary* (Oxford, Clarendon Press, 1922). [Designed for use with Kenneth Sisam's *Fourteenth Century Verse and Prose*. Issued separately for use with the 1921 edition of that book, in subsequent editions of which it appears as the glossary. It was also reprinted separately.]

1923 Poem 'Iumonna Gold Galdre Bewunden' ['The Hoard'] in *The Gryphon*, New Series, Volume IV No. 4, January 1923, p. 130. (Published by Leeds University).

Review headed 'Holy Maidenhood', *Times Literary Supplement*, London, Thursday 26 April 1923, p. 281. [A review of Furnivall's E.E.T.S. edition of *Hali Meidenhad*. Unsigned, but Tolkien's authorship is established by a reference in his diary.]

Poem 'The City of the Gods' in *The Microcosm*, edited by Dorothy Una Ratcliffe, Volume VIII No. 1, Spring 1923, p. 8. (Issued privately in Leeds).

Obituary: 'Henry Bradley, 3 December 1845–23 May 1923.' (Signed 'J. R. R. T.'), *Bulletin of the Modern Humanities Research Association* (London, Cambridge University Press), No. 20, October 1923, pp. 4–5.

Poems 'Tha Eadigan Saelidan (The Happy Mariners)', 'Why the Man in the Moon Came Down Too Soon', and 'Enigmata Saxonica Nuper Inventa Duo' in *A Northern Venture: verses by members of the Leeds University English School Association* (Leeds, at the Swan Press, 1923), pp. 15–20.

Poem 'The Cat and the Fiddle: A Nursery Rhyme Undone and its Scandalous Secret Unlocked', in *Yorkshire Poetry*, Volume II No. 19, October–November 1923, pp. 1–3. (Leeds, at the Swan Press). [An early version of the poem that appears in *The Lord of the Rings*, Book I Chapter 9.]

1924 Chapter on 'Philology, General Works' in *The Year's Work in English Studies*, Volume IV, 1923, pp. 20–37. (London, Oxford University Press, 1924).

1925 'Some Contributions to Middle-English Lexicography', *Review of English Studies*, Volume I No. 2, April 1925, pp. 210–15. (London, Sidgwick & Jackson).

Poem 'Light as Leaf on Lindentree' in *The Gryphon*, New Series, Volume VI No. 6, June 1925, p. 217. (Published by Leeds University). [An early version of the poem that appears in *The Lord of the Rings*, Book I, Chapter 11.]

'The Devil's Coach-Horses', *Review of English Studies*, Volume I No. 3, July 1925, pp. 331–6. (London, Sidgwick & Jackson).

Sir Gawain and the Green Knight, edited by J. R. R. Tolkien and E. V. Gordon (Oxford, at the Clarendon Press, 1925). [Reprinted many times. Second edition, revised by Norman Davis, Oxford, 1967; issued as a paperback, 1968.]

1926 Chapter on 'Philology, General Works' in *The Year's Work in English Studies*, Volume V, 1924, pp. 26–65. (London, Oxford University Press, 1926).

1927 Poem 'The Nameless Land' in *Realities: An Anthology of Verse*, edited by G. S. Tancred, p. 24. (Leeds, at the Swan Press; London, Gay & Hancock Ltd, 1927).
Chapter on 'Philology, General Works' in *The Year's Work in English Studies*, Volume VI, 1925, pp. 32–66. (London, Oxford University Press, 1927).

1928 Foreword to *A New Glossary of the Dialect of the Huddersfield District* by Walter E. Haigh (London, Oxford University Press, 1928).

1929 'Ancrene Wisse and Hali Meiðhad', *Essays and Studies by members of the English Association*, Volume XIV, 1929, pp. 104–26. (Oxford, Clarendon Press, 1929).

1930 'The Oxford English School', *The Oxford Magazine*, Volume XLVIII No. 21, 29 May 1930, pp. 778–82. (Oxford, the Oxonian Press). [An article proposing a reformed syllabus.]

1932 Appendix I: 'The Name "Nodens"', *Report on the Excavation of the Prehistoric, Roman, and Post-Roman Sites in Lydney Park, Gloucestershire*, Reports of the Research Committee of the Society of Antiquaries of London, No. IX (1932), pp. 132–7. (London, Oxford University Press).
'Sigelwara Land': Part I, *Medium Aevum*, 1 (December 1932), pp. 183–96. (Oxford, Basil Blackwell).

1933 Poem 'Errantry' in *The Oxford Magazine*, Volume LII No. 5, 9 November 1933, p. 180. (Oxford, The Oxonian Press).

1934 Poem 'Looney' in *The Oxford Magazine*, Volume LII No. 9, 18 January 1934, p. 340. (Oxford, The Oxonian Press). [An early version of the poem printed in *The Adventures of Tom Bombadil* as 'The Sea-bell'.]
Poem 'The Adventures of Tom Bombadil' in *The Oxford Magazine*, Volume LII No. 13, 15 February 1934, pp. 464–5. (Oxford, The Oxonian Press).
'Sigelwara Land': Part II, *Medium Aevum*, 3 (June 1934), pp. 95–111. (Oxford, Basil Blackwell).
'Chaucer as a Philologist: The Reeve's Tale', *Transactions of the Philological Society* (1934), pp. 1–70. (London, David Nutt).

1936 *Songs for the Philologists*, by J. R. R. Tolkien, E. V. Gordon, and others (privately printed in the Department of English at University College, London, 1936). [A collection of humorous verses originally circulated in typescript at Leeds University. The verses are unsigned, but Tolkien was the author of 'From One

to Five', 'Syx Mynet', 'Ruddoc Hana', 'Ides Ælfscyne', 'Bagme
Bloma', 'Eadig Beo þu', 'Ofer Widne Garsecg', 'La, Huru',
'I Sat Upon a Bench', 'Natura Apis', 'The Root of the Boot'
(an early version of 'The Stone Troll'), 'Frenchmen Froth', and
'Lit and Lang'.]

1937   Poem 'The Dragon's Visit' in *The Oxford Magazine*, Volume LV
No. 11, 4 February 1937, p. 342. (Oxford, The Oxonian Press).
Poem 'Knocking at the Door: Lines induced by sensations
when waiting for an answer at the door of an Exalted
Academic Person' (signed 'Oxymore') in *The Oxford Magazine*,
Volume LV No. 13, 18 February 1937, p. 403. (Oxford, The
Oxonian Press). [The original version of 'The Mewlips'.]
Poem 'Iumonna Gold Galdre Bewunden' ['The Hoard'] in
The Oxford Magazine, Volume LV No. 15, 4 March 1937, p. 473.
(Oxford, The Oxonian Press).
'Beowulf: the Monsters and the Critics', *Proceedings of the British
Academy*, 22 (1936), pp. 245–95. (London, Oxford University
Press, 1937). [Reprinted separately by the Oxford University
Press, Oxford, 1958. Reprinted in the U.S.A. in *An Anthology of
Beowulf Criticism*, edited by Lewis E. Nicholson (University of
Notre Dame Press, 1963); and in *The Beowulf Poet*, edited by
Donald K. Fry (New Jersey, Prentice-Hall Inc., 1968).]
The Hobbit: or There and Back Again (London, George Allen &
Unwin Ltd, 1937). [Reprinted in 1937, 1942, and 1946. Four
colour plates were added for the second impression. Second
edition 1951; reprinted many times. Third edition 1966;
reprinted many times. First U.S.A. edition (Boston, Houghton
Mifflin Co., 1938). Second U.S.A. edition 1958. Third U.S.A.
edition (New York, Ballantine Books, 1965); reprinted many
times. Translated into and published in Swedish (1947 and
1962), German (1957 and 1967), Dutch (1960), Polish (1960),
Portuguese (1962), Spanish (Argentina, 1964), Japanese (1965),
Danish (1969), French (1969), Norwegian (1972), Czech (1973),
Finnish (1973), Italian (1973), Bulgarian (1975), Danish (1975),
Rumanian (1975), Serbo-Croat (1975). In preparation: Hebrew,
Hungarian, Portuguese (Brazil).]

1938   Letter about 'The Hobbit', *Observer*, London, 20 February
1938. [Tolkien wrote in reply to a letter published in that
newspaper on 16 January 1938.]

1940   Preface to *Beowulf and the Finnesburg Fragment: A Translation
into Modern English Prose* by John R. Clark Hall, revised by
C. L. Wrenn (London, George Allen & Unwin Ltd, 1940).

1945 'Leaf by Niggle', *The Dublin Review*, 432 (January 1945), pp.
46–61. (London, Burns Oates & Washbourne Ltd). [This short
story was later reprinted – see below – and translated into Dutch
(1971), Swedish (1972), French (1974), German (1975),
Japanese (1975), Spanish (Argentina, in preparation).]
'The Lay of Aotrou and Itroun', *The Welsh Review*, Volume IV
No. 4, December 1945, pp. 254–66. (Cardiff, Penmark Press).

1947 ' "Ipplen" in Sawles Warde', *English Studies*, Volume XXVIII
No. 6, December 1947, pp. 168–70. (Amsterdam, Swets &
Zeitlinger). (In collaboration with S. R. T. O. d'Ardenne.)
'On Fairy-Stories', *Essays Presented to Charles Williams*, edited by
C. S. Lewis (London, Oxford University Press, 1947), pp.
38–89. [Reprinted – see below – and translated into Swedish
(1972), Japanese (1973), Spanish (Argentina, in preparation).]

1948 'MS. Bodley 34: A re-collation of a collation', *Studia
Neophilologica*, Volume XX, 1947–8, pp. 65–72. (Uppsala, 1948).
(In collaboration with S. R. T. O. d'Ardenne.)

1949 *Farmer Giles of Ham* (London, George Allen & Unwin Ltd,
1949). [Reprinted many times. First U.S.A. edition, Boston,
Houghton Mifflin Co., 1950. Translated into Swedish (1961),
Polish (1965), German (1970), Dutch (1971), Hebrew (1968),
German (1975), Italian (1975), Japanese (1975), Spanish
(Argentina, in preparation).]

1953 'A Fourteenth-Century Romance', *Radio Times*, London,
4 December 1953. [Foreword to the BBC Third Programme
broadcasts of Tolkien's translation of 'Sir Gawain and the
Green Knight'.]
'The Homecoming of Beorhtnoth Beorhthelm's Son', *Essays
and Studies by members of the English Association*, New Series
Volume VI, 1953, pp. 1–18. (London, John Murray).
[Subsequently reprinted – see below – and translated into
Spanish (Argentina, in preparation).]
'Middle English "Losenger" ', *Essais de Philologie Moderne*, 1951,
pp. 63–76. (Bibliothèque de la Faculté de Philosophie et Lettres
de l'Université de Liège, fasc. 129, Paris: Les Belles Lettres,
1953).

1954 *The Fellowship of the Ring: being the first part of The Lord of the
Rings* (London, George Allen & Unwin Ltd, 1954).
The Two Towers: being the second part of The Lord of the Rings
(London, George Allen & Unwin Ltd, 1954).

1955 *The Return of the King: being the third part of The Lord of the Rings*
(London, George Allen & Unwin Ltd, 1955).
[Between 1954 and 1966 *The Fellowship of the Ring* was reprinted

in Britain fourteen times, *The Two Towers* eleven times, and *The Return of the King* ten times. Second edition of all three volumes, 1966; reprinted many times. Paperback edition of *The Lord of the Rings* in one volume (London, George Allen & Unwin, Ltd, 1968). First U.S.A. edition (Boston, Houghton Mifflin Co., 1954 (volume I), 1955 (volumes II and III). Second U.S.A. edition 1967. Ace Books edition, New York, 1965. Ballantine Books edition, New York, 1965; reprinted many times. Translated[1] into Dutch (1956), Swedish (1959), Polish (1961), Danish (1968), German (1969), Italian (1970), French (1972), Japanese (1972), Finnish (1973), Norwegian (1973), Portuguese (Brazil, 1974). In preparation: Hebrew, Hungarian, Icelandic, Spanish (Argentina).]

Poem 'Imram' in *Time & Tide*, London, 3 December 1955, p. 1561. [The poem that appeared in the unpublished manuscript *The Notion Club Papers* as 'The Death of St Brendan'.]

Preface to *The Ancrene Riwle*, translated into Modern English by M. B. Salu (London, Burns & Oates, 1955).

1962   *The Adventures of Tom Bombadil and other verses from The Red Book* (London, George Allen & Unwin Ltd, 1962). [Subsequently reprinted. First U.S.A. edition, Boston, Houghton Mifflin Co., 1962. Translated into Swedish (1972), French (1972), French (1975), Japanese (1975), Spanish (Argentina, in preparation).]

Ancrene Wisse: the English Text of the Ancrene Riwle, edited from MS. Corpus Christi College Cambridge 402, Early English Text Society No. 249 (introduction by N. R. Ker). (London, Oxford University Press, 1962).

1963   'English and Welsh', *Angles and Britons: O'Donnell Lectures* (Cardiff, University of Wales Press, 1963), pp. 1–41. [Published in the U.S.A. by Verry, Lawrence, 1963.]

1964   *Tree and Leaf* (London, George Allen & Unwin Ltd, 1964). [A reprint of 'On Fairy-Stories' and 'Leaf by Niggle'. First U.S.A. edition, Boston, Houghton Mifflin Co., 1965.]

1965   Poems 'Once Upon a Time' and 'The Dragon's Visit' in *Winter's Tales for Children: 1*, edited by Caroline Hillier (London, Macmillan, 1965), pp. 44–5 and 84–7. [Published simultaneously in U.S.A. by St Martin's Press, New York. Reprinted in *The Young Magicians*, edited by Lin Carter (New York, Ballantine Books, 1969), pp. 254–62.]

1966   'Tolkien on Tolkien', *Diplomat*, Volume XVIII No. 197, October 1966, p. 39. [Taken from a statement prepared by

[1]The dates given are for the publication of the first volume.

Tolkien for his publishers, this is a brief account of his life and
his motives as a writer.]

Contribution as a translator to *The Jerusalem Bible* (London,
Darton, Longman & Todd, 1966). (New York, Doubleday,
1966.) [Tolkien is named as an editor of this work, but his only
contribution was to make the original draft of the translation of
the Book of Jonah, and his work was extensively revised by
other hands before publication.]

The Tolkien Reader (New York, Ballantine Books, 1966).
[A reprint in one volume of 'The Homecoming of Beorhtnoth',
'On Fairy-Stories', 'Leaf by Niggle', 'Farmer Giles of Ham',
and 'The Adventures of Tom Bombadil'.]

1967   *Smith of Wootton Major* (London, George Allen & Unwin Ltd,
1967); (Boston, Houghton Mifflin Co., 1967). [Subsequently
reprinted. Translated into Afrikaans (1968), Dutch (1968),
Swedish (1972), German (1975), Japanese (1975), Spanish
(Argentina, in preparation).]

Poem 'For W. H. A.' in *Shenandoah: The Washington and Lee
University Review*, Volume XVIII No. 2, Winter 1967, pp. 96–7.
[A poem in Anglo-Saxon with a modern English translation,
in honour of the sixtieth birthday of W. H. Auden.]

The Road Goes Ever On: A Song Cycle. Poems by J. R. R. Tolkien
set to music by Donald Swann (Boston, Houghton Mifflin Co.,
1967); (London, George Allen & Unwin Ltd, 1968).
[At the time of the publication of this song-book, a long-
playing gramophone record was issued by Caedmon Records
(TC 1231) under the title *Poems and Songs of Middle Earth*. On
the record, William Elvin sings Swann's settings of Tolkien's
poems, with the composer at the piano, and Tolkien reads
some of his own verse.]

1969   Letter describing the origins of the Inklings in *The Image of Man
in C. S. Lewis* by William Luther White (Nashville & New
York, Abingdon Press, 1969), pp. 221–2. Reprinted in Great
Britain by Hodder & Stoughton, 1970.

1970   Poem 'The Hoard' in *The Hamish Hamilton Book of Dragons*,
edited by Roger Lancelyn Green (London, Hamish Hamilton,
1970), pp. 246–8.

1973   Ballantine Books issued a calendar containing a number of
Tolkien's drawings. In 1974 Allen & Unwin and Ballantine
issued calendars using the same illustrations. In 1975, 1976 and
1977 Allen & Unwin issued calendars using further drawings by
Tolkien. Several of the drawings have also been issued in the
form of posters and postcards.

1974   Poem 'Bilbo's Last Song' published in poster form, with decorations by Pauline Baynes (London, George Allen & Unwin Ltd, 1974). The poem was also published as a poster, with a photographic background, by the Houghton Mifflin Co., 1974.

1975   'Guide to the Names in *The Lord of the Rings*', *A Tolkien Compass*, edited by Jared Lobdell (La Salle, Illinois, Open Court, 1975), pp. 153–201. [Notes on the nomenclature in the story, originally written for the guidance of translators.]
Sir Gawain and the Green Knight, Pearl, and Sir Orfeo, translated into modern English; edited and with a preface by Christopher Tolkien (London, George Allen & Unwin Ltd, 1975).
[During 1975 two long-playing gramophone records were issued by Caedmon Records (TC 1477 and 1478) on which Tolkien reads from *The Hobbit* and *The Lord of the Rings*. These recordings were made by George Sayer at Malvern in August 1952.]
Tree and Leaf, Smith of Wootton Major, The Homecoming of Beorhtnoth reprinted in one volume; *Farmer Giles of Ham, The Adventures of Tom Bombadil* reprinted in one volume (London, Unwin Books, 1975).

1976   *The Father Christmas Letters*, edited by Baillie Tolkien (London, George Allen & Unwin Ltd, 1976); (Boston, Houghton Mifflin Co., 1976).

In preparation: *The Silmarillion*, edited by Christopher Tolkien.

APPENDIX D
Sources and acknowledgements

In this book I have quoted J. R. R. Tolkien's words usually without giving references to the sources of the quotations. Such references would have had to be numerous and therefore (I considered) tiresome to the eye, and since many quotations are taken from unpublished material, references would only have been of very limited interest. I have also eschewed the customary row of dots to indicate a passage omitted in the middle of a quotation; again, these would have had to be numerous and therefore (I believe) irritating without being enlightening. My aim here has been not to interrupt the narrative with what Tolkien himself once called 'the trail of the passing editor'.

In view of the absence of references, it may be of some interest if I give a brief indication of the nature of my sources. The account of family life in Bloemfontein is based on letters written by Arthur Tolkien to his parents in England. Childhood days at Sarehole and in Birmingham were recalled by J. R. R. Tolkien in manuscript notes and in newspaper and radio interviews. I was also fortunate to be able to meet his brother Hilary Tolkien, who told me much of their early days and corresponded with me at some length while this book was being written. Sadly he did not live to see it completed, for he died early in 1976. The events at Duchess Road were recorded in contemporary letters between Tolkien and Edith Bratt, whom he was later to marry, and their enforced parting was chronicled in a diary that he kept for a brief time at this period. After they had been reunited their correspondence continued until they began a settled married life late in 1918, and the several hundred letters that they wrote to each other during this time were the source of much information about Tolkien's undergraduate days and his war service. The origins of 'The T.C.B.S.' were recounted to me by Christopher Wiseman, whose assistance, encouragement, and friendship have been among the chief delights of my work on the book. Tolkien's itinerary in France during the First World War was recorded in a cursory diary that he kept at the time, and this, together with Major-General J. C. Latter's *History of the Lancashire Fusiliers, 1914–18* (Aldershot, 1949) and John Harris's *The Somme* (London, 1966), made it possible for me to construct a detailed picture of his active service. Between 1919 and 1933 Tolkien kept a diary at some length, writing it in his invented alphabets, and this was the principal source of information for my account of this part of his life. For the remaining years I drew chiefly on his correspondence with his family, his friends, his publishers, and readers of his books; and on the diaries kept by him with varying degrees of regularity from 1964 to the end of his life. I have also drawn much on the autobiographical content of his published writings, most notably the essay *On Fairy-Stories* and the lecture *English and Welsh*.

The diaries, letters, and other papers were made available to me through the generosity of Professor Tolkien's sons and daughter, and my greatest debt of gratitude is consequently to them: the Rev. John Tolkien, Michael Tolkien, Christopher Tolkien, and Priscilla Tolkien. Moreover they have each of them given me unstintingly of their time and attention; they have discussed their father's life with me, and commented upon the book in manuscript; and throughout my work on the project they have shown me unfailing kindness, encouragement, and friendship.

Similarly Professor Tolkien's executors have given me every possible assistance during my work on the book; and they and Messrs George Allen & Unwin have kindly allowed me to quote from Tolkien's writings, both published and unpublished.

Many people have talked or written about their memories of Professor Tolkien, either to me or to Ann Bonsor, who has generously allowed me to make use of the tape-recordings that she made for a series of radio broadcasts about his life. To these I owe my thanks: Professor Simonne d'Ardenne, Owen Barfield, the late John Bryson, Professor Nevill Coghill, Professor and Mrs Norman Davis, the late Hugo Dyson, Elaine Griffiths, Joy Hill, the late Rev. Gervase Mathew O.P., the Rev. Robert Murray S.J., Mary Salu, Donald Swann, Dr Denis Tolhurst, Baillie Tolkien, Rayner Unwin, the late Milton Waldman, and Dick Williamson. Several of those named have also been kind enough to read the book in manuscript and comment upon it.

My thanks are due to many members of Professor Tolkien's family other than those already mentioned, for kindness and assistance in many ways. I am also grateful for the loan of family photographs, and for permission to reproduce them.

Many other people have helped me in a number of ways, and my thanks are due to (among others): C. Talbot d'Alessandro, Jonathan Anelay,

Sir Basil Blackwell, C. H. C. Blount and Norman Craig of King Edward's School Birmingham, Alina Dadlez, Professor Glyn Daniel, the Very Rev. Pascall Dillon O.M.I., Charles Furth, Glen and Bonnie Good-Knight, Juliet Grindle, the Rev. Walter Hooper, Guy Kay, Jessica Kemball-Cook, Professor Clyde S. Kilby, the Rev. R. P. Lynch and the Very Rev. C. J. G. Winterton of the Birmingham Oratory, Mr and Mrs Michael Maclagan, A. C. Muffett, Mr and Mrs David Phillips, Oliver Suffield, Graham Tayar, Gwendoline Williams, and the Headmaster of St Philip's Grammar School Birmingham. Brenda Goodall of Supercopy (Oxford) has given me much assistance with photocopying.

My thanks are due to the executors of the late C. S. Lewis for permission to quote from his letters to Tolkien.

During my preparations for writing the book I visited Marquette University at Milwaukee in the United States, in whose archives are housed many of the manuscripts of Tolkien's works of fiction. At Marquette I received much kindness from Paul Gratke, the Rev. Robert Callen S.J., and the Rev. Raphael Hamilton S.J. My thanks are also due to several British libraries: the Bodleian, the library of the Imperial War Museum, Evesham Public Library and its librarian Keith Barber, and the Brotherton Library in the University of Leeds.

I have consulted a number of books which have been of assistance, most notably C. S. Lewis's *Surprised by Joy, The Four Loves,* and his collected letters, as well as the biography of Lewis by Roger Lancelyn Green and Walter Hooper. Other books that have been of service include *The Life of Joseph Wright* by E. M. Wright (Oxford, 1932), *The Rise of English Studies* by D. J. Palmer (Oxford, 1965), *Tolkien Criticism: An Annotated Checklist* by Richard C. West (Kent State University Press), and *A Guide to Middle Earth* by Robert Foster (New York, 1974). I also owe thanks to many journalists and broadcasters who interviewed Tolkien, and whose interviews I have consulted. I should mention in particular interviews by Keith Brace (*Birmingham Post*, 25 May 1968), Daphne Castell (*Glasgow Herald*, 6 August 1966, and *Christian Science Monitor*, 11 August 1966), William Cater (*Daily Express*, 22 November 1966, and *Sunday Times*, 2 January 1972), Don Chapman ('Anthony Wood', *Oxford Mail*, 9 February 1968), John Ezard (*Oxford Mail*, 3 August 1966), William Foster (*The Scotsman*, 25 March 1967), Denys Gueroult (*Now Read On*, BBC Radio 4, 16 December 1970), Philip Norman (*Sunday Times*, 15 January 1967), Charlotte and Denis Plimmer (*Daily Telegraph Magazine*, 22 March 1968), and Richard Plotz (*Seventeen*, 17 January 1967).

I must also add my thanks to members of my family for reading the book in manuscript and making valuable suggestions, and to my wife Mari Prichard, who besides being a constant adviser did much vital work in 'de-coding' the diary in invented alphabets that Tolkien kept between 1919 and 1933.

I have already mentioned Christopher Tolkien, but I cannot leave unrecorded my especial debt to him. As his father's literary executor he has been faced with the immense task of ordering *The Silmarillion* for publication. In the midst of this work he spared innumerable hours to assist me, and made radical and invaluable suggestions which have had a considerable influence on the final shape of this book. Moreover he, his wife Baillie, and their children Adam and Rachel, welcomed me into their house five days a week for almost eight months while I consulted the many papers and manuscripts that were at that time kept under their roof. Thanks to the unfailing warmth of their welcome, my task was made a delight to me.

INDEX

Characters and places in Tolkien's stories are printed in inverted commas. The titles of his works, published and unpublished, will be found indexed under 'Tolkien, J. R. R.'.